THE
INVISIBLE CHILDREN

THE
INVISIBLE CHILDREN

School Integration
in American Society

RAY C. RIST

HARVARD UNIVERSITY PRESS
Cambridge, Massachusetts,
and London, England   1978

Library of Congress Cataloging in Publication Data

Rist, Ray C
    The invisible children.

    Includes bibliographical references and index.
    1.   School integration — Oregon — Case studies.
2.   Brush School.   I.   Title.
LC214.22.07R57   370.19'342'09795   77-24554
ISBN 0-674-46588-1

Foreword

BY CHARLES V. WILLIE

Ray C. Rist calls his book *The Invisible Children*. Years ago, Ralph Ellison wrote his great novel, *The Invisible Man*. The title of Rist's book obviously was influenced by the resemblance of his research findings to the experience of the characters in the Ellison volume, a fictitious autobiography of a black man and his trials and tribulations in a predominantly white society. The reader, then, may be inclined to examine the data of this study as a way of understanding the dangers and difficulties of black children in a predominantly white school and to determine whether or not school desegregation and integration are worth all the troubled effort. Such an approach to the reading of this book would be incomplete, however. It would lead to a limited and one-sided comprehension of a complex phenomenon.

The double-consciousness theory developed by W. E. B. DuBois —that the minority members of a society look at themselves and their circumstances from their own vantage point as well as through the eyes of the majority—is worthy of adoption by all, majority and minority both. Indeed, an analysis of the "invisible children" is incomplete without an analysis of their interaction with the "visible children." Also an analysis of the desegregation and integration experiences of all children is incomplete without an analysis of their interaction with adults, particularly their principal and teachers in school. The analysis presented in this book focuses on the adaptations of black and white children. But, most important, it describes teachers who are effective or ineffective in guiding the integration process and indicates the policy context based on actions and inactions of educational authorities which prescribe the conditions for interracial associations in school and community. These have as much to do with the ultimate outcome of school desegregation as the attitudes and actions of the children.

The activities of school-board members and the school superintendent, the principal, and the teachers are essential data for analysis in any study that seeks to understand the desegregation and integration processes. They are the dominant people of power in the educational system and have a great deal to do with setting the scene for the desegregation drama. The actions of black, brown, and white children — the subdominant people of power in the educational system — largely are responses to the direct and indirect initiatives of significant adults in the system. Rist recognizes this fact and gives a blow-by-blow description of what the teachers and principal say and do in addition to describing the activities of the children.

The dominant and subdominant categories of people with respect to power in the school desegregation drama are mentioned because it is important for the reader to recognize that he or she may identify with (or even be) one or the other. Karl Mannheim reminds us that perspective — how one views, perceives, and construes an object or situation — is a function of social position. The perspectives on school desegregation issues and proposals for their solution tend to differ for those who are in charge and those who are dependent on the initiatives of the dominants. For example, dominants — whether teachers over against students or whites over against blacks — tend to focus on the successes of their own kind and the failures of others. It is important in school desegregation research to recognize that teachers have weaknesses as well as strengths and that they fail as well as succeed. The same can be said for students and the same can be said for blacks as well as whites. The analysis in this book is about the full range of adaptations and is not limited to the perspective of those who are in charge, which is the perspective of most school desegregation studies.

This is a case study that uses the participant-observation method to gather data. The liability of this approach, chiefly the inability to generalize findings, has been well documented. What has not been discussed so fully is the positive aspect of the case-study approach. In no other way can one weigh and consider the effect of a combination of influences experienced as cross-pressures or serially, to see how one manages conflicting goals and competing claims and how changes in perceptions and definitions of problems and appropriate responses occur in time and space. There is the sacrifice of understanding the incidence and prevalence of specific behavior within the social structure when the case method is used. This sacrifice is unacceptable if an understanding of the stability and central tendency of the social structure, or homeostasis, is the basic purpose of social research. But if one is concerned about change as well as stability—homeokinesis as well as homeostasis—then a method which analyzes behavior in space and time is necessary. The case method reveals information that helps one to achieve insight into structure and process. This is the asset of the approach used by Rist in his study.

In balancing assets against liabilities of various methods of study, obviously the conclusion is that many studies of school desegregation using different kinds of methods are needed. Yet most studies analyze race relations in schools as if success or failure depended upon the kinds of adaptations observed at a particular point in time. Without the temporal perspective on school desegregation and integration events, the possibility of arriving at wrong conclusions is ever present. The literature is full of such conclusions based on cross-sectional statistical studies.

Rist gives us an excellent view of school desegregation-in-action. The reader gets the feeling of being there as it happens. The author made some one hundred and seventy-five classroom observations. He interviewed teachers and the principal, and attended Parent-Teacher Association meetings. These detailed observations were made from the beginning to the end of one schoolyear.

Analysis of the data from these many observations leads me to one conclusion: school desegregation has been the best thing that has happened to public education in this century in the United States. According to Rist, "teachers will face, perhaps for the first time, multi-racial and multi-ethnic classrooms and the need to decide how they will revise their curriculum to accommodate students from varying backgrounds." This study describes those teachers who have succeeded and those who have failed. How teachers have learned to cope, therefore, is the real meaning of the message contained in this book. Of less importance is the finding that some teachers blame the students for their own teaching incompetence. It seems that we have heard this song before. Rist points it out but goes on to describe the full range of adaptations of teachers to school desegregation and indicates the consequences for children of each form of adaptation. Because of its judicious objectivity, this is one of the few studies of school desegregation yet written that is worthy of being called social science.

Preface

The last twenty years have been rough ones for America. It is as if the country has been on a perpetual roller coaster ride, plunging into war, assassinations, Watergate, crime, and urban strife, and climbing to Camelot, moon walks, the civil rights and ecology movements. The plateaus have been few and far between.

Central to these years of turbulent social change has been the problem of how to redress the grievous injustices suffered by black Americans. The issue has changed during this period from whether black Americans shall have equal protection of the law and equal opportunity to how these principles are to be translated into reality. And perhaps more than any other institution, the schools have been asked to lead the way. It is in this sector of our public and collective life that we have most vigorously sought to apply our principles. In a society where racism and segregation find support in countless formal and informal arrangements, the schools have been singled out as the vanguard for change.

One has only to jump from the armed troops in Little Rock in 1957 to those in Boston in 1976 to realize that the efforts have spanned a generation. Even now they continue. The direction in which we are headed appears irreversible. The question is how quickly we are moving.

It is ironic that while we have debated, fought, and spilled blood over the role of the schools in integrating our society, we have spent little energy examining the outcomes. Surprisingly, we know precious little about the day-to-day experiences of black and white children in integrated schools. We do know about their test scores, their grades, and their responses to paper-and-pencil assessments of attitudes, but about their interaction and behavior, we can say very little.

This book has been written to help remedy that omission. It describes the life of one school during the time of its transformation from an all-white school to one that was "integrated" through the busing of a small number of black students. It traces what happened from the first day of school in September of 1973, when the black children came off the bus, to the last day of school in June 1974. Before that, there had never been a black student in the school.

There may be some question as to whether a school that receives only a small number of black students is, in reality, integrated. The answer depends upon the criteria used for ascertaining "integration." I shall frequently suggest that there are many assumptions about what constitutes an integrated school, and although from one standpoint, the school in this study was an example of the grossest form of tokenism, from another it was the epitome of a good integration program. For this reason I have not made the conventional academic distinction between "integration" and "desegregation." I prefer the generic term "integration," knowing full well it may have entirely different meanings to different readers.

The data for this study were gathered in Portland, Oregon, in 1973 and 1974 under the sponsorship of a grant from the National Science Foundation. I am indebted to the foundation and particularly to Donald Ploch, the program officer, for encouragement and support. A number of colleagues at Portland State University provided me with good advice and patient sounding boards as I gathered the material and began to analyze it. They include Leonard Cain, Jan Hadja, Wilson Record, and Robert Shotola. My graduate assistant, David Johnson, was indispensable, as was my secretary, Holly Johnson, who typed reams of protocol sheets.

The book itself was written during the time of my affiliation with the National Institute of Education, Department of Health, Education, and Welfare. My colleagues there have been a constant source of ideas and suggestions. They also have been among my toughest critics. Individually and as a group, they belie the notion that serious and rigorous thinking must be put aside if one comes to work in government. Most especially, Ronald Anson, Edward Barnes, Jessie Bernard, Martin Burlingame, Donald Bushell, Manuel Carlos, Paul Hill, Mark Lohman, Gregg Jackson, and Marshall Smith have provided the critical mass of intellectually exciting people it has been my good fortune to work with. Harold Hodgkinson, the director of the Institute, deserves special mention for fostering an atmosphere where good scholarship was integral to the success of the agency. Elizabeth Cohen and Charles Willie have my deep appreciation for their careful and thoughtful examination of the entire manuscript. I do hope I have done justice to their critiques.

This book is the second in a series I am writing to elucidate life in American schools. The two sites I have chosen for study thus far could not be more dissimilar. The first was a *de facto* segregated black school in Saint Louis, Missouri. There most of the children were desperately poor and the school had pitifully few resources with which to respond to their educational needs. This volume explores the day-to-day reality of life in an affluent white school located in Portland, Oregon. Here the school was brimming with materials and special programs aimed at enhancing the experiences of the children who were already reaping the benefits that went with their parents' social positions. Just as there were no white students or staff at the school in Saint Louis, so conversely there were no black students or staff at the school in Portland—that is, until the first day of the busing program.

Early formulations of some of the material presented here have appeared in the following of my articles: "Busing White Children into Black Schools: A Study in Controversy," *Integrateducation*,

xii   Preface

vol. 12, no. 6; "Race, Policy, and Schooling," *Society*, vol. 12, no. 1; "School Integration: Ideology, Methodology, and National Policy," *School Review*, vol. 84, no. 3; and "Race and Schooling: An Analysis of Policy Issues," *The Educational Forum*, vol. 15, no. 4.

I would also like to acknowledge by name the many students, teachers, administrators, and parents associated with Brush School and the Portland Public Schools who participated in this research effort and opened their doors to me. But in the interest of protecting their anonymity, I shall refrain. They will know who they are and they have my thanks. Without their generosity, this study would not have been possible.

Contents

We come then to the question presented: Does segregation of children in public schools solely on the basis of race, even though the physical facilities and other "tangible" factors may be equal, deprive the children of the minority group of equal education opportunities? We believe that it does.

Supreme Court of the United States,
Brown v. Board of Education of Topeka, 1954

Introduction

Education has been that child of the Enlightenment which for generations has helped to nourish and sustain the American vision. Now, the view has become cloudy. And nowhere now does it seem harder to find one's way than in ascertaining the interrelations of education, race, and equality. Consider the emotions generated by the use of such terms as "forced busing," "the destruction of the neighborhood school," "community control of schools," "power to the people," and "whites have rights." The heat that emanates from the struggle over what path should be chosen seems most intense when the issue is school desegregation.

Few debates related to domestic social policy have involved such a complex mix of law, social science, and cultural values as that over when and how dominant and minority children should come together in classrooms across the land. In the two decades since the monumental Supreme Court decision of 1954, *Brown* v. *Board of Education of Topeka,* the United States has been grappling with this issue in the courtrooms, in the classrooms, in the political arenas, and in the streets. To mention only federal troops at Little Rock in the 1950s, or the events in Boston and Louisville in the 1970s, is to gloss over a generation of conflict.

For there has been much violence, and in some instances failure, in the efforts to resolve the basic dilemmas of race and education in American society.

Whether nationally or locally, to move from a pattern of segregation to one of integration is to effect social change.[1] For dominant and minority-group members alike, support for or resistance to this change will ultimately rest on the evaluation of both objective and subjective components. Of immediate concern to parents will be the safety of their children and what may be happening to their "neighborhood" school. School officials will be concerned with federal guidelines and maintaining the support of the community. Teachers, perhaps for the first time, will face multiracial or multiethnic classrooms and the need to decide how they will revise their curriculum to accommodate students from varying backgrounds. What has traditionally concerned researchers may or may not coincide with the fears and concerns of parents, teachers, administrators, and school board members. What each group brings to a discussion of school integration is influenced by their position in the social system and the interests associated with that position. Without an understanding of these divergences in interests and perspectives, it may be incorrectly assumed by parents, principals, and policymakers alike that a commonality of meaning exists when one speaks of "integration," or "desegregation," or "busing," or "separatism," or "pluralism."

Thus, in any debate or struggle over the direction of a social policy to effect social change, there will be multiple perspectives and, perhaps more profoundly, multiple assumptions about the

1. The first national statistics on school desegregation became available in the late 1960s. In 1968-69, the nation had 23.4 percent of its black students in majority white schools (50 percent or more whites), as compared with 18.4 percent for the South alone. In 1970-71, the ranking reversed, with the South having 40.3 percent blacks in majority white schools, and the national figure being 33.1 percent. The 1968-69 survey also showed that the U.S. had 39.7 percent of all black students in all-black schools, compared with 68 percent for the South alone. The South dropped to the national figure of 14 percent in 1970-71 and dropped below the national figure of 11.2 percent to 8.7 percent in 1971-72. For the North and West, the percentage of black students in all-black schools in 1971-72 was 10.9, and the percentage of black students in majority white schools was 28.3 for the same year.

nature of reality itself. The answer to the question "What makes for a desirable situation in an integrated school?" clearly depends on a number of judgments on the part of the respondent. Those judgments relate to how one believes the world and the patterns of everyday life within it are ordered. As Berger and Luckman (1966:13) note: "The reality of everyday life is taken for granted *as* reality. It does not require additional verification over and beyond its simple presence. It is simply *there,* as self-evident and compelling facticity. I *know* that it is real. While I am capable of engaging in doubt about its reality, I am obliged to suspect such doubt as I routinely exist in everyday life."

Of direct concern in discussing school integration is that assumptions about the construction of reality are often unexplicated and, consequently, go unexamined and unchallenged. What is "taken for granted as reality" by white school board members may profoundly diverge from that "taken for granted as reality" by black parents. The need here, then, is first to examine a number of assumptions that appear to influence how integration is defined by different groups involved with the schools. Second, it is important to trace the consequences of these differing perceptions for the formulation of integration programs.

The justification for attention to the assumptions that influence definitions of situations is that they in part influence how we pattern our social interaction, what we believe to be good or evil, and ultimately what we believe about the inherent characteristics of human beings. Such assumptions are not the sole property of formally explicated theoretical models. Each of us individually carries a "metatheory" of the nature of everyday reality, and it is within this framework, however unexplicated, that we try to make sense of the world. The ongoing correspondence between the sense that other individuals and each of us tries to make of the world leads to "common sense." Common sense is the patterned knowledge about the nature of everyday life routinely shared with some others. It is important to analyze commonsense notions of the world to understand why, for example, some parents seek an integrated education for their children and others actively avoid it.

WHAT DO WE MEAN BY INTEGRATION?

Much of what has been written on integration tends to reify the concept. In this literature, it is as if there is an implicit consensus that everyone will "know" what is meant when the term is used. Yet if the arguments of Berger and Luckman or Gouldner (1970:23) are correct, one cannot assume that a commonality of meaning does exist, for every society has a diversity and heterogeneity of constructions of reality that result from how that society is internally differentiated. Thus, intelligent discussion as well as rational social policy must account for this differentiation, or else fail to effect a "goodness of fit" with the world it seeks to interpret. What follows is a brief discussion of the major axes along which concepts of integration appear to differ.

The Pivot of Color versus Class

The thrust of the 1954 Supreme Court decision was to outline *de jure* school segregation; subsequent Court decisions of the 1960s and early 1970s have moved to extend and define more precisely unlawful acts creating racial separation in the schools. The rationale for these decisions has remained remarkably the same: that black children are denied equal academic opportunity and equal social justice by being deliberately isolated in all or predominantly black schools. It is assumed that the actions of public officials to foster such separation, in and of itself, is unconstitutional and in need of remedy. Thus, the courts order the elimination of predominantly one-race schools and the physical mixing of black and white children within the same educational facility. The belief is that desegregation of student bodies enhances the opportunity for equitable educational opportunity. Consequently, the 1954 *Brown* decision explicitly said that "separate but equal" can never in reality be equal.

Of interest here is the "contact theory" of Allport (1954) and later elaborations by Pettigrew (1971) and Pettigrew et al. (1973). Allport's central concern was to stipulate means for achieving a reduction of racial and ethnic intolerance based on group-stereotypic beliefs. If such stereotypic beliefs could be undermined, it was assumed there would be a reduction of prejudice, since prejudice was believed to be essentially based on false perceptions. A reduction in prejudice was expected to result in less discrimination and segregation, leading to enhanced opportunity for education and economic mobility. Allport's concern with the contact theory was to postulate the conditions under which intergroup contact would lead to lessened stereotypic beliefs. Although the primary function of schools is believed to be the transmission of academic skills, the contact hypothesis suggests that an important outcome of desegregation would be the improvement of racial understanding and acceptance as a consequence of the diminishing of stereotypic beliefs.[2]

Some recent studies have shown that contact *per se* is not sufficient and that the *quality* of that contact is the key determinant of the outcome of the interaction. Many researchers — Amir (1971), Armor — (1972b), Carithers (1970), Cohen (1973), Cohen and Roper (1972), Katz (1968), Lohman (1970), Perry (1973), and Porter (1971) — have suggested that the conditions of the contact must be more carefully specified before any conclusions can be drawn about the anticipated outcomes. Allport himself noted that when the contact was among those of unequal status, and was casual or competitive, it might result in a reinforcement of stereotypes and thus foster further prejudice and a worsening of relations. Pettigrew and his associates (1973) have taken this analysis further, arguing that such conditions, combined with a lack of cross-racial acceptance, may be a critical variable in explaining the lack of achievement gains by supposedly "integrated" students. Thus, the quality of race relations in the classroom is viewed as central to any assessment of whether or not an integration program is successful.

Juxtaposed to the emphasis on racial desegregation is the argument by many that the critical issue is not color, but class. It is one's position in the socioeconomic hierarchy that most directly

2. It is the anticipation of the precise opposite of this hypothesized outcome of school busing that generates the intense opposition of black nationalists. To bus black children into white schools, they argue, is to allow whites to confirm the stereotypes they hold about blacks: that black people are unequal, inadequate parents, incapable of maintaining their communities, etc. (Hamilton 1972).

influences opportunity and achievement, regardless of race or ethnicity. For example, Orfield (1973:7) notes: "The only factor so far identified as having a significant impact on improving the educational performance of poor children is a certain kind of integration — placing children from poor families in predominantly middle-class schools." The U.S. Commission on Civil Rights study of 1967 bears out Orfield's contentions. It demonstrated that lower-class children do in fact benefit by contact with middle-class children in terms of scholastic achievement. Likewise, St. John (1972) concludes that "adopting the norms of peers will be functional for school achievement only if peers are of higher SES [socioeconomic status] background and display more achievement-oriented behavior." Jencks (1972:87) has also supported this contention: "Poor black sixth graders in overwhelmingly middle-class schools were about 20 months ahead of poor black sixth graders in overwhelmingly lower-class schools. Poor students in schools of intermediate social economic composition fell neatly in between. The differences for poor white sixth graders were similar."

People's attitudes about social class, however, do not appear to be easily swayed by academic research. Irrespective of data that indicate benefits accrue to poor children when they are in classrooms with middle-class children, there are strong social pressures in the middle class to raise children "among one's own kind." Consequently, deliberate efforts at creating school settings with students of differing social-class backgrounds can generate significant reaction among the parents, particularly those who are middle class.

The fact that social class shapes attitudes about what is correct and desirable means that parents hold certain assumptions about what the school will accomplish for their children. Furthermore, such attitudes also influence parent's views about the backgrounds of students with whom they wish their own children to associate. It is at this point, where parents express preferences as to the social-class composition of the peer group for their children, that one of the most thorny issues of the integration dilemma is raised, to wit: how to create situations where middle-class parents will agree to the presence of more than a minuscule number of lower-class children in the schools of their own children. For many middle-class parents, a school with a high low-income student enrollment is simply unacceptable. The result is frequently a movement of these families into private or suburban schools, where the class position of other children is comparable to that of their own children. Though attention has been focused on the response of white parents, the response of many middle-class black parents to the likelihood of their children being in a heterogeneous social-class school has also often been a movement into private schools, particularly Catholic parochial schools. In either instance, though, the point needs to be reiterated that the absence of middle-class students from public school classrooms diminishes the educational opportunity and quality of schooling experienced by poor children.

There is yet another and separate dimension to this issue of class and color: How do teachers' assumptions about the nature of everyday reality impinge on their behavior in the classroom? Every child can be portrayed in terms of many attributes—sex, race, social class, clothing, speech, physical attractiveness, manners, and more. Which of these traits become highly salient to teachers and how in turn do they respond to them?

My own classroom observations suggest that, in the interaction between teachers and students, a "flooding phenomenon" takes over, and certain critical variable(s) become dominant, with the remaining characteristics receding into the background. Those traits selected as dominant by the teachers relate to their "commonsense" notions of how children should appear and behave. (I have seen an attribute such as body odor supersede all else. In one classroom, the teacher put any child who smelled of urine into the coat closet for long periods of time.) The point is, of course, that teachers have different assumptions about salient attributes, and the consequences of such differentiation are profoundly dissimilar "integrated" experiences for the children involved. In this perspective, the *process* of integration cannot be defined as a uni-dimensional experience, for there is no unanimity of perception on the part of the teachers.

If, for instance, an individual white teacher, or perhaps an entire staff, perceives the dominant attribute of incoming black children as their racial category, then the teacher's racial attitudes and behavior are crucial to the success or failure of those students' experience. We know that what the classroom teacher does will affect the behavior of students, but the exact nature of that relationship has yet to be determined. Boocock (1969) reviewed twenty-five years of research only to conclude, "Very little seems to be known about the relationship between what teachers do in the classroom and the subsequent behavior of students."

Even though it is very difficult to demonstrate the connections between teacher behavior and teacher attitudes, one can make certain assumptions. If racism and prejudice are normative values for white teachers, and they believe blacks are less academically capable than are whites, then one can anticipate that this prejudice would be expressed, if only infrequently, in their interaction with black students. Likewise, if tolerance and affirmation of racial differences are a normative value, one could expect that attitude to influence classroom interactions. Though my only observation of black teachers has been in all-black schools, I assume they also would give expression to their commonsense notions about both black and white children within their integrated classrooms.

But what if the salient characteristic for the teacher is not the skin color of the students, but their social class? Even teachers who are relatively free of racial animosity may react to class-associated differences between their own and some of their pupils' orientations toward the value of schooling, the likelihood of reward for one's efforts, and the desire for a competitive atmosphere. The dominant motif in busing programs throughout the United States has been the busing of low-income black students into working-class and middle-income white schools. Such an arrangement arises from the existing economic, social, and political divisions within the country, and the consequence is that any teacher participating in an integration program is likely to have a group displaying differences not only of color, but also of class.

A frequently used approach in analyzing the impact of differences in social-class attributes between teacher and pupils is the "cultural gap" hypothesis. Davis (1952), Riessman (1962), and Rist (1972) have all proposed that the presence of such a gap influences the outcome of the schooling experience. Many researchers — Becker (1952), Bettelheim (1972), Bowles (1972), Coleman (1966), Hollingshead (1949), Leacock (1969), Rist (1970, 1973), Stein (1971), and Warner et al. (1944), among others — have demonstrated that the social-class position of the student does in fact affect his role within the social system of the school. These researchers have documented, both in elementary and in secondary schools, the critical importance of social-class position in relation to academic achievement, participation in school activities, formulation of peer cliques, and interaction patterns with teachers.[3] In sum, the findings suggest that academic success and self-esteem are both directly linked to the student's social class — the higher the class, the higher the probability of academic success and reward. If teachers think that assumed social-class characteristics supersede assumed color characteristics, beliefs by various participants in an integration program that the children are involved in a "race" issue would not be borne out in the classrooms themselves.

The Pivot of Assimilation versus Pluralism

As color and class represent *alternative definitions* of the salient attributes of the children within integrated classrooms, so assimilation and pluralism represent *alternative responses* to these same children.

There is a curious relation in the United States between the rise of public education and the arrival of large immigrant populations from Europe. As Katz (1971) has noted, the school became

3. Hauser (1971) and Boudon (1973) both suggest, however, that there is a progressive attenuation in the relationship between schooling outputs and the status characteristics of students. Boudon, in particular, argues that socialist Eastern Europe, Western Europe, and the United States are meritocratic societies where the impact of social class upon educational opportunities is increasingly minimal.

an institution of great importance in the attempts to "American-ize" these newcomers—all that was alien had to be stripped away, and American values and attributes had to be substituted. Much the same process has been applied to nonwhite minorities. How successful the schools have been in this matter is a point of controversy, but that they have tried is not. Katz (1971; xviii) writes:

> For the schools are fortresses in function as well as in form, protected outposts of the city's education establishment and the prosperous citizens who sustain it. In their own way, they are imperial institutions designed to civilize the natives; they exist to do something to poor children, especially, now, children who are black or brown. Their main purpose is to make these children orderly, industrious, law-abiding and respectful of authority. Their literature and their spokesmen proclaim the schools to be symbols of opportunity, but their slitted or windowless walls say clearly what their history would reveal as well: They were designed to reflect and confirm the social structure that erected them.

What were the values of the social structure? Who was in a position to create this definition of reality? Gordon (1964) suggested that the values and power to enforce them were held by the Anglo-Saxon Protestants, who, among all the early groups competing for ascendancy in the New World, finally won. Their central aim was "to maintain English institutions (as modified by the American Revolution), the English language, and English-oriented cultural patterns as dominant and standard in American life" (Gordon 1964). All those who did not possess such traits as a matter of birth and upbringing were expected to learn to conform to them—or remain social, economic, and political outcasts. It is quite likely that with whatever slight modifications it may have had since, this notion of Anglo-conformity has been the most prevailing and powerful influence on majority-minority relations during the course of the nation's history.

According to this tenet, assimilation is ultimately a matter of conformity to the majority's values. The basic premise is that in order to succeed, one must take on the values, life-style, and world-view of the dominant WASP group. Whereas the early concerns of the dominant group were religious, political, and cultural differences vis-a-vis the new European immigrants, the recent struggle has been focused on color. In the early years, when WASPs were concerned with the Irish, such groups as the black Americans, Mexican Americans, and Native Americans were in no position to present any challenge to the cultural and political hegemony of the dominant group. But that is, of course, no longer the case. What has emerged is a shift in the attention of WASPs from what Ogbu calls "immigrant minorities" to "subordinate minorities": "By subordinate minorities I mean those minority groups who were incorporated into the United States more or less against their will. Subordinate minorities include the American Indians who were already here before the dominant whites arrived and conquered them, the Mexican-Americans of the Southwest and Texas who were similarly incorporated by conquest, and blacks who were brought here as slaves" (Ogbu 1974:2). With this distinction between minorities in mind, one can argue that the concern with the assimilation of subordinate minority groups takes on a new dimension, qualitatively different from a concern with the assimilation of immigrant minorities, past or present.

In their attempt to impose on various minority groups the values and beliefs of Anglo-conformity, the dominant group maintains that minority groups will benefit by accepting these views. Indeed, the dominant group implies that they want others to take on their values and assimilate into their culture. But it is not clear whether dominants do in fact want assimilation of all minority groups or whether they merely display a pretense of wanting it so as to hold within current institutional arrangements the aspirations of minority groups to partake of the American Feast. From the point of view of the minority group, the subordinate minority group in particular, the question is whether to accept Anglo values and seek assimilation, to reject them in favor of separatism, or to opt for a bicultural approach and hope that will suffice for entrée and perhaps acceptance.

The implications are immediately apparent for any integration program in a school whose values and curriculum are based on

Anglo-conformity. The task of the school is to legitimize those parts of the American experience which reflect Anglo values and culture and delegitimize those parts which do not. For any individual teacher, if that teacher accepts the validity of the dominance of Anglo values, the integration process within the classroom becomes one of instilling one perspective in all the students, regardless of their backgrounds. Those children who possess Anglo culture before coming to school need only reassurance. Those who do not possess it need salvation.

The development of the concept of pluralism within the study of majority-minority group relations came as a reaction against the implicit assimilationist assumption that some cultures are inherently superior to others. Pluralism was first propounded by Jane Addams in *Twenty Years at Hull House* (1914) and H. M. Kallen in *Culture and Democracy in the United States* (1924). Initially, the pluralist perspective was based on three central propositions. First, a person has no choice as to his ancestry, and it is therefore undemocratic to penalize him for what he did not voluntarily consent to have as a part of his permanent identity. Second, each minority and ethnic culture has within it valuable and positive attributes that could enhance American society; to deny these aspects of minority culture is ultimately to lessen the value of the dominant culture. Finally, as Kallen in particular emphasized, the idea that "all men are created equal" means not that there are no differences between people, but that all people merit equal respect and treatment. Together, these points suggest that pluralism as it was initially formulated represented an ideological struggle on the part of minority groups to maintain cultural and social traditions in the face of pressures for Anglo-conformity.

More recently, the concept of pluralism has undergone a bifurcation. Gordon (1964), for example, has written of the need to distinguish structural pluralism from cultural pluralism, suggesting that American society is characterized by both. Structural pluralism is seen as the development of institutions, organizations, and communities that are separated from others in the society along lines of religion, race, and ethnicity. And that both majority and minority groups opt for certain forms of structural pluralism is evident, for example, in the media, in religious organizations, in educational institutions (and even in cemeteries). Structural pluralism is not of direct concern to this analysis, because any discussion of either segregation or integration in American public schools must assume the existence of a unified school system, independent of its internal differentiations.

Gordon's analysis of cultural pluralism is of more immediate concern here, for it raises a critical question: Can unidimensional institutions (in his terms, those which are "structurally assimilated") retain cultural differentiations? Given the entrenched power of WASP culture to dominate public institutional arrangements and ideologies, the tentative answer in the American context appears to be no. Here is the crux of the current debate over the nature of the integrated school experience. Minority groups in particular have argued for the necessity and the right to maintain cultural distinctions within a single institutional framework. They interpret anything that prevents them from doing so as a manifestation of white determination to maintain cultural hegemony in all areas of interracial contact.

Cultural pluralism implies that if several distinct groups come together within a single institutional setting, they are able to maintain their distinctions over time.[4] There is no guarantee that such coexistence over time will remain peaceful, or necessarily must. Quite the contrary. It may be conflict ridden, but the groups seek to find means to maintain themselves, as appears to be the present situation in such diverse institutional settings as the military, the university, and the political arena.

An emphasis on cultural pluralism is reflected in a school program that represents the diversity of heritages and life experiences of all the children involved and that does not define any cultural system as inferior to any other system. For most members

---

4. This definition is complicated by the fact that cultural pluralism itself can have two distinctive meanings. On the one hand, there is the possibility of cultural pluralism among groups that stresses the autonomy of their values and presumes a high degree of equality among the groups. But there is also the notion of cultural pluralism that is based on segmentation with dominance, the extreme example of which would be South Africa. In the United States, the struggle, especially of subordinate minority groups, is to move from the latter to the former (see Kuper and Smith 1969).

of the dominant system, recognition of cultural pluralism necessarily implies the willingness to forsake Anglo-conformity as the basis of one's world-view. For teachers from the dominant group in particular, the struggle against Anglo-ethnocentricism, in most instances, is a struggle, against the prevailing curriculum, the views of entrenched school board members, and even the opposition or noncooperation of other teachers. The overwhelming pressures toward Anglo-conformity make the implementation of cultural pluralism rare in American education.

To recapitulate: it has been argued by various researchers that color and class play a critical role in how the integrated situation is defined. Research evidence suggests either may become the dominant motif in an integrated setting. As either class or color may in broad strokes define the situation, so also assimilation or pluralism are the available alternative institutional responses. Pressure on minority groups to accept assimilation within the framework of Anglo-conformity appears to be the most frequent response, because of the power and authority of dominants to create conditions they perceive to be to their own advantage.

WHAT DO WE WANT?

Though conceptually one does damage to any idea by trying to fit it neatly into a category to which it has only a rough approximation, here I attempt to provide a framework for distinguishing between the multiple definitions of what constitutes an "integrated education." The foregoing discussion has suggested as major foci for that framework the pivots of class versus color and assimilation versus pluralism. Each of the four alternatives will be discussed with respect to both their theoretical underpinnings and their policy implications for the creation of integrated school programs.

Integration as Racial Assimilation

This category of integration is the one most frequently espoused by the dominant white group as well as by segments of various minority communities. It essentially views integration as the means of socializing nonwhite students to act, speak, and believe very much like white students. The dominant group supports such a program because it leaves intact their own values, beliefs, and cultural forms. It also may affirm whatever notions of racial superiority they hold, for they may think that such integration helps nonwhite peoples to become fully human by instilling in them "white" ways of thinking and feeling. Valentine (1971) and Baratz and Baratz (1970) have, among many, attacked assumptions about the inferiority of nonwhite culture as assuming a "deficit model" that is without empirical substance.

The motivations that would prompt the support of this form of integration by minority groups is more difficult to ascertain. Several tentative explanations come to mind. Minority groups may believe that as their cultural styles come more and more to resemble those of the dominant group, they will be accepted by the dominants and invited to the Feast. The inverse of this is the fear that if they fail to take on Anglo values, they continue to risk present or future persecution and oppression. Or minority-group members who feel much self-hatred may manifest it by adopting the characteristics of the dominant group and rejecting those of their own culture.

To implement this type of integration there should be few nonwhite children among many whites. Thus, there would be no danger that sufficient numbers of black or other nonwhite students would have the opportunity to reinforce within their peer group any cultural or behavioral traits perceived as nonwhite. In short, one keeps the critical mass of nonwhite students low so as to ultimately render them "invisible," or nearly so, particularly to the dominant group. Likewise, the curriculum retains its traditional orientation to WASP values and myths with little or no attention to nonwhite contributions.

Many students of race relations and school integration do not regard racial assimilation as a form of integration. Mercer (1973), for instance, calls this alternative "token desegregation." Wilcox (1970:25) suggests much the same, inferring from his definition: "Desegregation—The physical mixing of pupils from a variety of ethnic backgrounds within one school without changing the structure and content of the educational program to reflect the presence of different cultural groupings through the provision of systematic opportunities for the sharing of those creative differences."

But distinction between "token desegregation" and "racial assimilation" is more than one of semantics. It relates to profoundly different social constructions of reality. For many whites, racial assimilation *is* integration and is the only kind they will voluntarily support. To imply that racial assimilation is not "real integration" suggests a different assumption as to what the integrated experience entails. Yet, the growing racial consciousness in nonwhite communities has emerged as a powerful counterforce to the socialization attempts by dominants to have nonwhite peoples think and act white. Thus, for many nonwhites, an educational program based on racial assimilation is entirely unacceptable. The critique is essentially that any form of integration which coerces minority children to deny their background solves none of their educational problems and may generate both self-hatred and further difficulties with schooling.

Integration as Racial Pluralism

Just as the dominant group in American society would most probably support racial assimilation as the framework for school integration, so it appears that significant numbers of minority group members would favor racial pluralism. This perspective allows for the affirmation of cultures other than Anglo-culture. It values what Anglo-conformity demands be hidden and denied. Further, it assumes nonwhite groups have developed cultures with an internal logic and way of ordering the world that deserve as much respect as does Anglo-Saxon culture.

Within the context of racial pluralism, there appears to be a continuum of integrated settings — from settings that impose very little stress on the culture of the minority group to those that impose very great stress, but stop short of complete separatism. As Valentine (1972) has suggested, black people are essentially bicultural in that they possess cultural traits of the dominant group as well as those distinctive to themselves. Thus, an extrapolation of Valentine's analysis implies the need to create integrated settings where those values and cultural forms valued by the minority group are retained, and where minority-group members are equipped to partake of the dominant culture as they desire.

Some form of racial pluralism appears to be the integration alternative most frequently described as an ideal goal by both members of minority communities and the white liberal community. For a school to be truly racially pluralistic, it would be necessary to structure patterns of social interaction and organization so that children, teachers, and parents of all racial groups receive equal status and are able to assume roles of equivalent power and prestige. Not to do so creates only a veneer of pluralism, while the actual control remains with the dominant group. It is obvious that the creation of such a school is a difficult process, for not only are there historical and cultural obstacles to overcome, but seldom do members of the dominant group willingly give up their control of an institution. In some instances, the struggle for racial pluralism in the school has been encompassed within the struggle for community control. In others, white and nonwhite participants in the life of the school have been able to work together toward achieving a system of shared power and responsibility. The infrequent appearance of truly pluralistic integrated schools attests to the fact that when they do occur, they do so in spite of the prevailing institutional arrangements within American society, rather than because of them.

But not all problems related to the creation of multiethnic or racially plural schools are those of power; many are problems of pedagogy. Two examples will give an indication of the complexity of such a school arrangement. Mercer (1973:42), for instance, writes that the program and curriculum of the school should "represent the heritage and life experience of *all* the children" (emphasis added). This is, of course, an overstatement of the issue, but the notion of the school responding to the diversity of the backgrounds of the children is an important one. The pedagogical problem here is deciding how to create the various categories of student backgrounds and, further, how many such categories to create. When are the categories to be based on color, when on class, and when on culture? An extension of the creation of diverse programs is the issue of how intensely the members of one group would participate in the curriculum developed for another. If there is a school language program that provides Spanish, Black American English, and the dominant Standard American English, do Chicano, black, and white students have lessons in all three languages, in two, in one? The question is not only how pluralistic the program of the school should become, but how pluralistic the children themselves should become.

Integration as Class Assimilation

The classical conception of education in American society has assumed that equal educational opportunity is provided to all children, regardless of the inequalities with which they may come to school. This view was voiced as long as 120 years ago, when Joseph White wrote in a report to the Massachusetts Board of Education (quoted in Katz, 1971:40): "The children of the rich and poor, of the honored and the unknown, meet together on common ground. Their pursuits, their aims and aspirations are one. No distinctions find place, but such as talent and industry and good conduct create."

More recently, notions of class assimilation have found expression in much of the writing about the education of groups termed the "culturally disadvantaged," the "culturally deprived," and the like. A close examination of this literature shows that it views American society as essentially open, mobile, and nonascriptive. Thus, for any person to remain poor or culturally disadvantaged is the result of personal cultural factors, not of systematic exclusion and discrimination.[5] Such was a part of the prevailing ratio-

5. This contention, of course, has been strongly attacked by a variety of social scientists and educators, among others. The critique of the open, mobile, and nonascriptive assumptions about the structure of American education has stressed the *class*-related characteristics of the school, not the *culture*-related characteristics of children. For only one example, consider this passage from Bowles (1972:50): "Class stratification within schools is achieved through tracking, differential participation in extra-curricular activities, and in the attitudes of teachers and guidance personnel who expect working-class children to do poorly, to terminate schooling early, and to end up in jobs similar to their parents."

nale for the creation of Head Start programs. What poor children needed was an initial boost of socialization to acquaint them with the values, behaviors, and ideas of the nonpoor middle class WASP, so that they would have aspirations to do well in school and thus "pull" themselves out of poverty. The arms of the affluent were said to be open to all those who sought to climb the ladder of mobility and join them.

Class assimilation as a framework for school integration functions essentially as if it were "colorblind." The colorblind perspective defines racial and ethnic differences as irrelevant to education. Each child is to be treated, in terms of racial categories, like every other child. Thus, all will have an equal educational opportunity. To make special responses to the presence of nonwhite students would be interpreted as "reverse discrimination."

By stressing class as against color, this alternative for school integration allows members of both white and nonwhite groups to support it.[6] If one has middle-class status, one can argue that it was achieved by self-determination, hard work, and perseverance. An emphasis on class assimilation may be particularly appealing to those who have recently moved up in status, for it allows self-congratulation upon arrival and the assumption of having gained a secure middle-class status for one's children. Further, for those who think "too much emphasis" is placed on issues of race in American society, a stress on class assimilation is appealing. Such a perspective is highly congruent with the notion of America as an open and economic mobile system with rewards for "those who want to work." It allows for the celebration of the economic and political system when mobility does occur and the opportunity to blame the poor for remaining poor.

6. To my knowledge, only one school system in the country has sought to eliminate class-segregated schools and integrate on the basis of socioeconomic criteria. One account of the formulation of the plan for Duluth, Minnesota, is in *Saturday Review of Education*, May 27, 1972. At the last moment the plan was canceled because of resistance from the elites in the community. There was an unwillingness to accept 30 percent as the proportion of low-income children to be brought into the middle- and upper-income schools. The plan remains unimplemented at this writing.

Integration as Class Pluralism

The notion of class pluralism is the least likely of any alternatives to find proponents and, consequently, is the least likely to be inferred as a meaning of integration; for in recognizing class-based differences, one must deal not only with the middle- and upper-class value systems, but with that of the poor as well. Such a perspective necessitates a legitimation of the values, attitudes, and culture of the poor — and in a society premised on economic mobility, poverty is a sign of failure, not of simply being different. Few parents or teachers would urge class pluralism, for the suggestion that lower-class children should have pride in their poverty and lack of resources is so completely antithetical to the commonsense notions of reality held by most Americans, white and nonwhite, that to opt for class pluralism as a model for school integration would be to invite disbelief and outright hostility.

In the now famous exchange between F. Scott Fitzgerald and Ernest Hemingway, Fitzgerald is said to have said, "The rich are different from you and me." Hemingway replied, "Yes, they have more money." To opt for class pluralism is to opt for Fitzgerald. If the rich are different, are the poor different also? To say they are implies that America is a multicultural system with a distinct lower-class culture. To say they are not negates notions of class pluralism and implies a unified value system with some persons in a less advantageous position to act on those values.

To grant that the poor possess a distinctive lower-class culture is not enough to achieve class pluralism in an integration program. There would have to be an affirmation of that culture and the desire to transmit it to one's children through the formal socialization processes of schooling. That will not happen. The desire, if not for one's self, then for one's children, to "get ahead" and to "make it" supersedes any notion in American society of the legitimacy of lower-class culture. Any effort to affirm lower-class culture would be interpreted by many poor persons as an attempt by the affluent to refuse poor children full opportunity — it would imply that the affluent are content for the poor to be contented.

DESIGN OF THIS STUDY

What follows is an account of an urban, middle-class white school during its first year of racial integration, 1973-74. Each day approximately thirty black students from the black community were bused to and from the school. The school had a white enrollment of approximately five hundred, and in the decade before busing began, there had been no black children in the school. There had, however, been a single black teacher at the school in the early 1960s. One black aide was added to the staff with the advent of the busing program.

From the four alternative definitions of school integration outlined above, this school clearly opted for a model of integration based on racial assimilation: few black students, no modifications in the curriculum, an emphasis by the principal and teachers that "those kids want what out kids want," and a pride by teachers and white parents alike that "none of the children ever talk about any of the students being black."

To observe the process by which a school institutes an integration program based on racial assimilation (or any of the other three alternatives), it is necessary to make oneself a part of the school and classroom milieu. The realities of a school and its classrooms involve the behavior of its participants as well as their attitudes, values, beliefs, and notions of self and others. One cannot discover how either staff or students view the world and how such views relate to their interactions with others by relying exclusively on abstracted measures of aptitude, attitude, or behavior. It is by juxtaposing beliefs and behaviors that the complexities of the educational process are most adequately elucidated. Further, it is important that the educational experiences for teachers and pupils alike be examined as a temporal process. A teacher spends nearly one thousand hours with his or her students during the course of the school year. Such intensive and continual interaction within the confines of a single room results in the development of an internal order and logic that only becomes apparent to those who make themselves a part of that classroom.

In its broadest scope, this study involved data collection from June 1973 to June 1974 through participant and nonparticipant observation as well as through interviewing, sociometric analysis, and the use of school records. A total of 175 classroom observations were made through the school year by the principal investigator and a graduate assistant in first- third- and fourth-grade classes. These observations varied by time of day, day of the week, and length of observation, with participation ranging from thirty-five minutes to the complete school day. During all the formal classroom observations, a handwritten account was kept of classroom interaction and activity. No mechanical devices were used to record classroom activities.

In addition to the classroom activities of the teachers and students, observations were also made of conversations in the teachers' lounge, at meetings of the Parent-Teacher Association (PTA), on field trips with the students, during special assemblies in the school, library periods, recess and noon recreation periods, in the halls between classes, and during the teachers' lunch periods. Interviews were conducted periodically with both teachers and the principal. Sociometric questionnaires were administered to the students during the fall and again at the end of the school year. The teachers also completed sociometric questionnaires in the fall on how they thought the students would respond to the same questions. Interviews were conducted in the fall and again at the end of school with the parents of many of the black students. The circumstances of the extra-classroom observations dictated whether notes could be made during the activity. Field trips and lunch with the teachers prevented note taking; but meetings of the PTA and school assemblies presented no difficulties. In those instances when note taking was not possible concurrent with the activity, notes were made as soon afterward as possible.

It would perhaps be well to clarify what benefits can be derived from the longitudinal and detailed study of one school and specific classes within it. The single most apparent weakness of the vast majority of studies on urban education is that they are episodic. The data that studies of this type generate are more like a single photograph than a film. There is little if any focus on process, but great concentration on products. Further, where direct classroom observations have been made, they have frequently been quite short in duration; Smith and Geoffrey (1968) completed their study in one semester, Leacock (1969) in four months, and Eddy (1967) in three months.

Second, the complexities of a school and its classrooms cannot be reduced to the evaluation of measurement scores, even if made over time. The reduction of classroom interactions and the belief systems of its participants to test results may do great injustice to the reality of the actual events. (Statistical realities do not necessarily coincide with cultural realities.) Finally, it is only with long-term participation in a social system such as the school that one becomes aware of subtle nuances, brief references that have meaning only within that system, gaps between the professed and actual, and disparities between official and unofficial pronouncements. To share gossip, frustrations, and discussions of the way things "really are" provides a dimension to the study of a school that is simply not possible without participation in the life of that school.

There is a legitimate concern about the degree to which one can generalize from data gathered in one school to other schools in the same city, to other urban schools in the nation, and to the process of schooling itself. The school reported upon in this study was selected by an official in the subdistrict where the school was located. The only criteria he was asked to follow in selecting the school were that it be in its first year of integration and that it be predominantly white. Several schools in the subdistrict met these constraints. The willingness of the principal at the school ultimately selected to allow the study appeared to be the deciding factor. It is difficult to know how the school in this study does or does not resemble other middle-class white schools across the country, for little such ethnographic work has been done in other schools. Perhaps the study that gives the most complete data on a middle-class white school is that of Leacock (1969). In comparison with the school described by Leacock, the school studied here does not appear to vary significantly (though it is older and has almost four hundred fewer students.) Both schools demonstrated approximately the same reading achievement scores at the sixth-grade level (7.7 for the Leacock school and 7.0 for the Portland school).

There are admitted limitations in the use of participant and nonparticipant observation as the major methodological technique in the study of schooling. Sample size is necessarily small, replication difficult, and the basis for generalizations limited. But benefits, accrue from the development of an extensive case history and the accumulation of large amounts of data on selected subjects; and what generalizations do emerge from a study of high specificity are grounded in the similarity of that sample to others removed in both time and place. Ultimately, one must choose a methodological approach that best suits the problem at hand. Direct observation seemed best suited to describing the reality of an urban school working through its first year of integration.

In a funnellike fashion, the following chapters describe that process of integration. Chapter 1 focuses on the city school system and Chapter 2 on the school itself, its social and cultural milieu as well as the approach it took to the presence of black children in the classrooms for the first time. Chapter 3 describes the first days of the school year with a particular focus on one classroom. Chapter 4 looks at several other classrooms and follows them through the fall. In Chapter 5 the ongoing patterns of interaction in the school are examined (as well as others that were disrupted) and the children are followed until the end of the first semester. Chapter 6 describes the persistent processes during the second semester and the decisions teachers made on promotion and retention during the last days of school. In the final chapter, the merits and liabilities of the approach the school took toward integration are discussed and an epilogue outlines the broader implications for social policy and further research endeavors.

1.

Schools in Portland: One-Way Integration

Individual classrooms in any school do not exist in a social, cultural, or political vacuum. They are tied in innumerable ways to the teachers and activities of other classrooms, to administrators and their policies, as well as to the larger school system of which they are one small unit. Though it has been in vogue for some time to tell "horror stories" of what children face in schools, particularly in urban schools, scant attention has been paid to an understanding of the school or to the system in which such abuse occurs. By ignoring these two additional levels of influence on the child, and focusing exclusively on the classroom, some recent studies leave unexplicated the bureaucratic, cultural, and political properties of the schooling process. What follows in this chapter is an attempt to elucidate important aspects of the Portland school system that ultimately impinged on the classroom situation itself. By this graduate funneling process of moving from the macro to the micro level of analysis, one can arrive at a study of individual classrooms with the context of larger systems.

DEFINITION OF THE PROBLEM

In Portland, in contrast to many northern and western cities, the growth of the black population has been slow and small. In

1940, the black population was 1,931; in 1950 it was 9,529; in 1960 it was 13,240; and in 1970 it was 22,110. Though in absolute numbers this increase is 20,000 in the past thirty years, as a percentage of the city population, the black community has never been more than a small part. In 1960, the black community was 4.2 percent of the city population (372,298), and in 1970, the percentage was 5.6 in a city population of 383,300. One other demographic characteristic of Portland of interest here is that during the past thirty years the white population in the city has steadily increased, as opposed to the more general trend of a decline in the number of whites in northern cities.[1]

The slow growth of the black community in Portland has been reflected in the schools. In 1940 only one of the fifty-five elementary schools in the city reached a black enrollment of 10 percent. Five other schools had black enrollments of less than 5 percent, and all the remaining schools had less than 1 percent or none. In 1950, six elementary schools had a 5 percent or higher black enrollment. The highest percentage was 45. By 1960, six of the ninety-two elementary schools in the city enrolled 75 percent of all black pupils, and those six schools had black student percentages ranging between 96 and 48. Between 1960 and 1970, the number of schools with more than 48 percent black enrollment grew to nine, and there were eighteen schools with more than a 10 percent black enrollment. At the same time there were sixty-nine schools with 0 to 5 percent black enrollment. (Among the forty private and parochial elementary schools in the city, there were 299 (3.17 percent) black students enrolled in fall 1972; 253 of them were in the Catholic parochial system.) In 1966-67, there were 4,649 (8.5 percent) black students within a citywide elementary enrollment of 54,812; in 1971-72 there were 5,029 (10.3 percent) black students among a total of 48,833 elementary students.

Gittell and Hollander (1968) suggest that an important indicator of a school system's willingness to innovate in the face of changes in the composition of the student body, and, more fun-

1. As only one example, the city of St. Louis, Missouri, lost 326,000 white residents between 1950 and 1970, a figure nearly equivalent to the entire population of Portland, Oregon.

damentally, changes in the very character of the community, is whether the school system will allow independent study and evaluation of its policies and practices. The more study and evaluation the system allows, the more open and concerned those in decision-making positions are considered to be. The Portland system would rank as a very open system if the following analysis is substantially correct. In 1963, the Portland school board created a blue ribbon committee of elite and influential citizens in the community and charged it to determine the following:

1. Does the Portland school district, to any extent, deprive the children of one race of education opportunities equal to those of other races? If so, what corrective steps should be taken?
2. What might be done to improve achievement of students in culturally deprived areas of the city in meeting the educational objectives of this school system?
3. What might the school system do through its educational processes to eliminate unreasoned prejudice in the minds of children of one race against persons of another race?

The Committee on Race and Education submitted its report to the Board of Education in the fall of 1964. It would be well to focus on the findings and recommendations of this report, for the board and administrators of the public school system appear to have been strongly influenced by the report, and the broad outlines of subsequent school policy for at least a decade are found in it. Thus, it is no overstatement to say that the conditions found in the elementary school studied here stemmed, in part, from the implementation of recommendations within this report.

The committee began with a statement of what was held as a "virtual unanimity of opinion." The key statement was: "Racial integration will have been achieved when citizens of all races shall have been assimilated into the educational, cultural, social, political, and economic spheres of life. This, for many Negroes, remains a goal unattained. The quest for racial assimilation parallels the one-time goal of ethnic integration, which has been virtually accomplished in our community" (1964:11). The committee also indicated their unanimous agreement with the statement that a concentration of black students in some few schools was "inimical to the furtherance of racial integration," and said that such conditions should be overcome with leadership and equal access to opportunities and services. But the committee noted that they could not agree on the means to further racial integration or on the appropriate efforts to be undertaken by both private and public agencies.

The report continued with a reiteration of the general policies of the school system, including support for neighborhood schools, restricted options for transfers between schools, a centrally controlled curriculum essentially the same for all schools, and the hiring of minority staff. For the following 120 pages, or half the report, there is an exploration of the problems facing disadvantaged schools, which are defined as serving large numbers of disadvantaged children living in disadvantaged neighborhoods. The tone of the report is strongly oriented toward a "culture of poverty" hypothesis, and there is frequent and favorable reference to the work of Martin Deutsch, Frank Riessman, and David Ausubel, three major proponents of that position. Sprinkled throughout this section of the report are statements like the following:

> The basic Albina [name of black area in city] problem is that respect for education and close-knit families is not the prevalent condition. (p. 54)
> There is an indication that the mean achievement of Negro children in Portland schools is lower than the performance of white children in the same schools. (p. 77)
> The mean achievement of Negro children in the lowest predominantly Negro disadvantaged schools is lower than the mean achievement of white children in the lowest predominantly white disadvantaged schools, even when the socio-economic background of the Negro and white children is substantially the same. It would appear, however, that the common denominator for low scoring, low achieving children, whether white or Negro, is a depressed socio-economic environment. (pp. 77-78)
> Disadvantaged schools in an urban area, then, occur where substantial numbers of children come from the lower end of the social and economic scale. These schools present unique

and serious educational problems to the school system. In many cases the children that these schools are receiving are not competitive with children in other schools within the school system. Such children do not respond to conventional teaching methods and conventional curriculum which is employed in higher socio-economic schools. (p. 85)

Having established what it thought to be the problems facing black and low-income children, the report turned to a series of proposals to ameliorate the described conditions. The first area to be examined was the transportation of black and white children to achieve integrated schools. It decided that such programs were often "educationally invalid" and that "racial considerations must not be the sole criterion for educational decisions, or for desegregation decisions" (p. 187). Thus, support was forthcoming for retaining the neighborhood school concept: "In general the concept of the neighborhood school is sound and preferable to any other system which has been suggested for the organization of school student populations. Experience elsewhere has demonstrated that indiscriminate dispersal of children on a quota basis is questionable educational policy as well as disruptive of school organization" (p. 195).

How, then, the committee considered, could integration occur? Would not present patterns of racial separation continue? No, said the report, for: "It is fortunate that the Negro wants to participate more fully in the mainstream of American life, rather than maintain a relatively separate existence in opposition to the values and goals of that greater society. Because the school has been successful in this role before, because the school reaches substantially every person in our land, because it reaches us when we are forming our first impressions of the world around us, the schools have a vital role to play in the assimilation process" (p. 187).

The answer was not to be found in planned attempts to integrate, because "widespread transfer on a quota basis could result in educationally unsound groupings, not simply of race, but more critically of economic and education-readiness groups, and would result in more educational and social difficulties and intergroup tensions than now exist" (p. 194). Rather, the answer lay in offering the "opportunity for both Negro and white parents to transfer their children voluntarily from their neighborhood school to fill existing vacancies in other schools [and such opportunities] should produce favorable contacts between children of different races or different backgrounds on an individual and personal basis" (p. 196). The report stipulated, however, that space must be available in the receiving school before a transfer could take place and, further, that the parents were to assume "responsibility for the child's transportation and attendance."

For those low-income white and black children who did not voluntarily transfer to a middle-income school, the report suggested the creation of at least six "model schools" that would address themselves directly to the conditions of culturally disadvantaged children. These schools would have additional teaching personnel, a full-time nurse, a revised curriculum, community agents, preschool programs, vocational counselors, and administrative autonomy.

The Portland school board accepted the report almost *in toto*, and began to plan immediately for the implementation of its recommendations. A voluntary transfer program was begun in the fall of 1965 with approximately two hundred elementary black students providing their own transportation to attend white schools. (Not until the beginning of the third year of the program was the cost of transportation paid for by the school system.) Plans were adopted for the creation of the "model schools." These schools, relying on large amounts of Title I funding from the federal government, were in operation from 1965 to 1970. In 1970, a new decentralization plan was implemented that resulted in the elimination of the model schools district and the dispersal of these schools into newly established districts. They did, however, continue to receive Title I funding.

THE ADMINISTRATIVE TRANSFER PROGRAM: PORTLAND'S INTEGRATION STRATEGY

Lack of pressure from federal court decisions and adherence to the neighborhood school concept have meant that the voluntary desegregation program in Portland has achieved only partial success. It has been partial because the school system has relied exclusively on attempts to disperse black students away from predominantly black schools. And though the number of black students participating in the voluntary program has increased each year, the net effect on the twelve predominantly black elementary schools has been to reduce their absolute numbers of students, while making only marginal reductions in the percentages of remaining blacks. Thus, for example, in 1966-67, 58 percent of all black elementary school students were in schools with more than 50 percent black enrollment. Another 10 percent were in schools with black enrollments between 25 and 49 percent. Seven years later, when the voluntary program was transporting a full quarter of all black elementary students in the city (26 percent), 44 percent of all black elementary school students were still in schools with black majorities, and another 7 percent were in schools with black student enrollments of 25-49 percent. (During the 1974-75 school year, 11 percent of the total 66,402 students in the public schools were black, and 11 percent of the elementary school students were black). In 1971-72, there were approximately 700 black elementary and secondary students involved in the transfer program; in 1972-73 the figure was nearly 1,000 students higher with 1,682 participating; in 1973-74, the year of this study, 1,962 students were participating (1,420 elementary, 455 secondary, and 87 in suburban school districts.)

A program for desegregating schools that falls entirely on the shoulders of the black community—black parents having to volunteer their children for busing to predominantly white schools—can carry a school system only so far. The first and most immediate issue is: What happens when no more black parents volunteer their children for the program? Does desegregation end? Do white parents carry the load for a while? Do the courts step in to establish quotas? It may be that the current program is near the end of the road, and such questions will be of more than hypothetical interest. Though the school administration sought and anticipated 460 new black students for the program in 1973-74, the actual number of black children who joined was closer to 280.

The second and more long-term implication of such a program is that ultimately there could no longer exist viable neighborhood schools in the black community. Thus, the neighborhood school concept espoused by school officials would work in white neighborhoods, but not in black ones. And if the administrators continue to support both the neighborhood school concept and school integration simultaneously, a collision of these irreconcilable forces appears inevitable.

That Portland has not yet come to that point appears to be the result of the school administration's policy of allowing the black community to have it two ways, but at a price. The black community can opt for as much school integration as they are willing to volunteer for, at the expense of not having neighborhood schools. Alternatively, black people in Portland can have as many neighborhood schools as they wish, but at the expense of not having school integration. The black community, however, cannot simultaneously have it both ways as does the white community. Yet, giving these choices to the black community appears to have defused both potential integration and potential neighborhood school controversies.

But things are not always as they appear. If, for example, black parents demanded that one white child come into the black community schools for each black child that left to attend a white school, a stormy battle could ensue, for then the white community would be integrally involved in the school integration issue. The dispersal of black students presents no threat to the white community and its neighborhood schools, for no more than 45 black students have been bused to any single white elementary school. In fact, some white schools of 400 and 500 pupils during the 1972-73 school year received as few as 10 or 15 students, and one white school of nearly 400 pupils received only 4 black students. The tactic of the school administration has been to be discreet and keep the numbers low. But in addition to all this, perhaps the most critical element contributing to the present sense of calm is that white parents have been able to keep their children off the buses. In the Portland schools, black people come to white people for integration, not vice versa. Some hard moral and political questions have yet to be confronted in the white community.

But even if the questions have not been asked in the white community, it appears that the school administration is already providing some purely political answers. The policies of the school system do as little as possible to antagonize a 96 percent white majority for the sake of a 4 percent black minority, perhaps largely because the system is heavily dependent on that majority for both financial and political support. For the white community, the costs are low and the benefits high. Thus, the necessary political compromises are made and the system persists. Black people get some of what they desire, as do white people, but for the former the price is higher. At this juncture one confronts a major reality of American schooling, the political overriding the pedagogical.

ALTERNATIVE INTEGRATION STRATEGIES: THE PATHS NOT TAKEN

In October of 1971, at the beginning of the seventh year of the voluntary one-way busing program in Portland, a confidential report entitled "Portland Schools and Integration — Some Alternatives" was circulated among top administrators of the school system. The report included seven "basic alternatives" and two "supplementary plans" suggested as "the most viable alternatives at this time for largely ending *de facto* segregation in the Portland schools, and for the improvement of educational experiences that are essential to the ultimate development of racial understanding and harmony in the community" (p. 4).

The report spelled out the problem facing the Portland schools in 1971 as follows:

> The dimensions of the problem of desegregation facing this District are quite different in magnitude but not in importance from those common in many large cities. Many cities have concentrations of minority students in excess of 60% in a large percentage of their schools and would be envious of the logistic potential for desegregation involving relatively few of our

schools. Nevertheless, Portland's problems are real, and are regarded by present Board policy as critical in all instances where there is more than 23% minority student enrollment. (p.4)

And summarizing the current efforts of the school system to overcome *de facto* racial isolation, the report stated: "Beyond the contributions of Early Childhood Centers and the possible contribution of Middle Schools [the plan for Middle Schools was subsequently voted down by the voters] to desegregation, *the District's administrative transfer program for all grades has been the primary instrument for improving racial balance in the schools. That transfer program is limited in effectiveness as an instrument for achieving total integration because of its voluntary nature"* (p.5; emphasis added).

The report suggested as the seven basic alternatives:

1. K-8 clustering with 12-month year.
2. K-8 two-way interchange, regular school year.
3. K-9 random interchange, 12-month year.
4. 6-8 one way exchange, regular and 12-month year.
5. 6-8 two-way interchange.
6. K-5 class interchange.
7. 9-12 closing Jefferson High School or making it an alternative facility.

The two supplementary plans were:

1. Voluntary transfer grades K through 5.
2. Voluntary transfer from those schools with concentrations of minority students greater than the city average to schools where space exists at the appropriate grade levels, grades 6 through 12.

For each of the seven basic alternatives the report first discussed the approach in general terms, then gave specific examples of how it might be implemented, and finally listed its advantages and disadvantages. For example, considering approach number two, K-8 two-way interchange, regular school year, the report notes: "A K-8 interchange would disperse black students from schools with black enrollment in excess of 25%, and replace these students in equal numbers with white students. Since building capacities are not a factor in a one-for-one interchange plan there are countless possible solutions all of which carry the same set of advantages and disadvantages. This is a common desegregation approach used by districts acting within short time restrictions" (p. 12). The specifics of this alternative were then laid out. In 1971, implementing this option of ensuring no school had more than a 25 percent black enrollment would necessitate the busing of 2,008 black students and their replacement with an equal number of white students. With the support of state funds and the use of school-owned buses, it was estimated this program would cost approximately $186,000. (It ranks fourth of the seven in total cost). Finally, both the advantages and disadvantages were listed:

Advantages
1. It achieves a change in racial distribution in all schools with the transfer program without disrupting the total enrollment in any school.
2. It can be achieved in a very short time with a minimum number of changes in buildings or programs.
3. It is the least costly of any nine-month school year alternative. The only significant costs are transportation expenses which are partly offset by State and Federal funds.
4. It distributes the burden of lost time and distance between black and white students in approximately equal shares.

Disadvantages
1. The logistics of bus scheduling are more complex since the optimum use of buses is counter to the ideal time for student arrival and departure at school.
2. It is likely to meet considerable community opposition.

At the end of the report, several paragraphs were devoted to the two supplementary program proposals involving transfers. They essentially summarized the shortcomings of the administrative transfer program that had been in effect since the fall of 1965.

It is the present policy of the District, in seeking to assure the best educational opportunities for all students, to encourage students to transfer on a voluntary basis to and from schools in a manner which increases the heterogeneity of student populations according to racial, ethnic, social and economic factors in each school. This voluntary transfer program has involved over the years approximately 600 students and continues now to involve 611 students. *However, though this program is making a contribution in this area, it is clearly inadequate when it continues to involve, in spite of the promotional efforts of administrators and community agents, only about 8% of the black population.* Though this transfer program is effective in encouraging small numbers of isolated black students to attend schools that are not impacted, *it is clearly not in and of itself an answer.* It should be used, however, in a manner supplementing other alternatives for desegregation. (p. 29; emphasis added)

Because the report was and remains confidential, there is no public record of the discussion among school administrators about the merits and liabilities of various strategies. Thus, one can only surmise from their subsequent actions how the administrators responded. Their actions suggest several conclusions:

1. No new initiatives were undertaken that would involve the transportation of a single white pupil. Alternatively stated, there has been no movement to implement any of the first six basic alternatives.

2. There was a decision to implement alternative seven, the transformation by the beginning of the 1974-75 academic year of Jefferson High School from a general curriculum high school to one specializing in the fine arts and communications. It was hoped in this way to draw students from throughout the city. Jefferson had been the high school with the largest concentration of black students (41 percent in 1972-73). Black students in attendance before this shift in emphasis could either remain or choose another high school. The hope appeared to be that some black students would leave and some white students would come, both factors working to reduce the percentage of black students in the school.

3. In spite of the reservations expressed in the report about the effectiveness of voluntary transfers as a means to achieve integra-

tion, the school administration reaffirmed voluntary transfers as the major effort to integrate elementary schools. In fact, the administrators not only affirmed the transfer program, but decided to expand it greatly. In the summer of 1972, the school system hired a number of persons to go into the black community and gain new recruits for the program.[2] In the fall of that academic year (1972-73) the program was expanded by more than 1,000 additional black students.

TITLE VII FUNDING: A BASIS FOR A NEW INITIATIVE

For a number of years, the Congress of the United States has been grappling with the issue of school integration. Each legislative session finds bills and amendments being offered, for example, to limit the use of busing to achieve school integration, or to abolish busing altogether, or to establish barriers that would hinder the effectiveness of federal court rulings. The outcomes of the struggles in Congress have resulted in a number of pieces of compromise legislation.

One of particular interest here is the passage by the 92nd Congress and approval by the President in 1973 of the Emergency School Aid Act (P.L. 92-318). This legislation essentially employed a "carrot" philosophy for achieving integration by giving large sums of money to those school systems that were integrating their schools. The funds were to provide remedial and basic skills assistance in the newly integrated schools, not only for the black children who would be coming, but for the white children already there. The funds could not be used for the transportation of pupils, nor could they be used for programs in racially separate

---

2. By a fortunate circumstance, one of these recruiters subsequently enrolled in one of my classes. She indicated to me that she was given a quota to fill for the transfer program. Though she said she had had no difficulty in finding students, some recruiters did, and resorted to such tactics as telling black parents there was no longer room for their children in the black community schools and that they, the parents, had to sign up their children for the transfer program. In my own interviews in the black community, I found two families who said that was the story they were told and why they had put their children in the transfer program. I only learned of this at the end of the school year, and when I told the parents they had the right to send their children back to the black community school if they wished, neither family indicated they wanted to.

schools. Essentially, the legislation financially rewarded school systems opting to integrate. In Portland, the funds all flowed into white receiving schools.

The voluntary program under way in Portland fit the guidelines established by the legislation; thus, in the summer of 1973, Portland received $449,000 for the 1973-74 school year. The sum equaled approximately $375 for each of 643 black children in the transfer program and each of 575 white children in receiving schools.[3] As the figures would suggest, not all the black transfer children or all the white children in receiving schools were involved. The program's emphasis on providing remedial and basic skills instruction meant that only those children who scored low on one or more standardized tests were assisted. A brochure on the program called it "desegregating for equal educational opportunity," and described its goals as:

1. To improve the basic skills among academically disadvantaged students and to provide basic skills and remedial instruction for receiving schools in the voluntary Administrative Transfer Program.
2. To develop in teachers and administrators the skills necessary for delivering instruction in the basic skills to children from educationally diverse backgrounds and for management of interracial conflict situations.
3. To assist in the development of parental skills necessary to function effectively in support of their children's educational development in the home and the school.

To achieve the first of these goals, 83 percent of the funding was allocated to establish "skill centers" in twenty-five of the fifty-nine white elementary schools receiving transfer students. Each of these centers employed full-time "instructional specialists" to work with children designated as in need of help with basic skills. Federal guidelines also stipulated that no child could spend more than 25 percent of the school day in such centers and that none of

3. For the 1974-1975 school year, nearly $600,000 was requested in Title VII funding. The $150,000 increase was to be used for the creation of skill centers in the receiving high schools. However, the request was denied, and federal funding was set at $378,017 for the academic year.

the skill classes could be racially segregated. Both regulations hindered any attempt at resegregation within the receiving school. In each of the remaining receiving schools, one teacher was designated as either a "half-time specialist" or as an "extended responsibility specialist." In the former instance, the teacher was to be released from regular teaching responsibilities for a half day to teach those children qualifying for assistance with basic skills. In the latter, teachers were not released from any regular teaching duties but were paid $600 in additional salary and were allowed to have a paid substitute in their classroom for ten days each year so that they could work with individual children and assist the principal with the transfer program. For the two remaining goals of the program, 17 percent of the monies were divided between staff training (9 percent) and working with parents (8 percent). The observers for this study had no contact with attempts at generating parent effectiveness, but an in-session teacher-training program to create "cultural awareness" was observed and will be discussed in later chapters.

The importance that the Portland school administrators attributed to this new program was underscored by the calling of a citywide conference on August 30, 1973. Administrators, principals, some teachers, and special instructional staff from the fifty-nine receiving schools attended. In addition to viewing two films and participating in small group discussions, the conference heard presentations on the origins of the program, its goals, what administrative and instructional staff were to be involved, and finally, how the superintendent himself viewed the program. His comments are of interest, not only for what he chose to emphasize, but also as an example of how the political in Washington, D.C., becomes the pedagogical in Portland, Oregon. My notes summarized his presentation as follows:

> The superintendent began with a review of the funding and the number of elementary schools to be involved. Quickly, though, he shifted emphasis and began to discuss intergroup relations. He said that intergroup relations are important in urban America and that for any educational professional not to have some knowledge of how to deal with intergroup rela-

tions in a "pluralistic America" is tantamount to being incompetent. That is why conferences such as the present one are important, so that educators can become aware of the dynamics of intergroup relations and gain sensitivity to the problems that will emerge between blacks and whites in the transfer program. He said he thought Title VII important because it has the advantage of "dealing with concrete educational problems. If children have reading difficulties, Title VII is providing funds to work at those difficulties." With Title VII, he suggested, the issue is no longer black and white, but simply children who need assistance. Thus, a program of this type will allow children to "grow with their human relations when they are no longer held back with educational deficiencies." He told the group he thought it important to stress to the white receiving schools that many of the black children who will be attending them will not need the assistance of the skill centers, for they are "competent, capable and will have no difficulty holding their own with white students." Funding such as Title VII, he notes, has enabled Portland to "turn the corner on a number of the problems facing the schools."

BUSING WHITE CHILDREN INTO BLACK SCHOOLS: THE PORTLAND CONTROVERSY

During 1973-74 there was one major dispute that arose within the city over the issue of school busing. It began with an account in the city's largest daily newspaper of an interview with the white principal of Boise School, an elementary school with a 90 percent black enrollment.[4] The reporter was examining the effects of the Administrative Transfer Program on the predominantly black sending schools, particularly the impact the reduction in enrollment due to the busing of black children had had on Boise School. In the course of the interview, the reporter asked the principal whether the exodus each day of 200 black students to white schools would now allow white students to come into the school to fill those empty seats. The principal commented:

The idea of busing white kids in here is unthinkable. They would get eaten alive. [This school has a strong pecking order

4. The name of this school, Boise School, is not a pseudonym. Since the controversy is a part of the public record, anonymity was not deemed necessary.

in which physical prowess and the ability to socialize according to the rule of urban Black culture are the main determinants of status. Most white students, even those who are strong enough to defend themselves physically, aren't used to the social rituals of a Black school—the dancing, the clothing, the jive. Whites may be accepted, but they do not become leaders.][5] A white kid cannot excel here. In fact, we've had several requests from white parents to have their kids bused out, which we can't do. (*The Oregonian*, September 24, 1973)

The roof fell in. There were immediate cries of racism from black parents, the local chapter of the NAACP, and the black press. A resolution calling for the principal's resignation was endorsed by at least seven organizations active in the black community. The superintendent of the Portland public schools and a member of the school board both publicly "completely disavowed" the principal's remarks. An investigation of what he "actually" said was begun by school officials, and there were hints he should resign to restore "public confidence in the schools."

On the surface, much of the controversy surrounded the language the principal used—"They would get eaten alive." The crux of the matter, though, was not what he said but what he implied—that black schools were not like white schools and that the talk of busing white children into black schools meant the sacrifice of white children at the altar of "urban black culture." People took from the principal's comments what suited them and responded accordingly: whites who wanted no two-way busing; blacks who believed there are no "real" differences between blacks and whites; school officials who hoped to avoid federal mandatory regulations by supporting a voluntary program of allowing blacks, but not whites, to be bused; white parents in the receiving schools who wondered what was happening in their neighborhood school with the black children who were being bused in; and the black parents from the principal's own school who denied that they or their children possessed any distinctive black culture that meant white children had to fear for their

5. The material inside the brackets was not in quotes, as were the first two and last two sentences. From the context, it appears to be a paraphrasing by the reporter of further comments by the principal, but this is not certain.

physical safety. Over and above all this, the black community newspaper condemned the principal for the "glorification of the seamier side of ghetto culture" (*The Portland Observer,* September 27, 1973).

Having slowly twisted in the wind for several months, the principal held to his position. He was able to muster some support in the black community, and the school administrators decided that the "incident does not indicate he should be transferred from his post" (*The Portland Observer,* October 11, 1973). Although school officials seemingly took the stance that the interview was best interpreted as a "nonevent" that never really happened, for a brief moment it was possible in this controversy to view the schisms that are continually defined and denied, to observe contending positions argued with passion, and to see the subtlety of ideology emerge from under the rocks of objectivity. A closer look is in order.

The events unfolded as follows:

September 24, 1973

ITEM: The principal of Boise Elementary School in Portland gives an interview to the larger of the two daily newspapers, *The Oregonian.* The article explores what has happened to this school since it has lost over 200 black students who are being bused to receiving white schools. The article is encouraging when it describes what can now happen at Boise School with no overcrowding and the resultant drop in student-teacher ratios. The consequences are described as higher levels of teacher-pupil interaction in smaller classes. The question is posed to the principal whether the decrease in the total number of students would open opportunities for whites to be bused into Boise School to achieve more integration. His answer was that given above.

September 25

ITEM: The following day in the same newspaper a report is given of the meeting of the Portland school board the prior evening. The article is entitled "Removal of Boise Principal Urged over 'Racist' Remarks." The president of the Portland NAACP had come to the board meeting and called the remarks of the principal "vindictive, prejudicial and racist." He also called for the principal's ouster. In response, the board members noted the issue was a "personnel matter," but both the superintendent and a board member said that they joined the president of the NAACP in "completely disavowing" the principal's remarks. The superintendent also said that the comments were "extremely re-grettable." The NAACP spokesman said he had received twenty or twenty-five calls from parents angered by the principal's comments.

September 27

ITEM: The black weekly newspaper, *The Portland Observer*, carries as its banner headline "Community Calls for Boise Princi-pal Removal." The article states that members of the black com-munity "reacted violently" to the comments of the principal and demand his immediate resignation. The NAACP representative expanded on his previous remarks at the school board meeting and commented that he had "heard similar comments from George Wallace, members of the KKK, as well as citizens here in Portland."

When asked to comment on the charges and demands for his resignation, the principal said that the article had been correct, but that much of the positive description of the school had been omitted, thus giving a "biased" slant to the picture he wished to portray. He did, however, reaffirm his belief that white students could not excel at Boise because of "the group pressure against learning created by the black students." He added that the stu-dents who do well academically are not accepted by the remain-der of the students and that this pressure is more intense on the white students. Asked why he thought this was the case, he re-sponded that he had not really thought it through, but that it must be the outcome of something "lacking in the home or environment."

A black female aide at the school is also quoted in this article, and she disagrees with the principal. She says that any child who has a "good character and a good home" can achieve at any school. Thus, she feels white children who have these qualifications can excel at Boise.

ITEM: In the middle of the same article, there is boxed in heavy type an announcement that the Portland branches of the Urban League and the NAACP have scheduled a community meeting this same evening to discuss the conditions at the school. The meeting is to be held in Bethel AME Church.

ITEM: The same issue of the black weekly paper carries an editorial calling for the removal of the principal on charges of racism. The editorial claims the principal has "indicted" black students and has attempted the "glorification of the seamier side of ghetto culture." The principal does not demand a "standard of behavior which will enable them to continue in school, or in work, or in the professions of their choice." Instead, "the children are allowed to set their own acceptable standards."

ITEM: The same issue of the paper includes three "Letters to the Editor." Two are highly critical of the principal, one suggesting that he has heightened racial tension and the other implying that he is one of the "bigots insensitive to culturally deprived and underdeveloped communities." The third letter is from a teacher at Boise School who defends the principal and argues that the article containing his initial interview failed to give all the pertinent information. She contends that to assume "children are children" and thereby "ignore the historical and social context" is naive. She adds, "Some white children at Boise appear intimidated, and their apparent weakness compounds their problems of relating in a group in which self defense is important."

September 27

ITEM: The principal at Boise School distributes to his teachers and to a number of community residents a mimeographed letter expressing his apologies for the wording in his interview. Copies of the letter are also sent to the city newspapers. The letter reads as follows:

> In an article on Boise School, there are included several quotes from me that have justifiably outraged the community,

the parents and students and damaged the image of Boise School. While admitting certain key statements, there were other concepts developed in the article for which I am not responsible. In looking back, I realize the words were badly chosen and did not, in fact, convey what I really feel, especially in attributing to Blacks generally the characteristics of some whose behavior we treat affirmatively and actively when it occurs. I must emphasize that defiant behavior is not accepted or condoned by the school staff. I wish to formally apologize to the members of this community and to all concerned citizens. I am more proud of Boise School, its students, its patrons and its staff than any effort in which I have ever been associated. Very Respectfully Yours.

October 1

ITEM: Today *The Oregonian*, which carried the initial interview with the principal, carries his letter of apology.

October 3

ITEM: There is a long article in *The Oregonian* headed "Beleagured Boise Principal Finds Supporters among Parents Who See Deeper Problems." An account is given of a meeting of the Boise Citizens Improvement Association where the principal was "grilled" by community residents and parents of children at Boise School. The outcome of the meeting is described as one where parents and principal alike share a sense of "deeper, more significant issues involved in black-white relations." The article states: "While the principal has the support of many parents and a united staff, it is not at all clear the school administrators are going to forgive his blunt words." The article then suggests five reasons why the principal has been "disavowed":

> They [the administrators] feel the principal is guilty of stereotyping because in talking about the problems at Boise, he gave the impression, they feel, that ALL black children use foul language, behave in a rowdy manner, and refuse to learn.
> The administrators feel [the principal] was patronizing, especially in his admission that teachers at Boise permit some student behavior which might not be tolerated at a white school.

Administrators object to the principal saying whites would face a tough time if they were bused into Boise.

Administrators feel [the principal's comments] provided "Ammo" for racists who oppose the busing program.

The administrators don't say so, but above all they charge the principal with the capital crime of being controversial. The politics of schooling are clear cut. A principal isn't supposed to say controversial things, at least not for the record.[6]

The article deals with each of these five points in turn, essentially calling into question much of the rationale of the administrators. For example, in reference to the third point, the reporter notes that it is somewhat ironical for the administrators to criticize the principal for not giving a positive assessment of busing white students into black schools when they themselves will not undertake such a venture.

October 4

ITEM: The black community newspaper runs another banner headline, "Community United on Ouster of Boise Principal." The accompanying article is an account of the community meeting at the Bethel AME Church the previous week. There a resolution was passed noting, first, that conditions exist at Boise School that require a different principal with a "high degree of teaching and supervisory competence, empathy, insight and sophistication"; that the present principal has "failed to enforce the necessary discipline to make for a quality learning experience"; and that the principal through his choice of words has "reflected adversely on the Black population in the Portland area, subverting school district policy and losing the personal credibility necessary to perform his job." The resolution called for his immediate removal and was signed by seven organizations, including the NAACP, the Urban League, and the Black Ministerial Alliance. The article concluded with the observation that the participants

---

6. The principal of the school in this study told me at the time of this controversy that seeing what had happened to the principal at Boise made him decide never to grant newspaper interviews. He also said that the school administration was "passing the word informally" not to talk to the newspapers.

at the meeting had agreed that "the same educational process and the same opportunities should apply to black students as to white."

ITEM: The same issue of the black newspaper carried an editorial suggesting that the school board had created at Boise a "ghetto school in a district that is ninety percent white . . . a school where a white student can't excel and a Black student doesn't want to." The argument is that while large numbers of black students are bused out, no whites are bused in. Moreover, in the busing out of black students, the best are "creamed off," leaving those with "academic or social problems." The editorial again calls for the resignation of the principal on grounds "of his insensitivity to the needs of Black children."

ITEM: The single entry in the "Letters to the Editor" in this issue of the black newspaper is from the principal. It is his letter of apology previously noted. The newspaper prints "Excuse Me Please" above the letter.

October 11

ITEM: A front-page story in the black newspaper states that the superintendent of schools in Portland has decided to retain the principal in his position. The article recounts the Board of Education meeting that same week. The superintendent, after noting that he had given "careful review" to the matter, said he had decided on the basis of three considerations that the principal would remain. An edited version of his remarks follows: (1) The superintendent and another member of the Board were disavowing the principal's comments to the degree "that careful investigation established his responsibility." They noted as particularly disturbing the stereotyping of all black students as "having a particular urban culture, which is obviously not true," and the inference that instead of correcting "clearly improper behavior," Boise tolerated such behavior, in direct conflict with board politics. (2) The superintendent attributed "two, possibly three, of the unfortunate comments in that article" to the principal. The comments on "a monolithic black culture and tolerance of misbehavior were not made by him." (3) By acknowledging the general accuracy of the article to two news sources, the superintendent said, the principal has demonstrated "responsibility" and also "courage and humility in apologizing to the school and the citizen community."

ITEM: In the same article, the superintendent reflected on "inner city schools" in the aftermath of the controversy at Boise. He said:

> No matter how capable the staff of a particular school, no matter how much is spent by a school district, any school attended by a vast majority of low income children is unsound educationally. Further, it is my social as well as educational conviction that this is especially damaging in the case of a low income school that is also black.
>
> For this reason I have recommended, and the Board has supported the creation of, additional pre-kindergarten through grade 2 early childhood centers in schools such as Boise. I am convinced these centers would attract, voluntarily by reason of their quality, middle class children in sufficient numbers to provide a healthy balance of student enrollment. This would give additional response to those who feel that our administrative transfer program is too much one way.

ITEM: These remarks of the superintendent were not carried in the major daily.

ITEM: The lead editorial in the black paper is for the most part a summary of points of controversy to date. It notes that people are beginning to have second thoughts about their earlier condemnation of the principal, with some factions arguing that he is doing an acceptable job, others that he should be forgiven for his racist remarks, and yet others saying that he is the scapegoat for an entire school system that perpetuates elementary schools with 90 percent black enrollments. The editorial also quotes the superintendent's statement that low-income schools that are also overwhelmingly black are "especially damaging." Thus, the editorial concludes: "This gives the school district two alternatives: close Boise or transfer in an equal number of white upper and middle class children. Black children and their families have borne the burden of the transfer program. Now let the white families share the responsibility to provide an equal educational opportunity for all of Portland's children."

October 18

ITEM: The only relevant comment in the black newspaper is one "Letter to the Editor" from the Boise Citizens Improvement Association in which the principal is thanked for his letter of apology and support is extended to him and his policies at the school.

November 1

ITEM: The black newspaper carries an article written by the only black person on the Board of Education, a woman who is a professor of sociology. The following are pertinent passages from her article:

> However, as a person, especially one deeply committed to public schools in Portland, my immediate reaction was one of anger and outrage that any adult in this system could utter some of the negative remarks in that article. And when he admitted to some of the remarks in that story, it was no comfort that some of the positive remarks were omitted. The principal is guilty of carelessness and insensitivity that shall not go unrecorded. Obviously the principal was aware of that when he made public apology through a letter to the editor plus copies to various members in the community. Such remarks did reflect a bad image of one of our schools, a school where children are enrolled with the promise of being provided a good education.
>
> . . . while my attitude towards his remarks will remain the same, I am satisfied to accept the stance of his staff and parents and the best judgment of the Superintendent, who assures us that he would not hesitate to bring charges against any employee who demonstrates a continuing pattern of incompetence.

November 6

ITEM: *The Portland Public Schools Achievement Profiles* for all elementary and secondary schools in the city are published.

The data are from the 1972-73 academic year. The following are some of the data supplied for Boise School:

Grades: K-8
Enrollment: 404
  white: 20 (4.9%)
  black: 367 (90.6%)
  oriental: 5 (1.2%)
  Spanish American: 4 (1.0%)
  Native American: 9 (2.2%)
Certified Teachers: 29
Administrators: 2
Aides: 6
Average years of experience of staff: 10.4
  white: 30 (83%)
  black: 7 (17%)
Percent student turnover: 12.3%
Ratio of pupils to Certified Teachers: 13.9 to 1
Median family income: $6,121
Percent family incomes under $4,000: 35.6%
Percent of children in welfare families: 73.0%

Grade Four achievement scores: (year equivalents)	City Average
Reading: 2.8	3.4
Math concepts: 3.3	3.9
Math problem solving: 3.3	3.6
Math computation: 3.3	3.6

Grade Eight achievement scores	
Reading: 5.3	7.4
Math concepts: 5.9	7.5
Math problem solving: 5.4	6.6
Math computation: 5.8	7.2

November 15

ITEM: The black community newspaper entitles its lead editorial "Portland Schools Fail Black Students." The editorial discusses the data from the *Achievement Profiles* and notes that when one examines both poor white and poor black schools, the students in the black schools are doing less well. The editorial concludes from this that poor academic performance by black students cannot be attributed to social-class factors, but must be attributed to the "inadequacies of the public school system." "We don't believe the deciding factor is the community, or even the home, for every parent, no matter how poor or deprived, wants an education for his child. The principal of Boise Elementary School said the Boise parents are more cooperative than in any school where he has been assigned—yet he thinks the parents must be blamed for the school's lack of achievement. The time has come for the Portland Public Schools to get down to the business of educating black children."

So what is to be made of this controversy? Was the principal merely a naive white man who used poor imagery? Or was he in fact racist in his expectations about black students? Or did white students face being "eaten alive" in an urban black school? Needless to say, the reaction provoked by the principal had elements of these arguments and many more. What is perhaps even more interesting is what was often avoided and left unsaid in the discussion in Portland of busing children to achieve racial integration. This sequence of events could be interpreted in several ways.

The comments of the principal and his critics suggest that they hold contrasting views of the life and experiences of black people. The principal argued that there did exist a distinctive social system in his school and that it was distinctively black. There a set of norms different from those in middle-income, predominantly white schools governed success and acceptance. Further, if white students came into this school milieu, they would have difficulty, perhaps from physical harassment, but more surely through being denied peer recognition. The principal's critics, however, suggested that there was no basis for arguing that white children faced any threat, for in a school that had sufficient discipline and respect, all children could learn. Thus, for the principal to say white children could not make it was to reflect not on the black students, but on his failure to keep the school in order. In the life and behavior of the black students there was nothing that would make a joint educational experience unattractive to white children.

Of the alternative definitions of integration discussed in the previous chapter, the principal's remarks suggest that he had opted for a racial pluralism approach. Though he thought black and white children could not do well together in his school, this was not because they were so much alike, but because of their differences. For him, black and white children would bring such distinctive and diverse cultural systems into the school that accommodation would be difficult if not impossible. No one would be "eaten alive" if there were a mutually compatible set of behaviors and values for black and white alike. The alternative argument, as posed by the superintendent, was that the integration experience is primarily one of class, not of color. Hence, the superintendent's comment that "any school attended by a vast majority of low income children is unsound educationally" implied the need to integrate these same children into middle- and upper-income schools. The gist of these remarks is to opt for integration as class assimilation. One puts skin color aside and attempts to overcome social-class barriers and handicaps that hinder children who have the same values and aspirations as others, but have not been free to achieve them. From the perspective of the principal, color drags class; from the perspective of the superintendent, class drags color.

What compounds the issue, however, is that it is not an either-or situation. In Boise School, as I suspect one would necessarily find in similar schools, there is an interaction of color and class. In schools like Boise, where some few whites are in attendance and where busing would bring many more, neither class nor color can be ignored. For example, in the black community newspaper the principal was criticized for using racial categories and for the "glorification of the seamier side of ghetto culture." Had he glorified aspects of color or of class, or of both? Is the reverse to imply that there was a healthy side to ghetto culture? How similar might both be to presumably different cultural systems in the white community? Have any of these systems a relation to the comments of the principal about a social hierarchy in his school related less to an emphasis on academic success than to physical survival? One of the letters criticizing the principal mentioned "culturally deprived and underdeveloped communities." What relation do communities of this type have to schools located in their midst, and how is the culture of the community manifested in the culture of the school? Could both white and black schools exist in "culturally deprived and underdeveloped communities"? How would they be similar, or different? The answers are, of course, not easily found. But simply to pose the questions suggests the complexity of juxtaposing color to class in a discussion of school integration.

This controversy ultimately was one of ideology — of alternative ways of defining reality and the nature of the social system. The principal's view may or may not have been correct. It presented an empirical question subject to verification. In a broader context, though, the principal's comments imply that those who conduct research in minority schools need to view those schools in terms of their own internal order and logic, and not in comparison with some assumed absolute from the dominant white society. One must forcefully reject the traditional white perspective of viewing subordinate minorities in general, and black people in particular, as incomplete, as having some white culture, but not grasping it sufficiently to be considered fully cultured and therefore fully human.

The alternative view emphasizing the social-class basis for encouraging school integration has made much of "cultural deprivation," the "culture of poverty," and the "disadvantaged child." This perspective carries a latent message that middle-class children and middle-class schools have more to offer the poor than vice versa, for it is in contact with the culturally "advantaged" that such handicaps can be overcome. At one level, the proponents of this view are persuasive, for as James Coleman has noted (1966:290-325) in the massive *Equality of Educational Opportunity,* low-income children do begin to achieve at a higher rate when placed in classrooms with large numbers of middle-class children (a caveat, though, is that Coleman's measures of achievement are rather narrow, based largely on communications and calculating skills). The danger here is that people may slide from an assessment of educational skills to an assessment of moral worth. The result of such a slide is often a middle-class hegemony, with its officially sanctioned values and a corresponding deprivation of low-income children.

Yet it would be glib and grossly paternalistic to say that those in the black community who opt for integration based on considerations of social class are ultimately experiencing false consciousness. Both middle-class black people and those of the lower class who aspire to the middle class may view the school as the mobility escalator by which to achieve and maintain middle-class status. In these circumstances, the aspirations are not reserved for black people alone. White people as well have looked to the schools as their source of mobility.[7]

The strongest reaction to the principal's statement came from the middle-class segment of the black community. The newspaper and the Urban League joined in demanding his resignation, while the NAACP termed his comments "racist." The principal also was disavowed by some whites, I suspect because he suggested the existence of a black school in the public school system that was not under the control and domain of whites. Further, his comments on busing forced a different interpretation of the current activities of the school administrators. To have recognized a "racially pluralist" model of integration as valid would have meant placing race, as opposed to class, at the heart of the integration debate. This would have necessitated the establishment of means to introduce, legitimate, and institutionalize the black experience in all its diversity—something that Portland administrators have consistently failed to do.

In summary, any interpretation of a school integration program necessarily should be multidimensional; there are issues of ideology, of assumed characteristics of institutions and individ-

7. That schools cannot, as they are presently constituted, increase mobility is what I understand as one of the major conclusions of Jencks's (1972) book, *Inequality*. The classroom has little direct bearing on the activities of the political arena and the economic marketplace, other than, in broad terms, to reinforce the inequalities already there.

uals, and, finally, of the particular mix of color and class specific to the community in question. Further, it is important to be cognizant of the *processes* at work. The principal introduced an element of complexity into the equation on integration that up to that time had been missing in Portland—he juxtaposed color to class and found color the stronger variable.

In a situation of multiple realities and interpretations, what the Urban League may desire as the optimal integration situation may not be the goal of the white superintendent, or of white parents in the receiving schools, or of the low-income black parents whose children are being bused. The fears of parents, whether they be black or white, that their children would be "eaten alive" is an imponderable in any equation, yet it is there and cannot be ignored. For any attempt to do so ultimately implies that the comments of the principal at Boise School were irrelevant—and it is doubtful that any of the participants thought that.

2.

Brush School: Its Social and Cultural Milieu

In an upper-middle income neighborhood of Portland, where the lawns are nicely manicured and the homes spacious, there stands Brush School. The building sits far back from the street and has a large playground in the front and on either side. There are a number of commercial establishments within easy walking distance from the school, but the favorite of the students is an ice cream shop they sometimes sneak away to on their lunch hour. For the seventh- and eighth-grade boys, there is also a nearby restaurant where they go after school to buy cigarettes.

The 1970 Census indicated that there were less than 3 percent nonwhite residents in the tract including Brush School. The racial composition of the school clearly reflects this demographic characteristic, for there had been no black children at the school for at least a decade prior to the beginning of the Administrative Transfer Program in the fall of 1973. Likewise, teachers who had been at the school for as long as fifteen years said that there was only a single black teacher and never a black aide before the transfer program.

What follows is a description of several of the dominant patterns of interaction among the teachers, principal, and parents. Because the life of the school was so closely interwoven with the activities of the parents, considerable attention is paid to them. It is perhaps this ability to superimpose a cultural ethos on the school that distinguishes schools where parents are middle and upper middle class from those where parents are poor and low in status. Further, taking account of parental activities adds an important dimension to analysis of the classrooms, for what happens there cannot be separated from the larger social forces operating in the community.

This chapter will also examine some of the preparations made at Brush for the arrival of black children. The "definition of the situation" provided by these activities gave the staff a perspective from which they could interpret what was to happen at their school. As will become evident as the school year progressed, the early assumptions were held through to the end and never fundamentally changed or challenged. Instead, each new event was interpreted in the light of what had gone before. And in the beginning were the cultural definitions.

The students, a key set of participants, are not examined closely here, because following chapters will focus in depth on life in the classrooms for the students and on how the realities of the system and the school came to impinge upon them.

TEACHER-PARENT RELATIONS

Whereas many urban school districts within the past two decades have witnessed the relatively affluent middle and upper-middle classes leaving city schools for those in the suburbs, in the Brush district the affluent have stayed. Indeed, not only have they stayed, but they have been able to maintain an influence on the school in ways reminiscent of the debates over "community control" of the later 1960s. Here is an urban school where affluent whites chose to remain in the public school system because they felt that the school was responsive to their values and to their aspirations for their children. There were no apparent factors to "push" the parents, in their own view, from the school and perhaps the neighborhood; what is of interest is what "pulled" them into the public school when many of the families could afford the reputedly quite good private and parochial schools in the area.

My first observation of the rapport between parents and teachers took place at an "open house" meeting in late September in the first-grade room of Mrs. Brown. As should be apparent from the following, Mrs. Brown's *professional style* seemed eminently to please the parents. Her discussion of the rationale she used for her patterns of classroom organization, her lecturing to the parents from a child psychology textbook, and her emphasis on instilling self-motivation in the children all seemed consonant with the values of the parents, a group whose affluence and education would make them receptive to a "professional" pedagogical approach. Thus, from a first-grade teacher who spoke to parents with the language of child psychology, to a fourth-grade teacher who cooked a Japanese meal (wok and all) for her entire class and their parents, to the seventh- and eighth-grade music teacher who organized a string quartet, the motif at Brush was one of teacher professionalism and emphasis on the parent's cultural values and interests.

When I entered Mrs. Brown's room at 7:25 P.M., there were perhaps twenty or twenty-five persons, some drinking coffee, others talking informally, and some looking at the children's pictures on the bulletin boards. Shortly, Mrs. Brown said the meeting should begin, and the parents took seats. I counted thirteen women and twelve men, excluding the teacher and myself. Mrs. Brown began a rather long talk, which was to take thirty minutes. She first talked of what she hoped to accomplish with the children during the year: more self-reliance, more self-motivation, an ability to carry out directions by themselves, more sensitivity to social situations, and, finally, how to get along with others in the room. She said she thought she could summarize her goals by saying she wanted a "more developed social maturity" in the children by the end of the year.

She next covered how she organized the class day, indicating that she planned reading and mathematics in the morning, social studies and printing in the afternoon.

She told the parents that in late October she would send home a note to them telling them it was time to make an appointment to come to talk with her about the performance of their child during the first grading period. She said there would be no grades given at the end of the fall quarter. Instead, there would be these teacher-parent meetings. Grades, she added, were really poor indicators of a child's performance so early in the year, because at that point the children had not yet "settled down." Several of the parents nodded approval of these comments.

As Mrs. Brown was talking, the principal came in and sat in the back of the room. He stayed perhaps fifteen minutes and then got up and left. At no time was he introduced by the teacher. (I made a note as he left: "No introduction. Is apparent she has an agenda of her own this evening.")

The lunch program was discussed, and the problem involved in buying more than one lunch ticket at a time was brought up. When the group got to this issue, it sparked some considerable comment from two parents who expressed strong resentment that the school had this year for the first time introduced a chocolate drink to the menu. Both women who spoke indicated that they were going to speak to the principal and district officials as well. Mrs. Brown said she was in no position to do anything about it, but if the parents would send a note saying that they wanted their child to have only white milk, she would order only white milk for them. She encouraged any of the other parents who were upset about the introduction of chocolate drinks to talk to the principal.

Mrs. Brown then told the group she was sure they were interested in her philosophy of teaching and what she thought important to stress in her dealings with the children. She took from the top of her desk a child psychology textbook and told the group it was one of her "very favorite books." I could not see the title from the back of the room, and she did not give it. She began to summarize and lecture from the book. She said that it was important to provide opportunities for the children to experience a positive sense of fulfillment; that there was a need to demonstrate concern and interest in the children; that adults should respect the rate at which children develop and maturate, for each child would be unique; that comparisons between children was often more harmful than beneficial, because each child had the right to be different and to be himself. Finally, she said, she thought it critical that the children experience love and support, because that would give them the sense of self-worth necessary to be "healthy human beings."

What was happening among the parents as she was reading and talking from this textbook startled me. The parents were writing down everything she was saying on anything they could find. One father was writing on the back of a bank deposit slip, another had an envelope out, one mother was using a paper from one of the children's desks. I estimated that at least half of the adults in the room were taking notes. Several times the teacher was asked to repeat herself for the benefit of someone writing down what she had said.

When she had finished, there was a moving incident: One mother stood and said she was pleased her child was in Mrs. Brown's class. She said she hoped Mrs. Brown would not leave Brush School so that in three years her next child could also have her as a teacher. At this, a number of the parents began clapping. Mrs. Brown seemed moved and stood in the front saying nothing, only smiling. Shortly, she dismissed the group, saying that she had talked enough and that the parents were welcome to stay and have coffee, talk with her, and look at the work of their children. When she dismissed the group, not a person left the room.

In most areas, the teachers of Brush School welcomed the interest and enthusiasm of the parents. To have a large number of educated and articulate parents who strongly supported cultural events at the school, who worked to raise large sums of money for educational equipment not available through the regular school budget, and who took an active interest in the academic performance of the children was described as the "most one could hope for." But the involvement of the parents in the life of the school was not without friction. Though both the setting and the magnitude were different, the realities Ravitch (1973) described for the New York City schools had their counterpart in the Brush situation: the tension between the teachers' views of professionalism and the parents' views of prerogatives. The teachers felt that they should control the classroom. Parents could at best be advisory, but surely not coequal or above the teachers in determining the activities of the class. The parents regarded the teachers as essentially their substitutes, working with their children *in loco parentis*. Thus, the final authority should be the parents, for it was they who would "know best" for their own children, and, besides, they paid the teachers' salaries.

Throughout the school year, skirmishes between individual teacher and individual parent were observed. These most frequently involved the parent disputing the grading or grouping of the child. But there occurred in the spring of the year what was interpreted by the teachers as a major effort by an organized group of parents to intrude into the life of the classroom and determine the methods and content of instruction. What prompted the teachers' concern was the development by a group of parents of a "Curriculum Study Group" that was going to assess the curriculum of Brush *in comparison* with other schools' curriculums and then recommend changes at Brush. This move struck at the heart of the teachers' belief in their own autonomy as professionals. They viewed the parents' group as an attempt at increased supervision as well as redefinition of appropriate classroom instruction.

As an indication of the hostility such a move generated among the teachers, it would be well to recount the reaction Mrs. Brown first had to the proposal.

I had just taken my seat at the rear of the room for an observation when Mrs. Brown came over to me and said in an angry voice, "Do you want to see something that really burns me up?" I said I did, and she showed me a questionnaire entitled "Curriculum Study Group Assessment." As she handed it to me, she commented, "This damn group of meddling mothers has gotten me so mad, I feel like leaving this school." I read the covering letter, and it essentially said that a group of "concerned parents" at Brush were going to assess the curriculum at between ten and fifteen other elementary schools in the metropolitan area, and would then return to Brush with a set of recommendations to be implemented. Such recommendations would be used to ensure that a "continued high quality education" would be available to the children.

When I finished reading, she continued, "I'm so damn mad. Who do they think they are telling me what to do. With my training, what business do they think they have got coming into my room and telling me what ought to be done. Can you imagine that bunch of meddlers coming into my room, sitting themselves down, and watching what I'm doing. And then they think they are going to tell me whether it was right or wrong. They've really got some kind of nerve. I think maybe I ought to get out of here before they decide they are so good they can run the whole show."

I asked if she knew any of the mothers personally, and she responded, "Sure. They are a bunch of middle-class do-gooders with nothing to do but go around messing in other people's business."

I asked if she had talked to any of the other teachers. "Are they mad! I heard them talking in the lunchroom, and I agree. We don't go around telling doctors or lawyers what to do, so these mothers have no business coming in here and trying to tell us what we should be doing. Most of the teachers think they are nothing but a bunch of busybodies."

If the teachers at Brush resisted this strongly the efforts of a group of college-educated parents to influence the learning activities of the school, imagine how much greater would be the resistance to poor, perhaps nonwhite, parents. And it is such skirmishes that lead to struggles like that of the Ocean Hill-Brownsville school district and the New York City teachers union.

Some two months after the parents had informed the teachers of their plans for the curriculum study, it was completed. The parents called a special meeting with the teachers to explain their findings. I picked up the gist of the teachers' reaction the next day during an informal conversation in the lounge.

When I first entered, the teachers seemed to be in good spirits. One of them had mentioned how the change in weather (to sunshine) had brightened up her students. Another teacher said, "I wish someone could brighten up those parents." With this comment, a sudden change in the tone of the conversation occurred, and they began discussing the parents and the curriculum study group meeting the previous evening. "If I have to go through another night like last night, I'm going to need a whole week off. Those parents gave me a real pain." Another teacher said she was still at the meeting at 11:15 P.M. "That's nothing" added another, "I was there until ten till twelve. And the whole night, not one damn useful thing came out of all that talk."

This last comment struck a responsive chord, and several teachers expressed their agreement. One added, "I sure wish there was something else we could get those stir-crazy housewives to do besides bothering us." Again, other teachers agreed. "You know, they're so well off they haven't got anything else to do with their time but go out and try to stir up trouble." "Amen," responded a second-grade teacher. She continued, "From what they said,you'd think we weren't teaching their little darlings. But look at the scores, We do better than most. You'd think they'd be content to leave us alone as long as the scores stay up." "That's just the problem" responded Mrs. Brown. "They're never satisfied. They all think their kid is the one to go to Harvard."

In the spring of the year, I observed yet another way in which the parents' ethos of achievement impinged on the life of the school. Each of the classes had completed the tests taken as part of the citywide assessment of school performance. The scores had come back to the teachers, and I was with them at lunch when they were looking at them for the first time. A number of comments were made on the performances of individual children, and several teachers said that they did not look forward to having to explain the low scores to some of the parents. Here a third-grade teacher said, "These parents are just like a bunch of lemmings. Every spring they all come running over here. It must be instinct." The group broke up. Some of the teachers were laughing so hard at the lemming comment that they were almost choking. Added another teacher, "I wonder if we can find a handy cliff."

PRINCIPAL-PARENT RELATIONS

The principal at Brush prided himself on the relationship he felt he had with the parents of his students. On several occasions, he mentioned to me he thought he had "somewhere between 95 and 98 percent of all the parents behind him." He said that if his support ever fell below 80 percent, he would resign voluntarily and no one would have to ask him to leave. Once when I pressed him about what he thought was the basis of his relationship with the parents, he paused, and then said he was sure it was his "straight talk." It was not his way, he said, to "beat around the bush." Parents knew when they came to see him that they would not get "double talk." He added that the one other aspect of how he conducted himself as principal that he thought pleased the parents was his "fairness with the kids." He said he doubted that "there is a child in this school who thinks I play favorites, and I doubt their parents think that either."

It is difficult to assess the validity of the principal's comments because neither the children nor the parents were asked to comment on their perceptions of the principal. But from observations throughout the year, it was apparent that parents worked with him on various projects, ranging from the Host Parent program, to the parent car wash, to the monitoring of the cafeteria, to organizing and seeing into print a school directory. But it's an open question whether the parents at Brush were so actively engaged at the school and interested in their children that they would have helped regardless of who was the principal.

What follows is my first opportunity to observe the principal in interaction with a group of parents. The occasion was an October "open house tea" for the parents of new children at the school. It was sponsored by the PTA.

When I entered the room, the principal was speaking to the parents about the option of Brush School's going on the "year-around" school program the following fall. Apparently, the school district had asked schools to volunteer for the experiment. I glanced around the room and noted approximately forty persons, all women save the principal and myself. There was one black woman in the group. Many were very fashionably dressed. In one corner was a large silver service and several trays full of pastries, cookies, and sliced cake.

The principal tells the group that no school in the city is currently on the year-around program, and it is voluntary if a school wants to try it. He says Brush has tried new things in the past and if the parents are interested in trying this program, they have his word that he will do his best to make it work well. He repeats that "no one is forcing or telling us to do this. It is up to us. Personally, I think it is worth a try." The major reason he favors the program is its reduction of the number of students in school at any one time. According to the figures he cites, it would reduce the enrollment by 30 percent.

He tells the new parents that he discussed this issue yesterday afternoon with the parent advisory group and that the group had two major concerns. One was whether there would be more busing, given more space, and two, whether the school would be air-conditioned for the summer months. He says he told that group and will tell these parents now that they have nothing to worry about so far as more busing is concerned. "All I can say is that there simply won't be any more. We will keep the group we have now, but that's it. The program is not going to be expanded." He also says he doubts that there would be funds for air-conditioning, though he might be wrong.

He tells the parents that before he opens the meeting for questions, he wants all the new parents to know that he is a "kid-oriented principal." He says, "The decisions I make are in the best interests of the children, and not necessarily of the parents. You may not like everything I do, but you should know I did it because I thought it best for your child or all the children here. One other thing, if something is bothering you, come see me. Don't sit at home and stew about it. It is better to talk about it than to just stay home and get all worked up."

The principal opens the meeting for questions and the first parent called on asks if he is sure there would be no increase in busing if the school goes to the year-around program. He repeats his earlier statement. There is only one other question, whether he thinks there was any chance for a stoplight at the corner. He says parents have been trying for several years to get such a light, but they are not giving up. After answering this question the principal says, "Well, that's all I have to say. I hope you enjoy yourselves." With that, the parents begin talking among themselves, and some begin to leave.

I speak briefly with the single black parent at the meeting. She tells me her daughter is Diane, in Mrs. Hill's fourth-grade room. The mother mentions that she had difficulty staying awake at this meeting, and I respond, I could see why with the room so warm. She says, "Oh, it's not that. I have been up all night working." She tells me that she is on a factory shift from 11:00 P.M. to 7:00 A.M., and that she rushed home to get her children ready for school and then she had to get herself ready for this meeting. She says it is while the children are at school that she tries to sleep. Her host parent soon joins her and they leave together.

INTEGRATION AT BRUSH: BEFORE IT ALL BEGAN

Integration was something new for the teachers and principal at Brush School. As I later learned, at least ten of the twenty-five teachers at the school had never taught a black student. The same was true for the principal, Mr. Norris. Consequently, the advent of the Administrative Transfer Program precipitated some apprehension and uncertainty about what to expect and how to proceed.

With the absence of personal experience on the part of some teachers, and with no one else at the school taking the lead to work with the staff to help define the situation and clarify expectations, the teachers and principal were essentially left to their individual perceptions and assumptions. Three of the teachers had attended a summer workshop on interracial education, but the fruits of their learning were to be doled out in small portions over many months as they directed an in-service training seminar for the other teachers. Nothing, though, was shared in the first month of school.[1] Likewise, the school system had specialists in interracial affairs, but they did not make an appearance at the school until they served on a panel discussion at the first of the in-service training sessions. As a consequence of the lack of collective attention to the up-coming integration, the perceptions and assumptions of the principal came to have great importance. More than anybody else at the school, he was able to translate his notions into programatic responses. Thus, the formal orientation of the integration experience at Brush School was largely defined by him, and the outcomes were largely the result of his positions.

In the week before the beginning of the school year, I had a long informal conversation with the principal and attended the first principal-faculty staff meeting. What follows is an account of both, which I hope will elucidate how the busing program was coming to be understood and the implications this understanding had for the early activities undertaken by principal and staff. The reality the black students were to confront at Brush School as they came off the bus was one constructed in the absence of contact with black people, and one where white adults were deciding what to do to and for black children.

The Principal

After arrangements had been completed with district school officials for my presence at Brush School, I made an appointment

---

1. An account of this in-service training program will be interspersed in the narrative of the school year. By indicating when teachers received new information and how they responded to it during the school year, the impact of the training program can, I hope, be more accurately assessed.

to meet with Mr. Norris. I made note of my first impressions when we got together several days before the beginning of school.

Very congenial. He also appeared well organized and systematic. Almost immediately he began pulling out papers and files, sharing with me the names and addresses of the children, as well as his initial correspondence with the A.T. parents. He also had completed room assignments for the in-coming students and that list was also quickly produced. I asked if I could have Xerox copies of the names and room assignments. He called in his secretary and my copies were ready almost instantaneously.

After we exchanged some pleasantries and I thanked him for the opportunity to observe in his school (he responded that he thought it good for the school to have a university researcher around), we began to discuss the up-coming arrival of the black students. He immediately mentioned that he had personally met with eleven of the twenty or so black families who would be sending their children to the school. He also said that the president of the PTA had gotten in touch with a number of the black parents. When I asked him what his impressions were, he responded:

I told the parents I am going to treat their children just like I treat any of the other kids. I am also going to tell this to my teachers. Kids are kids, and there is no basis for making any sort of distinctions on the basis of color, any more than there is a basis for making distinctions on the basis of height or weight. I talked last week with some of the other principals who have had A.T. students and they told me they liked to bunch all their black kids from the same grade together in one room. But I don't think I will do that because then it appears that their skin color was important in where I placed them. I am going to try to spread them out as much as I can. I am not sure this is the best way, but I figured it is worth a try.

I asked if he had sensed any resistance from the parents of students at the Brush School to the coming of the black children.

Absolutely not. In fact, some parents have told me they are glad the school is going to be integrated. But, you know, I have deliberately downplayed this whole business. I figured it would do more harm than good to go around talking much about it, so I've said as little as I thought I could get away with. To make a big deal of thirty black children would probably only make those kids feel even more unique than they really are and also make the white students think of them as different. The important thing is to let these kids relate to one another as kids.

In response to a question of whether he was "doing anything out of the ordinary since the black students were coming," he said:

I've been working closely with the president of the PTA to establish a host family program. What we'd like to do is to have one family in this neighborhood adopt one of the black families and serve as a home away from home for the children. Since they are some distance from their own homes, we thought it a good idea for them to have someone close by to contact if anything comes up. If one of the kids would get sick and need a ride home or to the hospital and we could not reach the real parents, I hope we can call on the host parents to help out. I also hope as the year goes on that the host families will get to know the black families and maybe start to do things together. It would be nice if the black parents could feel a part of the school.

I then asked, "What in general terms can you tell me about the teachers here at Brush?"

They are good. In fact, I would guess they are as good or better than any elementary school staff in the city. And they like it here so well none of them want to leave. In the four years I have been principal, not a single teacher has requested a transfer out. I have lost a few, but that has been because they have gotten promoted or pregnant. I think we have a good working relation, and I feel I've gotten good support from them. I think you'll like them.

I then asked, "'Are there any black teachers here?"

No, but this fall I hired a black aide. I got her both because she seems competent and because she is black. I think it's important when the black kids get here that they see a black adult. You know, I bet many of these white children have never talked to a black person.

"Have you got any worries about the black students coming?" I asked.

Only one. I hope they can make it academically here. You know, the students at this school are really good. I would guess that a third of them have IQs above 130. There may be only twenty or twenty-five children in the whole school with an IQ below 85. And these kids really get pushed, not only by the teachers, but by their parents. Everyone expects these students to be achievers. What worries me is that I have looked at the records on the new transfer students and of the whole group, and it looks on paper like only three or four are going to be able to keep up. What I mean is that they are the only ones with an IQ above 110, and I figure you need at least that to make it here. Last year we scored high in the city testing, but I am afraid these new students are going to pull us down some.

After I had closed my notebook and was ready to leave, we shook hands and I started for the door. As best I could later reconstruct his parting words, he then told me he was sure he was going to make mistakes. He said he had never dealt with the A.T. Program before and that he had never taught any black children before. He thought the best way to proceed was simply to treat them all as kids. I was welcome any time at the school, he said, and he hoped I would let him know if there was anything he could do to help. Finally, "If you ever write anything up about us, try and go easy. Remember, it is our first go at this."

The Staff Meeting

Several days before the beginning of school, Mr. Norris called his first staff meeting.

As I entered the cafeteria, the informal and friendly conversation of the teachers was immediately apparent. They were drinking coffee, eating doughnuts, and seemingly catching up on a summer's worth of news. After the principal had called the group to order, I counted thirty-one persons, excluding myself. The single black person, the teacher's aide, was present. Of the total, seven were males—the principal, five teachers, and the janitor.

The first hour of the meeting was spent on several procedural matters: how to better organize the lunch hour and the use of the cafeteria, how to refer children for various types of testing, how to reach the school nurse, and how to deal with the lunch and milk money. On this last point, after the principal said the milk money envelope should be sent to the office along with the lunch money, he continued:

You know, I guess we had better not call it chocolate milk any longer. It would probably now be more appropriate to refer to it as black milk. He was laughing as he said this and went down to where the black aide was seated. He stood behind her, put his arm on her shoulder, and said, "You'll have to tell me when I start to use the wrong language. I'm new at all this." The aide and others in the room laughed.

When the Administrative Transfer Program came up for discussion, Mr. Norris began, "I firmly believe this. I want you all to know where I stand on this before we begin. Students are students, they all get the same treatment." Having made this initial statement, he dropped any discussion of the A.T. Program *per se* and, instead, began speaking about how to handle "problem students." (It was as if he equated black students with problem students and the discussion of one was synonymous with discussion of the other.) I summarized in my notes his comments as follows:

The principal says problem students are not really problems if the teachers will spend the time to find out what is bothering the student. He says learning, emotional, or psychological problems may all influence a child's behavior in school, and it is up to the teacher to assess the causes. No child should be sent to him, he says, until the teacher has first talked to the parents. "If you send any child down to me, and you have not first contacted the parents, I am not going to deal with him. And I am going to check with the parents to find out if you checked with them. You are going to have to deal with your problems. Don't expect me to come around and straighten out your messes."

Having made these comments, the principal then introduced the new black aide, indicating he wanted this aide treated as a part of the faculty and consulted on how her time was to be used. He said that he was able to hire her with Title VII monies, but that she was not at the school just to deal with the black students. Then he returned to the A.T. Program:

Mr. Norris mentions he has spoken with eleven of the black families. "You know, those parents want the same things for their children that all whites want for theirs." He emphasizes again for the teachers that he was impressed with the black parents' expressing the same views as white parents. He says that the black parents told him they want to know if their child misbehaves. "Several told me explicitly they did not want any special treatment for their children, just because they were black and in a new school. They really want their kids to be treated like all the others. You teachers would not want special treatment for your own children, and I don't want you giving it to these new students."

The principal asked if any of the teachers had questions or comments about the A.T. Program.

One of the teachers said her own children are at another elementary school where there is busing. She said she had talked with one of the teachers there, and the teacher said that the black parents were hesitant to initiate any communication with the school, regardless of whether it was a complaint or a question. She said that since the program was just beginning at Brush, the teachers here should be willing to go out of their way to make contact with the black parents to let them know the teachers want to hear from them. Another teacher raised the question of whether the black parents recognized that the teachers were not going to give any special treatment to the black students. The principal again reiterated that black parents want what white parents want. He then called on the black aide and asked if she has any comment. The aide said she had worked in the Portland schools for several years and had never heard of any black parents who did not want a good education for their children. She knew she wanted her own children treated like any other children. She also said that more white than black teachers were prone to treat black students differently from white ones.

When the aide had finished speaking, the principal called for a short break.

I was barely up and out of my seat when I was surrounded by six or seven teachers. Several began asking me questions at the same time. One asked if I was going to supervise the A.T. Program at the school, and I said no. Another asked if I was working for the public school system, and again I said no. Other questions related to how I selected Brush School, how long I was going to be coming, whether I was also studying other schools, what influence the affluence of the students would have on the study, and whether I had any children in the public schools. All these questions I answered directly.

Another category of questions suggested to me that the teachers were uncertain and a bit apprehensive about the A.T. Program. One teacher said she had heard that black children do not like to be touched or hugged. She said she was "always putting my hands on children." She asked if I thought it permissible for her to hug black children. I answered, it was. Another question was whether I thought she would be able to understand the language of black children. She said she had heard black people on television once and "could not understand a word they said." I responded that she might find some dialectical differences but nothing that would be likely to block communication.

Question followed question. Did I think that black parents would allow the white teachers to be as strict with the black students as they were with the white students. I said that I thought they would, as long as they believed the teacher was being fair to all the students. What would I do if I heard the A.T. students using four-letter words? This teacher said she knew that "dirty words" were a part of the way blacks spoke and she would not be surprised to hear them, but she did not know what to do about them. I said that four-letter words did not discriminate by race, but if she did not want them used in her room, she should tell all the students precisely that. Did I know what was going to happen on the first day of school? Did I expect any big fights? To the former I responded that I suspected it would be somewhat chaotic as it is on opening days at most schools; and to the latter, no. The last question before the end of the break was: Had I ever driven through the black community? I said I had, and the teacher commented that after school began, she wanted her husband to drive her through the black community so she "could get a better understanding of the children" by looking at the homes they lived in. I said I would be careful in drawing any conclusions from simply looking at the outsides of homes. After the break and for the remainder of the meeting, there was no further discussion of the A.T. Program.

The stage was set. Integration was coming to Brush.

3.

The First Days:
Defining the Situation

In a passage that captures much of the ongoing reality of American education, Philip Jackson (1968:1) has written:

> On a typical weekday morning between September and June some 35 million Americans kiss their loved one goodbye, pick up their lunch pails and books, and leave to spend their day in that collection of enclosures (totalling about one million) known as elementary school classrooms. This massive exodus from home to school is accomplished with a minimum of fuss and bother. Few tears are shed (except perhaps by the very youngest) and few cheers are raised. The school attendance of children is such a common experience in our society that those of us who watch them go hardly pause to consider what happens to them when they get there. Of course our indifference disappears occasionally. When something goes wrong or when we have been notified of his remarkable achievement, we might ponder, for a moment at least, the meaning of the experience for the child in question, but most of the time we simply note that our Johnny is on his way to school, and now, it is time for our second cup of coffee.

And so it has been at Brush School as well. For more than twenty years children in the neighborhood have been coming to the school, and in some instances, a second generation is now there. The arrival of the black children constitutes the first time Brush School has had nonneighborhood students in its halls.

What follows is an account of the first days of the 1973-74 school year as they unfolded in one classroom in particular, a first-grade classroom with one new black student. Though other classrooms will be included in the analysis in later chapters, this first-grade room will remain the cornerstone of the study. The decision to focus on one classroom in more depth than the others was made in an effort to present the situation in the school in an understandable and logically sequential manner. This particular room was chosen not because of any unique characteristics of the teacher or students, but rather because one room had to be chosen and this was the one the principal first arranged for me to visit. How it compares with other classrooms in the study can be judged after reading the protocol material in the book. One other point is that while observations were under way in this room, a variety of interesting events was going on elsewhere. But one observer cannot be in two places at once. Further, my concern was to discover long-term patterns of interaction, not to move through the school trying to uncover exotic episodes.

The emphasis here on the first few days of school is a result of my previous work. In my study of a St. Louis public school, it was within the first eight days that the basic patterns of interaction and the structure of classroom organization were established. These then persisted for the remainder of the school year (cf. Rist 1972, 1973). As the data accumulated during the course of the school year at Brush, it became apparent that the same process was repeating itself in Portland.

THE EARLY DAYS

Day 1

Public school in Portland begins on the day after Labor Day. On this first day, it has been the practice, at least in the lower grades, for a parent to accompany the child to meet the teacher and complete a number of forms. When I entered Mrs. Brown's first-grade room at 8:25 A.M., she was seated at her desk, and three parents were standing in line waiting to speak with her. The children were in various parts of the room. Another woman (who I learned had served as the "room mother" last year) was trying to match the children with apple-shaped name tags the teacher had prepared. Only a brief time was needed to fill in the forms, but the teacher had to spend considerably more time with each parent explaining the complexities of the lunch and milk money exchange. The parents were, without exception, well dressed. Several of the fathers who came to register children were wearing gray pin-striped suits. I went ouside at 8:45 to wait for the bus.

When I got to the front entrance of the playground where the bus would stop, I found a group of seventh- and eighth-grade students, each of whom had been assigned by the principal as a guide for one of the new black students. The bus came into sight, and the white children became visibly excited. One of them kept shouting, "Here they come! Here they come!" The bus stopped about fifty feet from the gate, and a white middle-aged woman was the first person off. She was carrying a clipboard and began to call the names of children. The twenty-eight children came off the bus one at a time and began walking toward the playground entrance. When they were almost there, they stopped and waited. The white students then approached them and began asking names, trying to find the student each was responsible for. The bus pulled away immediately. The group began to disperse, with the white and black students starting to move off toward the various entrances of the building. When the black child named Donald plus his seventh-grade escort and I reached Mrs. Brown's classroom, there were seven parents and fifteen children present. As we entered, I heard one girl say to her mother, "He's black." The mother made no comment.

When Donald entered the room, he found an empty seat. At approximately 9:15, when the last of the parents had left, the teacher initiated her first interaction with Donald. She asked if he would be buying his lunch at the school. Donald said he did not know. She called him up to her desk, gave him a name tag, and asked him which of the empty seats he wanted. He pointed to the far-left seat of the second row. The teacher said he could have it and he went over and sat down. Donald was the last of the children to get a seat assignment.

At 9:20, Mrs. Brown came to the front of the room. She asked if all the children had name tags. Two of the boys said they did not. The teacher apologized and immediately found two more, put their names on them, and passed them out. Her first discussion with the students:

She asks the class why she made the name tags in the shape of an apple. But before anyone responds, she says, "Aren't these name tags bright and pretty?" She now repeats her question, "Why did I do that? Why did I make these name tags look like apples?" One of the girls says, "Because red is a pretty color," "Yes, isn't it," responds the teacher. "Now who can tell me the colors I've used in decorating the room?" The children begin to call out colors, and she responds, "Yes, yes, yes" to all the children's answers and to no one in particular. As the noise dies down, she asks, "Who knows our principal, Mr. Norris?" Several of the children raise their hands, and she responds, "Isn't he a nice man?"

"OK, now let's see who's here and who's not. Raise your hand when I call the roll." As it turns out, all the children are present but one boy, who Mrs. Brown says has chicken pox. When the roll is finished, she asks, "Do any of you have money for me to keep? I know many of you will be bringing money, and you can either keep it in your desk or I will keep it for you." No hands go up. She continues, "You know, I don't ever want to hear of anyone losing money out of their desk. Your desk is like your home, and it's not right to come into anyone's home and take things from them, so don't let it happen here."

Mrs. Brown leaves the front and goes to stand by her desk on the right side of the room. "Will all the boys stand?" When they do, she asks, "Is there a girl in the room who could count all the boys for me?" A girl is selected and the boys are counted correctly. Mrs. Brown says nothing to the girl when she is finished, but tells the boys are to sit and the girls to stand. The same question is repeated to the boys. Tim is called by name to count. He counts correctly, but by the time he is finished, the teacher is no longer watching, but is back at her desk working on the packet of lunch money. When Tim is finished, he goes back to his seat. Mrs. Brown tells the children to sit and then begins to double-check on those children buying lunches and milk. When this is completed, she selects two boys to take the money to the cafeteria. She also tells them she has a note for the office. (I learn later it was a question as to what to do about Donald and his lunch.)

With the lunch money task completed, Mrs. Brown made her first movement toward establishing a pattern of classroom organization. What follows gives some glimpse of what she thought important, in terms of both classroom behavior and performance.

As Mrs. Brown walks from her desk toward the front of the room, she says, "For a while, you know, we're going to be moving slowly so I can get organized. It will be easy at first, but then it's going to get harder and harder. We want it to be easy now, but it's going to get better when the work gets harder. It will be exciting too."

When she reaches the front, she turns and faces the class. "OK, let's all look here at me. I want all of you to turn around and face me. Let's all sit straight and all sit in a line." The children shuffle a bit. "What did you think about when you started school this morning?" Donald and others raise their hands. Mrs. Brown first calls on Donald, and then slightly changes the question. "Donald, how did you feel about starting school today?" Donald answers, "I feel fine." She responds in a feigned tone of exaggeration and surprise, "Oh, you wanted to come didn't you."[1] Other children are called on and answers are given like: "I felt scared." "I felt fine." "I felt fine too." When one child says, "I felt excited to come," Mrs. Brown, again in an exaggerated tone of excitement, says, "Oh, I like that word 'excited.' That is such a good word to use. It is nice when we can use big words. You know, I was excited this morning too. Isn't it exciting when the school year begins?"

In the midst of asking other children about their feelings on beginning school, the teacher changes the tone of her voice and says, "I don't want to see any of you playing with your name tags. You can wear them, but if you begin to play with them, they'll break. I don't want that. I only let you wear them today because

1. It is important to stress this exchange, for time and again throughout the year, Donald, in particular, would receive this sort of overreactive response from the teacher. It is not that exaggerated responses are necessarily inappropriate, but when they are given predominantly to one child, and that one child is already unique in the class for some other reason—such as skin color—the effect is to reinforce that child's sense of being out of the ordinary.

it's a special day. I want to have them so we can wear them on other special days as well."

At the end of this short lecture on the care to be taken with the name tags. Mrs. Brown went to the science table, where she had arranged a display of seashells. She talked with the class about the shells, when she had found them, the animals that used to live in them, and the like. She told the children that if they had shells they would like to bring and put on the table, that would make her "very happy." The children were then introduced to the "I choose" board. Mrs. Brown showed the class that she had a name tag for each student and said that during the periods of free choice, they could put their name card in one of the slots designating different activities. When they do this, it means they have chosen an activity during the free time. She asked first the girls and then the boys to come up and find their own card. Every child knew his or her name and selected the correct card. When the boys were up finding their cards, she said to the class: "Oh, you are all so smart. Some of you are reading already, I have never had such a smart class. Never. Can't I catch someone. Isn't there at least one person who doesn't know their name so I can catch them?"

When all the boys were back in their seats, another activity was introduced to the class—going to the bathroom.

All right, I want to tell you all something. We are going to go to the bathroom. This week I will take you, but after that you are on your own. When you learn the rules, you're free to go anytime. I want to tell you there is no playing in the bathroom. You go to the bathroom, you wash your hands, and then you come straight back. It's not a place where you can play. You're not in school to play, but to work.

The system of passing to the bathroom was explained. By the door was a two-pocket folder with a card in each pocket. Each card was red on one side and green on the other. Below one pocket was written "Boys" and below the other, "Girls." Anytime the card in the pocket of one's own sex was green, one could go. But if it was red, one had to wait until the person returned. There was never to be more than one person in either bathroom at a time, except when the entire class was dismissed at recess periods.

When the explanations were completed, she said to the boys, "OK, boys, come over here and line up." She was standing by the door, and the boys came over to her. She counted off the first five and excused them to go down the hall to the bathroom. She stood in the doorway with the remaining boys. Donald was the last boy in line. She asked the remaining boys how many were in their line. Donald called out, "Five of us." Mrs. Brown responded, again in a somewhat exaggerated tone, "Oh Donald, you are so smart." When the first five returned, the remaining five boys were allowed to leave. When this group returned Donald did not go to his seat, but went to the wall by the door and turned the bathroom card for the boys back from red to green. He was the only child in the class who turned a card on this first trip. When the boys were all back, the same routine was repeated with the girls.

When all the children are back in their seats, Mrs. Brown comes to the front of the room, puts up a chart entitled "Our Room Helpers," and says to the children, "Let's see who in this room is a reader. Who can read?" Almost all of the children in the room raise their hands, Donald among them. "Stand up if you can read this sentence." She points to "Our Room Helpers" and seven or eight students stand. She points to one of the girls, who then reads it correctly. She puts her finger by the list of activities on the chart and explains that each week a different child will be responsible for one of the assignments. The first word on the list is "Leader." She asks anyone who can read that word to stand. No one stands. She says, "OK, let's spell it out," which she does. She then pronounces the word in syllables, and now a number of children call out the word. "Brad," she says, "you know the word. You be our leader." Much the same process is followed for the next six or seven words. When the word "duster" is reached, Donald stands up. Mrs. Brown calls on him and he says, "door." "No, Donald, it's not door. But you know, door is the next word so why don't you be our door monitor this week."

Toward the end of the list was the word "lights." When Mrs. Brown reached it, she changed her routine and began a discussion with the children about the lights in the room.

"Do you know why the lights are not on in the room today?" Several of the children call out, "To save electricity." "Yes, that's one reason. Did you see on TV that we need to save all the electricity now that we can. Can you think of any other reasons?" A girl responds, "It's bright outside." "Yes, that's true. Can you think of any others?" A boy answers, "'Cause you didn't want to." "Yes, but why didn't I want to?" One girl calls out, "I don't know." "Well, there are other reasons. I knew it was going to be hot outside today. What would that have to do with me not turning on the lights here in the room?" Craig raises his hand. She calls on him and he says, "The lights make it hot in the room." Mrs. Brown seems relieved at Craig's answer and says, "Oh Craig, you are so smart. You can be the classroom scientist."

The next word on the list was "chairs." She began a long elaborate discussion of the proper way to carry a chair. She also demonstrated all the improper ways she did not want to see used. Two of the boys were selected to pick up their chairs and walk around the room demonstrating the correct procedure. When the last of the assignments had been made, she said to the class, "You know, everyone in our class is going to have a turn at these jobs, because everyone in our class is important and everyone should help. Next week we will have new assignments and those who didn't get one this week will be first on the list next week."

While Mrs. Brown had her class out on the playground for the morning recess, I went to the cafeteria to check on whether I could buy lunch there and so eat with the teachers.

When I enter the kitchen, there are both teachers and students with lunch money envelopes. One of the teachers is counting out his money for lunches and milk. He says he wants seven chocolate and four white milks. Then he says, "Oh, I forgot myself. I mean I want seven black milks and four white milks." He looks at me. "I think I'm going to have trouble remembering to call that chocolate milk black. I've been calling it chocolate milk all my life. Now that the principal wants it called black I guess I'm going to have to change." One of the cooks who is nearby says, "You better remember if you don't want him on your back." And he responds, "I'm trying, I'm trying." He shakes his head and leaves.

I return to the playground just as Mrs. Brown is taking her children back into the building. The last one in line is Donald, the new door monitor. He closes the door behind him as he enters the building. Mrs. Brown, switching glances between Donald and me, says to him, "Oh Donald, you are getting stronger all the time. You are such a big boy." As she finishes, she turns to me and smiles. Donald walks back to his seat.

This last incident deserves a brief discussion, for it points up one of the very real imponderables of conducting observational research, to wit: to what degree does the presence of the observer change the social situation under study? I had little doubt that Mrs. Brown was making exaggerated and seemingly inappropriate comments to Donald at least in part because of my presence in her class as a university researcher conducting a study on school integration. The first day of a new busing program was probably anxiety enough for her, and to have me there also only heightened whatever uncertainty she might have had. It is for reasons such as this that it is important to study classrooms *over time,* so as to observe the unfolding of the patterns and processes of classroom interaction. As Malinowski wrote in 1922, it is only with a "prolonged, intensive, and direct exposure to the actual conditions of life" that a researcher is able to "replace superficial impressions with more accurate insights." If a teacher attempts to overcompensate or mask his or her behavior when in view of a researcher, it can only be assumed that with the passage of time, this will diminish. Both the difficulty of maintaining such masking behavior in a variety of social contexts and the building of a relation between the researcher and the teacher may have the effect of reducing the "atypical" behavior. (One need only observe a teacher after a particularly tiring day to decide if that teacher is perpetuating a "front" for the sake of the observer.)

In this regard, I do not consider these first exchanges between Donald and Mrs. Brown of undue significance. What matters is whether they persist. If one could surmise that they occurred repeatedly and in the absence of the researcher as well, then they point to a possible difficulty in newly integrated white schools — white teachers "bending over backward" so as not to appear hostile or uncaring and thus creating patterns of interaction with black students that are absent in interaction with whites.

Between 10:30, when the children came in from the playground, and 10:55, when they were to line up to go to the cafeteria, Mrs. Brown devoted her attention to two items: a short introductory lesson on mathematical set theory and how the class was to be organized for the lunch period. The latter took most of the time, with the detailing of where to find the milk, where to find the trays, where to find the first-grade table, and the like. At 10:55 she called first the girls and then the boys to line up in front of the door.

Just as the children are about to leave, two of the boys start to pinch each other. Mrs. Brown walks over to them and says in a firm voice, "Mrs. Brown is lots of fun and she's a good teacher, but she does not want her children to act naughty. How many of you understand that?" She seems irritated at the interruption. All the children raise their hands. "How many of you understand that Mrs. Brown does not like her children to act naughty?" The children's hands are still raised, and the teacher says "Good, now let's go."
On the way to the cafeteria, Donald comes to Mrs. Brown and tells her he does not have a lunch. She says she knows that, but Donald does not have to worry because there is going to be a lunch for him. She says that tonight she will send a note home to his mother telling her about the lunch program.

When the children reached the cafeteria, it was immediately apparent that Mrs. Brown would need help with her class. (The room was so chaotic I would have felt guilty standing and watching her alone dealing with the disorganization of the food-distribution and seating arrangements. The major problem was that the tables had been switched without Mrs. Brown's knowing it. The table where she had told her class to sit was already occupied by a second-grade class. Once we had served the children, we went into the kitchen and bought lunches, which we took to the teachers' lounge. The discussions that ensued there on the first day deserve close attention.

When I took a seat in the teachers' lounge, Mrs. Brown sat down beside me. The teachers immediately began to discuss the A.T. students. One of the second-grade teachers said she had only "one little colored child" in her room. Mrs. Brown said she also had only one black child. The second-grade teacher commented, "Oh that's right. Now we have to call them black, don't we?" The teachers then began asking one another what they thought of their black students. Another first-grade teacher, Mrs. Evans, said, "My two little girls are just precious." Mrs. Brown said of Donald, "I've got one that looks to be no problem at all. He seems to be a nice boy." When Mrs. Brown said Donald would be no problem, one of the secretaries who was also eating in the lounge said, "I don't think with this small number of A.T. students that there should be any problems. Now if there were seventy-five or a hundred, it would be different. But I don't think twenty-eight will make any difference at all. We probably won't even know they are here." This comment was greeted with nods of agreement from the other teachers, and the topic changed when the P.E. teacher began to complain about the amount of time he had to take that morning filling out the lunch and milk forms. This seemed to be a common complaint of all the teachers in the room, and they talked about it until they were ready to leave. As Mrs. Brown and I were walking to the cafeteria to return our trays, she commented, "It will get easier tomorrow. The first day is always almost impossible."

After the children had been called back into the room at the end of the noon break, Mrs. Brown passed out paper to the class and told them she wanted them all to draw pictures of their family. She said she did not want pictures of trees or of houses, but of their family. Her next comment, in the form of a question, generated an interesting exchange:

"Now when you draw your family, who will be the tallest person in the picture?" A number of children raise their hands, and Mrs. Brown begins calling on them. Without exception, the children answer, "My father" —until she reaches Donald, who answers, "My uncle." "Donald, does your uncle live with you?" Donald responds, "No, but he's in our family." "Well, I just want you to draw a picture of those who live in the same house with you." Donald makes no response.

As it turned out, this assignment to draw a picture of the family was to be done during the time the student was not a part of one of the small groups being tested by the teacher for letter and word recognition. The afternoon was to be devoted to determining which of three possible reading stages each child was in. The three stages were described to me as "reading," "ready to read," and "still working on letter recognition." As was to become apparent in the days ahead, *this division was to become the major, if not exclusive, organizational pattern around which the activities of the class would revolve. The major instructional activity of each day was related to reading; when and what a student was taught depended on which groups that student was in.*

After an hour of working with different small groups, Mrs. Brown began to organize the children to go to the bathroom. The lines were formed at the door, and groups of five were allowed to leave. At one point she returned to her desk and took out a bottle of medicine for one of the students. She mentioned to the boy, David, that she had forgotten to give him his pill in the morning. She told him he should come and take it now. While she and David were at the water fountain, she handed me a letter from David's mother saying that David was on a tranquilizing drug, Ritalin. The letter said he was to have the drug each morning between 11:00 and 11:30. Mrs. Brown said softly to me that she was not to administer the drug directly or to remind him of it. The child was to make the request. But she said she tries to make sure that he will have it when he is supposed to. She said that she had had children in previous years who were on this drug, and if they had not had it by lunch, they were a "mess" for the rest of the day.

One of the boys walked up to the fountain while David was taking his pill and asked why he was taking it. Mrs. Brown responded that David had a sore throat. The boy said he took pills too. Mrs. Brown asked if he took them because he had a sore throat. The boy answered, "No, it's my calming-down pill." The boy left, as did David, and I asked Mrs. Brown if many of the children at Brush were on medication. "Oh, yes. We get lots of them here. The parents are very concerned about the performance of their children, and if someone tells them pills will help, pills they get." She said that she did not approve of all the pills children in the school were taking. "Sometimes I feel more like we are in a drugstore than a school."

Day 2

It was this second morning, as the bus was arriving with the black students, that I heard the first racist comments directed toward them.

I was standing at the entrance to the playground as the bus came into sight. Soon it stopped, and the children began to disembark. One white boy, about fifth or sixth grade, climbed up on the fence and began to shout, "Here come the Black Sambos! Here come the Black Sambos!" None of the black children coming off the bus said anything in response. But one girl on the bus called out through the window, "Look at the white honky." The boy on the fence was beginning to shout back when I told him to be quiet and leave. He glared at me and asked if I was a teacher. I said I was not, but it didn't make any difference because he was going to be quiet and leave. He did. The children were now all off the bus and beginning to walk toward the entrance of the school. There were no teachers in sight, and none of the seventh- or eighth-grade guides of yesterday was present.

The bell rang at 8:50 for the children to go into their rooms, and the playground quickly emptied. Mrs. Brown told the children to go to their seats. Almost immediately she began the lunch count. She was still working on it twelve minutes later when she called on Donald to ask what he was going to do for lunch.

"Donald, do you have your lunch in your lunch box?" Donald shakes his head no and opens it for her to see. He has his school supplies in it. He says he's going to buy his lunch today and goes to the teacher's desk and gives her a nickel. Mrs. Brown leaves her seat and comes over to me. She shows me the nickel and says, "What am I supposed to do with this. Lunch is forty cents. Do you think this is all they pay in the poor schools?" I say I don't know, but the principal would know. She says she thinks so too, and she will try and see him at recess. About this time Donald is up out of his seat. He goes and turns the bathroom sign for the boys from green to red. Mrs. Brown asks him where he is going and he says to the bathroom. She says "OK," and he leaves.

Mrs. Brown tells me she thought she was going to get one more A.T. student in the room, but it looks now as if she won't. She says, "You know, this is not going to make it any easier for Donald, him being the only black child in the class." She turns and goes back to her desk to resume work on the lunch count.

During the time Mrs. Brown continued to work at her desk, she had one of the girls count all the boys and vice versa. She also had a short period of "show and tell." When the lunch count was completed, two girls were selected to take it to the lunchroom.

Mrs. Brown comes to the front of the room. "OK, who brought their pencils today?" The children hold up their hands. When Donald does so, his unsharpened pencils are in his hand. Mrs. Brown sees him and says, "Donald, I think I should sharpen these for you or you won't be able to use them." She sharpens them both for him and then asks if others in the room also need their pencils sharpened. Three boys and one girl come over to her. When she is finished with all the pencils, she walks first to Donald's desk with his two. She sees he has two boxes of crayons. She asks if one is the box she lent him yesterday when he had none. Donald answers no. She repeats the question, her voice raised a bit, "Did I give those to you yesterday?" Donald nods yes, and she responds, "Well, I think I'll take them back now since you have your own." She looks over to me and frowns.

Mrs. Brown decided to continue the show-and-tell period and told Brad, who was class leader for the week, to go on with the activity. Brad called on Peter, who then came to the front to tell how his family went to a Chinese restaurant last evening. He had brought along a pair of chopsticks and told how he tried to eat with them, but could not. As Peter was talking, Mrs. Brown walked by me and said softly, "Peter is a repeat." A girl, Debbie, was called on next, and she came to the front with some seashells. Mrs. Brown called out, "Oh look. You remembered about me saying you could bring shells for our science table. You know, our Oregon coast is full of seashells." Debbie responded, "But I didn't get them at the coast." "Oh, were you in California?" Debbie answered, "No, two of them came from Hawaii and one from Tahiti. We went there on vacation." Mrs. Brown asked, "Did your whole family go?" "Yes, and my grandma went too."

Brad chooses Donald to come to the front. Donald comes and begins to tell a story. "Yesterday I went outside and was going to help my daddy with his car when a big bear come by. We run in the house. After we run in the house we come back out and fix the chain on my bike. That all." He sits down. Mrs. Brown asks the class, "What do you think about that? Were you interested in Donald's story?" Several of the children say yes.

After the show-and-tell period had ended and the pledge of allegiance had been said, and as Mrs. Brown had begun passing out paper so the students could draw another picture of their family ("even prettier than yesterday"), the principal made his first appearance in the room.

When Mr. Norris enters, Mrs. Brown immediately asks him about lunch for Donald. He says she should send him down with the rest, because he's going to be put on the free lunch program.

Mrs. Brown speaks to the class and says, "Boys and girls, do you know who this man is?" Donald calls out, "He the principal." "Well, what does he do?" she asks. One of the girls calls out, "He works in the office," and another says, "When children are real bad, they have to go see him and he spanks them." Mr. Norris asks a direct question of Peter: "Peter, why do I sometimes have to spank the boys and girls who come to the office?" Peter responds, " 'Cause they be good." The principal seems momentarily taken aback by the answer and then says, "Yes, and I sometimes have to spank them when they are bad too."

He continues, "What really worries me though, is when the boys and girls in my school fight. I don't like my children to fight. That's when I get mad and start to give spankings." Mrs. Brown calls out, "How many of you boys and girls have ever had a spanking?" Nine children stand. "How many of you have never had a spanking?" Ten stand now. The principal says to them, "Well, if any of you who have never had one want to come see me and have me give you one, I'd be happy to do it for you." He laughs as he says this and turns to leave the room, meeting a mother who is coming in. He starts talking to her, and Mrs. Brown organizes the class for a trip to the bathroom.

I was about to leave the room to look at some of the children's drawings hung in the hall when the principal called me over to him and said, "She's really good, isn't she?" I said I enjoyed watching her teach. He responded, "She's one of the very best I've got." He waved and then walked toward the office.

When I returned to the room, the remainder of the children had come back from the bathroom and Mrs. Brown was dismissing them to go to the playground. She came over to me after the last child was gone and brought Donald's permanent file. She said she thought I would like to see it. The material in the file was very sparse. It listed his mother's name (but not his father's), his address, his phone number, where he had attended kindergarten, his vision, his hearing, and a short evaluation from his kindergarten teacher. There were three categories on the form: "Social Adjustment" was marked "good"; "Emotional Stability" was marked "good"; and "Significant Personality Traits" had the comment: "Donald is an active and intelligent boy who has a short attention span."

In the period after the morning recess, Mrs. Brown continued testing the children to see which reading group each child belonged in. On the side board she had written "Yellow," "Blue," and "Red." The Yellow group would be the most advanced and the Red the least. Thirteen children had so far been screened. Four were in the Blue, seven in the Yellow, and two in the Red. Donald and a girl (who later in the year would be assigned to a special education class) were the two in the Red group. As the teacher was about to begin testing another small group, she said to me, "You know, a lot of people don't like grouping in the classroom, but I've always used it, especially at the beginning of the year when the children aren't yet able to study on their own. And in a room like this I feel I really need it. I've got children in here who can read and write short stories and others who don't know all the alphabet. There's no way one can teach them all at once."

The children in the test group had been shown how to divide their sheets of paper into quarters and told they were to put "one of something" in the first box, two of something in the second, and so on for the third and fourth. Mrs. Brown then told the group to begin working on their papers, and called five children to come where she was seated. At 10:55 she ended the identification test and told the class to prepare for lunch. The two children who were each day to go early to the lunchroom to make sure the silverware and napkins were in place at the first-grade table were excused. I told Mrs. Brown I would go along to help, given how chaotic it had been yesterday. She seemed relieved and twice thanked me for being willing to help. I left the room with the two children at 10:57.

Day 3

There were no incidents as the black children came off the bus. In Mrs. Brown's classroom, the routine was beginning to take shape: the first fifteen minutes were allocated to dealing with the lunch and milk count while the children simultaneously went through counting who was present, having a short show and tell, and bringing up to the teacher any money they wanted her to keep for them. When the lunch count was finished, the pledge followed. Then came more show and tell (this morning another girl with shells from Hawaii, two stories written by the children, plus a doll from Japan and a bird's nest).

A point made repeatedly about American elementary education is the persistent emphasis on keeping classrooms orderly and neat (see Eddy 1967, Henry 1963, Jackson 1968, Katz 1971, and Silberman 1970). This emphasis was present in Mrs. Brown's classroom. Whether it was having the desk straight, the papers neatly arranged when they were passed to her, all the books in the shelves stood straight on end, or lunch boxes neatly tucked in one corner of the coat closet, order was stressed and achieved. One example occurred this third morning:

Mrs. Brown is standing in the front of the room. "Oh, I see something that makes me unhappy. See how the doors to the coat closet are still open. That makes me sad. Boys and girls, why is it that we should keep these doors closed?" Peter calls out, "So no one will take our lunch." "Well, I'm not worried about anyone here taking someone's lunch. There's something else that worries me." Tina gets up from her seat and closes the two doors. "Oh, thank you so much Tina. Now boys and girls, how does the room look different? How does it look that is different from the way it looked before?" Brad calls out, "Now the doors are closed." Mrs. Brown ignores this response and says, "See now how neat the room looks. Can't you tell that now it is neat? We'll all have to work together to keep our room neat. A neat room is a happy room."

Later in the morning, Mrs. Brown came to where I was seated and again told me that Peter was repeating the grade. This had been prompted, I suspect, by Peter's telling one of the other boys that he was older and smarter. I asked Mrs. Brown if any of the other children were repeating, and she replied that Brad was. She also said that Bruce had repeated kindergarten and that that was why he was larger than many of the other boys.

In this discussion, Mrs. Brown volunteers the information that she has never held back a child. She says it is only under one very specific set of circumstances that she would consider doing so. I ask what circumstances. She says that if a child is "particularly immature for his age and his social development is lacking," then that child would be held back. She says she takes retention very seriously, and does not like what often happens — the retained child starts to bully the new classmates.

Yesterday afternoon (the second day) Mrs. Brown had completed her testing of the children for reading skills. She had formulated the three groups: in the Yellow group, which consisted of those children already reading, there were ten; in the Blue group, which was described as the group "ready to read," there were ten; and in the Red group, where the focus was on letter recognition, there were four students. At 9:55 Mrs. Brown told the Red group to go to the reading area so she could work with them until recess at 10:20. She called the names of the four students in the group, Donald, Tim, Pam, and Trish. Before Mrs. Brown came to the group, Donald began to read a list of words that had been printed on the side board. The words were: "man," "fan," "can," "ran," and "dan." Donald did not read them correctly; indeed, he seemed to be guessing. I was seated nearby and asked him to point out for me the word "ran." He pointed to "fan."

Other than the single mention of Donald being black when he entered the room for the first time on the first day of school, I had heard no mention of race or Donald's color at any time in the room — until Donald and Tim began to talk while waiting for Mrs. Brown to come and start their reading group.

Donald says that he is black and he knows everyone else in the school is black too. Tim says he is wrong because everyone is white, including Donald. Donald then says he is not white, but he is an Indian. Tim tells Donald that if he is an Indian he should be careful because white people like to kill Indians. Donald asks, "What happen to black people?" Tim responds, "They can't get killed 'cause they not Indians. If you go over to Warm Springs [an Indian reservation in central Oregon] you see all those old dead Indians."

Donald tells Tim that when he was little he was white. Tim asks, "Did you get black when you got bigger?" Donald says, "Yeah, and now I'm black all over, even on my feet." Tim says, "You mean your feet are really black?" "Yeah, you want to see them?" Tim answers, "yeah." As Donald is taking off his shoe, he tells Tim, "When I was little I had white feet." "Do you want to be white now?" Donald answers, "No, I wanna be a Indian. And maybe some day I will be white again." Mrs. Brown sits down with the group and the conversation ends.

When the children in the Red group were ready to start their reading lesson, I left the room and went to the school office. The principal was in his smaller inner office, the door was open, and I called in greetings to him. He asked how the research was coming along, and I told him I thought quite well. We began an informal conversation, and one of the first items he mentioned was that he thought the A.T. program was going "smoothly." He asked if I had any impressions about the school in general, and I said I was somewhat taken aback by the affluence of the families of the white children. I told him about the seashells from Hawaii and Tahiti as well as the shirts some of the children brought to use while painting. I said I thought I should trade in some of my own shirts for those painting shirts in the first-grade room. He said, "That's really minor. Wait until Christmas vacation and the trips to the Riviera." That prompted him to continue to talk about the parents. He said that though the parents were quite affluent, they were not what he would characterize as permissive. He said the two things they expected of their children in the school were to behave and to work hard at their studies. "I bet you won't find a quieter school anywhere in the city," he added.

The principal mentions that I should try to get the views of two new staff members at the school, the black aide and the third-grade teacher who has come this year to serve as the coordinator of the A.T. program. He says that last year she taught in a pre-dominantly black school. She came up to him the first day of school, he relates, and said, "I can't believe it. I can't believe it." The principal says he asked her what she meant, and she responded, "When I asked them to sit down, they did."

As I am about to leave, I thank the principal for the opportunity to talk briefly with him. He says he is glad I have come this year and not during one of his first years as a principal. I ask why, and he mentions that some years back when he first was promoted from teacher to principal, he had difficulty in getting teachers to accept his new authority. For that reason he did not think his first years as a principal were conducive to having a "smooth-running school." "But now that is all behind me and I am happy to have you here. Every year gets easier and easier."

Day 4

The observation on this day began at 2:05 P.M. and continued until the A.T. children were on a bus back to their homes. Almost immediately as I came into Mrs. Brown's classroom, she began to talk to me, relating her first difficulties with Donald.

I have barely sat down when Mrs. Brown comes and says, "You should have been here this morning. I had a little problem with Donald. I saw him pushing other children at the water fountain. He didn't want to drink himself, but just to cause trouble by breaking into the line. I finally had to talk with him when he kept it up. I do hope that is the last of it. But, you know, Donald is not the only one having trouble. I was talking to Mrs. Evans at noon and she said she has had to move one of her black students twice now because she is always talking and bothering the other students. Mrs. Evans said she now has the two black children sitting together because it seems it is only the one black girl who can stand the other."

As Mrs. Brown and I stand talking at the back of the room, Donald, who is seated in the first row, calls out to Mrs. Brown, "Teacher, are we suppose to do it now?" Mrs. Brown looks up and answers, "Yes." She also tells the rest of the class to "get busy" on the assignment. A seventh-grade boy, who one hour each day serves as a helper in Mrs. Brown's room, goes over to Donald and begins to help him with the lesson. After several minutes, the older boy moves away to another desk, and I hear Donald call out, "Now I sure am dumb." I do not know what prompted this comment.

One of Donald's attributes that began to be apparent was his considerable facility for dealing with adults. He appeared to have no reservations about talking to Mrs. Brown, other teachers on the playground, or me. What is more, Mrs. Brown appeared to encourage this to some degree, for she often accepted Donald's comments even if they were unsolicited and perhaps inappropriate. For example:

Donald is out of his seat, standing by Trish's desk. He calls out to Mrs. Brown, "Trish put her book away." Mrs. Brown, from across the room replies, "Was it graded?" Donald answers, "No." "Well, tell Trish she should take her book back out and finish the lesson."

At least two aspects of this exchange are interesting. On the one hand, the teacher was willing to respond to Donald and listen to his message. On the other, the message was a "squeal" on another student, which the teacher took at face value and legitimated by allowing Donald to act as her surrogate in telling Trish to get back to her work. The teacher herself never checked to see whether Donald was telling the truth. And as Henry (1963) among others, has noted, to legitimate a student's criticism of and tattling on another student tends over time to expand that behavior rather than to decrease it, for such behavior is in harmony with the cultural emphasis on individual achievement and aggrandisement. Perhaps I am making too much of one incident, but at the least Trish was left as a nonentity in an exchange about her own performance.

Donald's interaction with adults continued as he shortly came to where I was seated and asked "Why you so late?" I explained that I wanted to see what his class did in the afternoon. He said, "Oh, OK," and went back toward his seat.

On the way to his seat, Donald stops by Peter and tries to pull his hair. Peter stands up and tries to get back at Donald. Peter calls out, "I can't get hold of your hair. It's braided." Donald says, "My hair ain't braided, but I braid yours." Peter says, "OK," and so Donald starts to braid Peter's hair. This continues for several minutes until Mrs. Brown calls Peter to the desk for a message she has for his mother. When Peter is at the teacher's desk, Donald goes down on the floor to hide from Peter under

Peter's own desk. Peter comes back and starts to pull Donald's hair. It must have gotten rough, for Donald yells, "Quit it Peter, or I gonna beat you up." Mrs. Brown hears this and asks Peter what he's doing. Peter says, "Nothin'," and Mrs. Brown goes back to her work with no further comment. Peter again starts to grab Donald's hair, and Donald says as he pulls away, "Boy, you quit it." Then goes back to his seat. (I made the following note after this incident: "In spite of this exchange, I think Peter and Donald are building a friendship.")

During the remainder of the afternoon, Mrs. Brown showed the children two film strips. One was about a little red car learning how to be safe in traffic and the other was about animals in the ocean. When the time was near for the children to be dismissed, the noise level increased and the children grew restless. Mrs. Brown had to turn the lights off twice to gain the attention of the class. When the lights were turned on the second time, Mrs. Brown went to the front of the room and said, "Well, you've been in school this whole week. Can you tell me what you've learned?" A number of children begin to talk at once, and even as Mrs. Brown pointed to individual children to respond, others continued to talk. Thus, it was difficult to hear clearly and distinguish who said what, but I noted the following exchanges:

Mrs. Brown points at Lori, who answers, "I learned how to paint." Kim is next and says, "I've learned to make friends." Mrs. Brown responds, "Oh, that is wonderful. It's a very nice thing to learn." All this time other children are calling out answers. Mrs. Brown points to Debbie; "I've learned how to be a nice hostess in the lunchroom." "I'm glad you have," responds Mrs. Brown.

The children were dismissed from the room at 2:45. While others were on their way home, Donald and other black children from the first three grades went to the corner to wait for the bus. The black children played among themselves, mostly tag on the sidewalk in front of the school. Donald later sat down by the fence railing and began to eat the remainder of his lunch. He said he had not been able to get his "milk jug" (thermos) open at lunch and asked me to open it for him. I did and stayed with him while he ate some potato chips and drank his milk. I asked if he had made any new friends since coming to Brush School, and he responded, "Yeah, I like Jeff." (Jeffrey was an Administrative Transfer student in Mrs. Wills's first-grade class.) I also asked if he liked Brush School, and he said, "Yeah, I do." Several of the other children waiting for the bus heard me talking with Donald, and when I asked if he liked the school, a third-grade girl spoke out, "I like it here a whole lots. Where I went before, those kids be so mean and always wanting to take my money and fight. These kids here nice. They play with me."

The bus arrives at 3:05, and the children begin to climb aboard. Donald is one of the last, and as he is about to get on, Peter comes running up to him and says, "Good-bye Donald." Donald smiles and says "Good-bye." When he gets to his seat, he starts to wave to Peter out of the window. Peter waves back and starts to run beside the bus until it turns the corner. I hear him shout one final "Good-bye."

Day 6

Again this morning there were no incidents when the black children came off their bus. They, along with the other students, played on the school grounds until the first bell rang at 8:50, the sign the building was open. (It is after the second bell at 9:00 that a student would be considered tardy.)

As Donald enters the room and moves toward his desk, he passes Kim's desk and sees she has a doll. He picks up the doll and turns to Brad. He holds it in front of his face and says, "Kiss it. Kiss it." Brad pushes him away, saying he isn't going to kiss any doll. Donald tries again and even makes a kissing sound this time as he tries to get it in front of Brad's face. He finally puts the doll down and goes on to his seat. Mrs. Brown calls out, "Who here knows their way to the office?" Donald and most of the other children raise their hands. "OK, Donald, if you know your way, you can go this time. Ask in the office for two Band-Aids." Mrs. Brown has one of the girls from the class sitting in a chair. Apparently, the girl has scraped her knee outside on the playground.

Donald returns in four or five minutes and the teacher tells him the Band-Aids he got are too small. She tells him to go and get the next larger size. Donald again leaves. Mrs. Brown goes back to her work on the lunch and milk money count. Several minutes later Donald returns with the larger size.

When Mrs. Brown finishes with the lunch count, she calls out, "Who is our lunch monitor this week?" Craig comes up to the teachers's desk. She tells him to take the envelope to the lunchroom. She also tells Tim that he can go along. Craig says he does not want Tim to go and pushes him away. Donald and Peter, who have been standing together in the back of the room and watching this exchange, tell Craig that they will go along. Craig says no and leaves the room. Donald and Peter follow anyway. Mrs. Brown makes no comment.

This morning, more than in any of the previous observational periods, Donald was in an almost constant state of motion. He had made three trips out of the room before 9:10, and in between trips, he was moving through the room — from one student's desk to another, to the teacher's desk, and on to another. Mrs. Brown began to let her displeasure be known.

Donald is out of his seat standing by Peter's desk. Mrs. Brown comes and stands directly behind him. She puts her hands on her hips and says to Donald in a firm voice, "Donald, what did I ask you to do?" She repeats it. Donald goes over to his seat and slouches in his chair. "Donald, sit up straight in that chair." Donald moves up a bit, but then begins pulling something out of his pocket. It is a string about ten inches long with a small red rubber ball on one end. Mrs. Brown is watching him all this time. I am also sure he is aware she is watching. Donald holds on to one end of the string and starts to twirl the ball around his head. Mrs. Brown, seemingly irritated by this, calls out, "Donald, put that away right now or I'll take it away from you." Donald sticks it inside his desk.

The routine of the room during the early morning period had become easily anticipated: putting away coats and lunch boxes, bringing money to the teacher, a short period of show and tell, the pledge, more show and tell, and then the organization of the class for activities. During the show and tell this morning there was a doll from England, a starfish, a short story written by Debbie (which was tacked up on the bulletin board), a narrative of a trip to the zoo, and a doll from the Netherlands. Also, the class spent some minutes with the hamster Paul had brought. When this was completed, the organization of the class began.

Mrs. Brown says, "You should all listen to me now. Let's all be quiet and take our seats. You can look at the hamster some more during recess." She continues, "OK, do any of you remember our big word from yesterday? If any of you remember our big word from yesterday, stand up and I'll call on you." Several of the children stand. Mrs. Brown first calls on Brad, who says nothing and then sits down. She then calls on Matt, who also makes no response. The same with Tim. Then she calls on Tina, who answers, "Pat." Mrs. Brown ignores this response and calls on Craig, who says nothing. Paul answers "Equivalent sets," and Mrs. Brown almost gushes out, "Oh, it's wonderful that you remembered. I'm so proud of you. Do any of you remember the other big word from yesterday?" Mary answers, "Nonequivalent sets." "Oh wonderful. You're all so smart. I've never had a class like this." Almost in the same breath, Mrs. Brown, seeing Donald again swinging the string and ball around his head, calls out, "Donald, this is the last time. If I see you with that once more during class time, it's mine for good." Donald puts it in his pocket.

One aspect of this brief interaction between Mrs. Brown and the class merits discussion. The first several children who stood in response to Mrs. Brown's question about the "big word" (though there were actually two words) could not answer when called upon. This pattern was to be observed throughout the year with some frequency. Why the children did this is not clear. But whether it was the pressure of competition among peers that encouraged them to volunteer, or the desire for attention from the teacher, or simply an almost autonomic response to the teacher's request, several children inevitably volunteered even though they could not give the answer when called upon.

The other side of this interaction was that the teacher essentially "fished" for the correct answer. Those who could not give it were bypassed in the search for the appropriate response. In this last example, Tina's answer "Pat" was not what Mrs. Brown wanted, and so it also was bypassed. An interactional game was being played out in that episode, with the students standing, maybe having the answer and maybe not. The teacher, in turn, would rapidly go through those who wanted to play until she found the response she was seeking. By analyzing such exchanges one might begin to draw distinctions between the activities of schooling and those of learning.

Mrs. Brown proceeded to organize the class activities for the morning with one of the three reading groups having free time, another working on the writing assignment, and the third having a reading lesson. At one time, while she was with the reading group on the left side of the room, she had to go to her desk for a paper. On her way back to the group, she stopped where I was seated and said:

"Do you hear all this seething in the room? I can't stand it. You'll have to come back later in the year to see what they'll be like once they've settled down. They're so excited now it's a task just to hold them to anything very long. It's a very difficult period."

It was at the end of the first morning period, when Mrs. Brown had all the children go to the bathroom and then onto the playground for recess, that we again had an opportunity to talk. Her comments suggested that Donald was a source of growing concern.

Mrs. Brown asks if I have noticed that she has moved Dawn out of the front row. I say I have. She says she had to do it because "Donald was tormenting her so." I ask what he had done and she began a list: taking Dawn's crayons and pencils, pulling her hair, marking in her book, and always talking to her. She says that once, yesterday afternoon, Donald pulled her hair so hard Dawn began to cry. Mrs. Brown says she is now afraid to put anyone else next to Donald because he "might start it all over again." That would worry her, she adds, because Donald might then get a bad reputation and no one would want to play or sit with him. So for the immediate future, Donald will have no one sitting next to him on the right. (He is first in the row so there is no seat next to his left.) Her last comment on Donald, "I know he's like all the other little boys, but he needs some work on calming down."

EARLY PERCEPTIONS OF THE TEACHERS AND THE PRINCIPAL

So far in this chapter, the focus has been almost exclusively on Mrs. Brown's classroom and the interaction between her and the students, particularly Donald. What follows is the result of a deliberate attempt on four consecutive days to learn the attitudes and perceptions of both the teachers and the principal concerning the Administrative Transfer Program and the individual black children involved. Four sources of information were used to learn about these perceptions: informal conversations with the principal and teachers; an interview with the teacher responsible for the coordination of the A.T. Program; the teachers' responses to a questionnaire on how they viewed the early adjustment of the A.T. students in their respective classrooms; and, finally, an evening meeting of the teachers, principal, host parents, and the parents of the A.T. students. The school year was under way; how was it being viewed by those who most directly influenced it?

Day 8: The Teachers

The observation this morning began during the morning recess (10:40-11:00) period for the third and fourth grades. I walked onto the playground and found the principal talking with several teachers. As I joined the group, one of the teachers was asking when the schoolwide testing program was to begin. The following week, he said. This same fourth-grade teacher asked if she was to give the test to the A.T. students as well. The principal said that she should and that she ought to score the tests of the A.T. students as quickly as possible so she "would have some idea of where they are." He said he thought it important to get test scores on all the A.T. students so that the teachers could "figure out where they are." He said that one of the permanent folders on an A.T. student had just come to the office, and the student was scored with an IQ of 81. He said he went immediately to this student's teacher and told her to "back off," not to put any pressure on the student to perform. He said he told the teacher that with a student who has an IQ of 81, there isn't much she could expect.

At Brush School, the cafeteria was small, which necessitated the staggering of lunch periods. The first and second grades had lunch at 11:00 A.M., the third and fourth grades at 11:30, and so on for the higher grades. Thus, when I had finished talking with the teachers and principal on the playground, I walked to the teachers' lounge, where the first- and second-grade teachers were having their lunch period. There were five teachers in the room. Mrs. Evans began to tell me of an incident in her room she thought I should know about. She said one of her A.T. students, Gloria, drew her first picture of her family using brown and black crayons. But the next two pictures of her family and herself she drew with yellow and orange crayons. All the members of her family were given blond hair, the teacher said. Mrs. West asked if I would be at the up-coming meeting between the parents of the A.T. students, the local host parents, and the school staff. I said I definitely planned to come. She responded, "Well, it's going to be a small meeting because I don't count on any of the A.T. parents showing up." Mrs. Evans said she understood that the host parents were going to pick up the black parents and bring them to the meeting. "In that case," Mrs. Brown responded, "I guess I better show up." I then asked Mrs. Brown how Donald was doing, and she said he was "beginning to try. It just takes him so long to settle down and get to work."

This last comment prompted Mrs. Wills, the third of the first-grade teachers, to say her one A.T. student, Jeff, was always "antsy" in the early part of the morning and then fell asleep. I asked Mrs. Wills if she knew whether Jeff had breakfast before he came to school. She said she did not know. She added, though, that he "was always trying to get in his lunch box. It got to be such a problem I had to put it out of his reach." Mrs. Brown said she noticed Donald doing the same thing. I suggested to them both that this activity might be due to the children's not having breakfast and consequently being hungry throughout the morning. Both teachers seemed quite amazed at this comment, and one said, "Who would ever guess there are children who don't get breakfast!"

During the entire lunch period, the teachers discussed with me and among themselves the A.T. students in their rooms. At one time, the teachers almost seemed to be vying among themselves as to who could tell the greatest "horror story" of what one or another of their A.T. students had done in the classroom. Mrs. Brown said Donald was always "tormenting" Dawn and pulling her hair; Mrs. Evans said Joyce was always talking and "pestering" the other children; and Mrs. Wills said Jeff spilled several boxes of crayons on the floor. But the *coup de maître* was delivered by Mrs. Briggs, a second-grade teacher, who said she heard one of her students use the word "damn" in her class. One of the teachers responded, "Oh no, I wondered when all that was going to start." Mrs. Briggs was asked what she had done, and she said she ignored it until one of the white children repeated the word. Both of them, she said, then were told to stay in for one recess period.

Mrs. Brown said, in reference to the discussion of cursing, that she "couldn't take it if it started in my room. I don't know what I would do if I started hearing all those filthy words." She turned to me and said, "I hope you are also keeping an eye on those kids on the playground." I asked why, and she said, "I think they're getting mean. Some of the bigger ones are starting to act like real bullies."

During the brief exchange with Mrs. Brown, the speech therapist, who came to the school several mornings a week, entered the lounge. We were introduced by Mrs. Evans, and the therapist said to Mrs. Evans, "Have you told him yet about the pictures your black kids drew?" Mrs. Evans said she had. What I find interesting in this conversation is the indication that the teachers were also talking among themselves about the A.T. students in my absence. I had been worried that the teachers might discuss the A.T. students only in my presence and that such discussion would essentially be an artifact of my being with them during informal periods in the day. But it was now evident that they discussed the behavior and performance of the A.T. students, at least intermittently, when I was not present.

Day 9: An Interview

As noted in Chapter 1, with the funding of the Title VII program in Portland, staff could be hired specifically to work with the desegregating schools. Some schools were to have full-time "Instructional Specialists"; others were to have such specialists half-time; and in other schools, one teacher was to be released from some duties to serve as an "Extended Responsibility Specialist." Brush School was in the latter category. Mrs. Miller, who served as the E.R.S. person at Brush, was a new third-grade teacher at the school and had taught previously in one of the majority black schools in the city. What follows are excerpts from an interview on the Friday of the second week of school.

Q. *How did you come to be associated with the A.T. Program?*

R. I was contacted by the principal during the summer, and he asked if I would take it on. I had no idea when I accepted the position here that I would be doing this.

Q. *Could you describe your duties in relation to the A.T. Program?*

R. If something goes wrong or if the teachers are having problems, I am supposed to be contacted to see if I can straighten it out. I am a go-between who is supposed to help everyone adjust to everyone else. So far, I haven't gotten to know any of the A.T. students individually, other than the children in my own room. I have been focusing mostly on the up-coming meeting of the A.T. parents and local parents and teachers. I hope they all get to know one another and feel free to talk about problems.

Q. *You mentioned problems. Are there any now you can see?*

R. None really. Except a number of the A.T. students are needing extra help. Most of them are not what you would characterize as high achievers.

Q. *What is your general impression of how the A.T. Program is going here at Brush School?*

R. I would say positive. Most of the teachers I have talked to are just great. I see them treating the black kids just like everyone else. Some of the parents in my room have asked why we are spending money to bus these kids out of their own neighborhood. I told them I am not sure either, but that I can see no problem with it.

Q. *What is the general impression you have of the adjustment of the black children here at Brush?*

R. Well, as I said, I don't know any of the black students except those in my own room. One of the boys was pushing when he first got here, but he has settled down a lot. He still talks a lot trying to get attention, but I think the students have accepted him. I think.

Q. *What is the general impression you have of the adjustments of the white children to the new black students?*

R. I don't see any difference with them. I have heard several of the white children refer to a "black boy" or a "black girl," but these have mostly been the older children, those in the fourth grade. One thing that really pleases me is the lack of fighting here. Where I taught before, black children were always fighting with one another, but here they don't fight with each other or with the white students. It is much better to see them work it out.

Q. *How would you characterize the response of the teachers to the program?*

R. They seem to be really putting out. I haven't heard one negative comment. They all seem to like the black children, and several have told me they are glad there are black children here at the school. I sense they all want to make it work.

Q. *How would you characterize the reactions of both the white and black parents to the program?*

R. Well, I haven't yet met any of the black parents so I can't say for them. The white parents I have talked to all seem quite pleased. One mother told me she was so pleased that both of her children are in rooms with A.T. students and neither of them has yet mentioned that any of their classmates are black. I don't expect there to be any adverse reaction because the numbers are too small to make an impact on the school.

Q. *Can you think of anything that should be, but is not happening with the A.T. Program here at Brush?*

R. Nothing that I can think of. I just think the important thing is for the teachers to get to know the students and to learn to have some understanding of their background. Some of the teachers seem to have no idea of the background of the black students, and they aren't prepared for the language and behavior they see. I would hope the teachers would visit in the homes so they could understand better.

Day 10: The Questionnaire

Each of the teachers in grades one through four who had Administrative Transfer students was asked to complete a short, seven-item questionnaire concerning the individual A.T. students. The response rate was 100 percent ($N = 18$), and all were returned within three days. The questionnaire was given in the lower grades only, for I had had little contact with the upper-grade teachers and had not planned observations in their rooms. The covering letter accompanying the questionnaire read as follows:

Dear Faculty Member,

As you know, I am at Brush School this academic year working on a research study concerned with the behavioral interaction between white and black children in a newly integrated situation. I have been conducting first-hand observations in some of your classrooms, but it is simply not possible to get to all of them. Consequently, I will have to rely on your observations and reflections to give me some understanding of how the year is beginning for the black children in particular and the classroom in general. Please leave the completed questionnaires in my mail slot in the office.

Because the number of questions was few, the number of students rather small, and the responses brief, what follows is a summary of comments given by the teachers on individual children in their rooms. Several teachers wrote only one- or two-word answers to the questions, and their responses are not included. The profiles will be given consecutively by grade level.

First Grade: Donald has one friend in the class. He might have more but the other children complain he takes their pencils and erasers — and he usually has them when I look. The only time he talked about his skin color was with Tim in the reading group. Donald does not have the background of the other children. He has a short interest span and finds it difficult to complete his tasks. He likes to move about the room. In many respects he is no different from two or three other boys in the room.

Jeff has made only a few friends at this time. He looks forward to the recess period when he can play with Donald. He reacts aggressively to the other children in the class, and they do not respond positively. He has made no mention of his skin color, nor have I heard any of the other students make comments. He is slow to achieve and does not follow directions. He seems many times to be confused and frustrated. He falls asleep almost every day. He is far below average and is unable to achieve many of the first-grade skills.

Gloria has been very cautious and shy. Until the other black girl came to the room, she opened up very little. She has one white friend in the class. She has made no verbal reference to her skin color, but her first picture of herself and her family was drawn with a brown crayon. The next two pictures were drawn with a yellow crayon. She is not different from the other children in any way I can perceive. She is attentive in class, anxious to do well, responds well to praise, and seems quite happy. She also seems to be proud that she is not on the free lunch program.

Joyce seeks only to play with Gloria. She has no other friend in the class. Other students seem to ignore her, and they are irritated by her constant talking. Gloria takes time from her own work to help Joyce. Joyce seems to have very little incentive to learn, yet she cried when she was unable to decipher any of the words on a recent test. She is anxious for attention. According to her mother, she is very happy in school, and the mother is pleased she is at Brush School because, she said, she was trying to bring Joyce up "right." The mother took many pages of unfinished work home and it all came back completed in two days.

Second Grade: Jan has been friendly, but has not gone out of her way to make friends. She requires much attention when she is given directions. She often acts as if she does not understand at first. She is below most of the class and has a short attention span.

Ann has no real friends as yet. She does talk with her seatmate. She does not have the background and enrichment that the others have. She is also quite immature, probably the most immature in the class. I think she will need to repeat second grade.

Third Grade: Melvin is outgoing and at times a show-off who wants to be the center of attention in the class. The other students have enjoyed this and have become very friendly with him. As a result, he has gained in popularity and has been elected to one of the class offices. He is an average worker and completes most of what he begins. I have not heard either him or any of the others in the class discuss his color.

Duke has not been the least bit sociable, nor has he tried to gain any recognition for himself. The rest of the students are not likely to include him in activities, not because they do not like him, but because they forget about him. He is a very sensitive boy and appears to take personally any adverse remark about him. His reactions sometimes lead the other students to pick on him. He has become the leading tattler in the room. He is very low academically and is far below third-grade work. He is certainly not third-grade material.

Bob tends to sit passively in the class. He also stays in the room during recess periods. The only student in the class who interacts with him sits next to him and is one of the best boys in the class. His parents have encouraged him to help Bob in any way he can. Bob performs far below class average and needs all the individual help he can get. He is listless and seems puzzled by class procedures.

Fourth Grade: Diane has not sought to make friends and apparently has none in the class. She seems to be a normal little girl who is perhaps overly shy in a new situation. She organizes her written work very well, but she is at the lower end of the class in overall performance.

Will stays primarily with the other black student in the room. He seems to lack some of the "understandings" of others in the class, about class routine and practices. He is willing to try and wants to listen. He will ask questions of me individually.

What the teachers had to say after ten days of school about their A.T. students is extremely important, for it suggested how the teachers viewed their early adjustment and performance as well as, in several instances, what could be anticipated in the way of future performance. In summarizing these comments, one gets the picture of a group of rather isolated children, with few or no friends, who were generally performing at the lower end of the class, and who seemed not yet to have caught on to the intricacies of the interaction within their white peer groups. The academic evaluations of the students fell within rather narrow limits: from those few who would hold their own, to the larger group who were already behind because of their lack of "background," to those who would not be able to stay with the class and would be repeating the grade level again next year. The general characteristics of the teachers' perceptions — the sense of isolation and low academic performance — posed a dilemma that was to become increasingly evident through the course of the school year: *If a school is to base its integration program on the assumptions of racial assimilation, how then does one neutralize the academic and behavioral performances of the black students, which are viewed in such a manner as to set them apart from their white classmates?* At Brush School no answer was found. The gap between the rhetoric of the school and the reality of the classrooms remained unbridged.

There immediately arises in this context a question of causa-

tion. Was it what the black children brought with them that generated a situation where they appeared to be on the outside looking in? Or was it what they found when they arrived that led them
to react in such a way to reduce the amount of interaction they
had with whites? Much the same could be asked of their academic
performance. Did they come to Brush School generally "behind"
the white students who were already there? Or did the teachers
scrutinize their performance with the idea of finding negative
evidence that would support previously held negative expectations about what could be anticipated from the students?[2] In
these first days, the observations were rather intense in Mrs.
Brown's classroom. First-hand observations of the initial adjustment of other A.T. students were limited, but observation of
Donald suggests that academically he was correctly pegged as still
in need of work with letter recognition. Behaviorally, he was
watched closely, but the teacher did not say to me that from what
she had observed she would label him negatively. For Donald,
perhaps more than for other A.T. students in the primary grades,
the book was still open.

Day 11: Parent and Staff Meeting on the A.T. Program

It had been decided by the principal and Mrs. Miller, the
A.T. coordinator, that a meeting of the parents of the black students, the local host parents, and the school staff would be a good
way of enhancing the A.T. Program. Both said they thought it
important that the black parents come to feel they "belonged" at
Brush and that they have the opportunity to meet other parents.
Thus, on the Tuesday of the third week of school, an evening
meeting was scheduled.

I arrived at the school at 7:55 P.M., five minutes before the
time the principal had announced as the starting time. When I

2. It is important to emphasize here that no data were collected on the new white
students in these same grades. Consequently, it is not possible to ascertain how various
teachers reacted to them during their initial days of enrollment. One might assume that
the reaction to the white youngsters would be similar or different from the reaction to
the black youngsters — similar if newness to the school is the determining factor, different
if race is the determining criterion. In any event, the lack of data on the white students
necessarily implies caution in interpreting teachers' reactions to the new black students.

entered the library, there were only six or seven people in the room, two of whom were black women. At 8:00, the principal announced he would wait a little longer before beginning. Coffee and cookies were available on one table and that was where the small group gathered. People began to arrive in large numbers and the group grew to perhaps forty by 8:20, when the principal called out he wanted to begin.

During the twenty-five minutes I was in the room before the beginning of the session, several teachers and I talked about how they thought the program was progressing in their respective classrooms. One of the fourth-grade teachers, Mrs. Hill, expressed her concern that her three A.T. students were already falling behind the others in the room. She stopped almost in the middle of a sentence and said, "But I shouldn't be telling you all my problems. You're not my psychiatrist." I said she need not worry about me even trying to be, but I was interested in her observations and comments on her class. Then, almost as if this exchange had not occurred, she went ahead with the sentence she had interrupted.

Mrs. Evans said that one of her students, Gloria, had come to her yesterday crying and trying to hold on to her. She said she asked Gloria what was the problem, and Gloria said it was Jeff from another first-grade room, who wanted to "beat her up." Mrs. Hill, who was still standing nearby, commented when she heard this, "You know, it seems these A.T. kids are having more trouble among themselves than they are with the white kids." Mrs. Evans concurred and said she had observed the A.T. students during noon periods frequently fighting with one another but never with white students. Mrs. Evans then completed her narration of the episode of Gloria and Jeff by saying that she had a talk with Jeff at the next recess period, and when it was over, Jeff told Gloria he was not going to bother her again. Mrs. Evans smiled as she told this, and said, "I'm so glad they worked it out."

A third-grade teacher also spoke with me briefly, saying she had the "cutest little story." She related how one of her black male students had brought a "cake-cutter" comb to the class and all the white students were amazed. She said several tried to get the comb to stay in their hair as could the black student, but none could. She told me she wished I had been in her room to observe that incident because "it is just fascinating to watch them work it out among themselves."

As the principal calls the groups together, I glance about the room and count nine black people out of a total gathering of about forty. He introduces everyone in the room by category, either as teacher, host parent, A.T. parent, or as visitor. He begins a rather rambling discourse on Brush School, saying he thinks it is a good school with qualified teachers. He mentions he is especially pleased that the teachers in the school do not have a double standard and he knows this would be welcome news to the black parents. "Because," he says, "I know you want for your children the same things we want for our children. None of us want to be treated any differently than anyone else." He continues speaking for at least fifteen minutes. (Note: I have the impression, after the first five, that he is searching for things to say.)

A curious aspect of the meeting was that it quickly became apparent that there was no agenda other than the short introduction and talk by the principal. When he finished, there was an uncomfortable silence, no one spoke or sought to pick up where he finished. Finally, the principal asked the black parents if they would like to have a tour of the school. Several nodded that they would. The principal said that they could have it immediately.

This signaled the disintegration of the meeting. The principal told the group the tour could begin with the science rooms across the hall. People began to rise; the teachers were putting on their coats and the general feeling was that the meeting had ended—if it had ever begun. The principal went across the hall and about eight or ten people followed. He waited in the science room for a few minutes and then came back into the hall, expecting to find people coming to the first stop on the tour. Instead, there were parents and teachers alike with their coats on walking toward the exits. The principal called out, "Hey, we are not done. Things are just beginning." Perhaps half of the people continued to walk toward and finally out the exit. Others turned back. He several more times spoke to smaller groups in the hall, telling them the tour was about to begin. He went back into the science room, and the audience was at best half of that when the original meeting began. Several teachers did not go into the room, but crowded around the doorway, where I also stood.

When the principal begins speaking in the science room, he mentions not a word about the science room, but begins another long discourse on discipline and how he deals with problem students. He says he supports his teachers in their efforts to deal with class problems and he generally wants to leave it up to the teachers to work them out. He says he is not going to treat a black child differently from a white child. Again, "I know you people want the same thing we want." After a ten- or fifteen-minute discourse on disciplinary matters, the principal turns his attention to academic problems. He tells the parents that if they are upset about the performance of their children, they should come to the school to talk to the teachers and himself rather than to "sit home and stew about it."

I asked a seventh- or eighth-grade teacher if she had heard these comments from the principal before. She responded, "At the drop of a hat." She had a deep frown on her face as she said this, and then added, "What a bomb this turned out to be." She continued by saying the principal must be able to give this talk in his sleep. I asked why. "He just gave this identical spiel yesterday at an assembly he called for all the upper grades. And wouldn't you know it, he named only two students during the entire talk who served as examples of what he did not like to see happen here, and both of the students singled out were black. I almost groaned out loud when that happened. I don't think he has the slightest idea of what he is doing with this whole program. All he can do is say the same thing over and over."

The principal is finished with his comments. He asks if there are any questions. There are none. He asks if anyone still wants to take the tour. There are no hands. He says, "OK, that about wraps it up. Thanks for coming." There is a mass exodus out of the building, as if he had called for a fire drill. One of the teachers says to me as we leave, "Jesus, we will never see another black parent at this school all year."

In retrospect a prophetic statement.

4.

In the Classrooms: Patterns
of Student Adaptations

A s the school year progressed, classrooms began to develop an internal order and logic of their own. In each of the
classrooms observed, teachers and students developed patterns of
interaction, levels of expectations, and organizational routines
that distinguished them one from another, even if only slightly.
In this and the following two chapters, the ongoing flow of the
school year is detailed through a presentation and analysis of a
variety of observations in several classrooms, at faculty meetings,
in the teachers' lounge, and on the playgrounds. In these chapters I give an overview of life at Brush School. In particular, I
emphasize the adaptations and interactions developed by the
black children in their new milieu. And the class that remains an
anchor point for our understanding of the dynamics of integration at Brush is Mrs. Brown's first-grade class.

Conceptually, the focus on the variations and adaptations
within a single school has taken on additional importance with
the reexamination of the initial findings of the Coleman Report
of 1966. In assessing the data from the original report, Smith reported in 1972 that 90 percent of all variations in the range of test
performance could be located within any typical school in the

urban North. This is crucial, for it suggests that there is greater pupil variability *within* the same school than *between* schools.

The classroom observations that follow will, I hope, provide a sense of the internal heterogeneity of Brush School and what the consequences were for patterns of classroom organization and interaction. Furthermore, they should reinforce our understanding of the school as a setting to which children bring a diversity of interests, talents, and backgrounds. From these observations, it should be apparent that it is no more correct to speak stereotypically of "white students" than it is to aggregate "black students." But in spite of the diversity among the black students, there is an added note of poignancy in the following descriptions, for, overwhelmingly, it was they who ended up at the bottom of the status-academic hierarchy in a "good" middle-class school.

This chapter presents, in an essentially ethnographic manner, a variety of episodes and interactions that occurred at Brush School during the fall of 1973. The episodic nature of the observations in this and the next two chapters and the change of focus from classroom to classroom and from grade level to grade level result from decisions made early in the study: (1) that it would not be possible to observe all day every day and (2) that a sense of the variability and diversity of experiences generated by the integration effort at Brush could be more accurately captured by focusing on several settings rather than exclusively on a single classroom.

The periodic references to Mrs. Brown's classroom provide the specificity a study like this needs, while the data from four other classrooms provide the scope that is also necessary. In this kind of analysis, the comparative adaptations of the black children become apparent, and the diversities and similarities of their situations are clearly outlined. Furthermore, the varying contributions of classroom climate, peer interactions, status and academic hierarchies, and teacher-student interactions can be linked to the experiences of individual children.

In the Introduction, four alternative perspectives for defining school integration were offered. A critical dimension to be considered in each is the impact on the values the children hold about themselves and others. Allport (1954), Goodman (1964), Pettigrew (1970), Proshansky (1966), Proshansky and Newton (1968), and Rosenberg and Simmons (1972) have all noted the importance of the preschool and early years of elementary school in the development of both the child's self-esteem and his evaluations of individuals and groups different from himself. As Proshansky and Newton (1968: 183) have written: "During this period the child becomes increasingly aware of racial differences and learns labels and affective responses associated with various ethnic groups including his own. The research indicates that the Negro child and his white counterpart become aware of color or racial differences as early as three or four and that within this awareness lies an inchoate understanding of the evaluations placed on this color by the larger society."

Thus, within the primary-grade classrooms, the children are actively involved in two processes: first, building an understanding of one's own identity and, second, ascertaining the *value* others give to that identity. Though analytically the conception and evaluation of identity must be distinguished, in reality they are inextricably interwoven. Both black and white children at Brush were learning of their color, the color of others, and the evaluative meaning of each. What becomes apparent in these observations is that the black children were learning of their color in a context where others were ambivalent toward them at best and willing to ignore them at the least. "Whiteness" was the norm at Brush; it pervaded the pictures in the classrooms and in the halls, the films shown to the classes, the textbooks, the teachers, and the administration. If identities are socially constructed, as I believe they are, what follows is the sketching of one part of the social world in which children were coming to know of themselves and what others thought them to be.

September 21

One aspect of American education that is seemingly universal is testing. There are spelling tests, reading tests, mathematics tests, and achievement tests, the last being generally misunderstood but highly revered. Each fall in the Portland public school system every elementary school tests all children with a battery of achievement tests designed to give the teacher information on individual performance, to give the principal information on his school as a whole, and to provide the administration with the basis for developing a composite picture of comparative perform-ance of schools throughout the city.

I was observing in Mrs. Brown's first-grade class the day she was administering part of the test to her students. The following observation raises a series of questions about the relevance and accuracy of test scores generated in classroom settings, as well as important questions about the ethical and pedogogical value of tests and their use.

Mrs. Brown comes to where I am seated and apologizes to me, saying she is going to have to take the remainder of the morning to administer a series of tests to the class. She says she is sorry there will be no class activities for me to observe. I ask if I can stay to watch the testing, and she says I can, but answers in a way im-plying that there will be nothing of interest to me. Before she leaves, she adds, "Every fall I have to give this damn test. There is no need for it because I know what all these kids are doing. But it's required and I guess I have to go along."

She goes to the front of the room, tells the class to put every-thing off their desks except a pencil. She tells them they have to get ready to take a test. "How many of you understand that this test doesn't matter? It really doesn't matter, but you should still try to do your best. How many of you really understand it doesn't matter?" Only a few hands go up. She starts walking through the room moving the desks apart, telling the class she knows they will not look at anyone's paper, but she does not "want any eyes to wander by mistake." When she comes by my seat, she hands me the test record sheet with the scores of the two tests the class com-pleted yesterday. The scores suggest a bimodal distribution. Don-ald scored toward the bottom of the lower distribution.

Mrs. Brown is back in the front of the room. "OK, I am wait-ing." Mary calls out, "Mrs. Brown, will you move Donald away? He wants to look at my paper." Mrs. Brown replies, "Oh no. Donald would not do that." But she moves his desk anyway. She asks Mary if everything is now all right and Mary says, "Yes."

"OK, I want you all to listen. Open your tests to page 6, where we will do test three. There is a blue line across the middle of the page. Donald, what does that line mean?" Donald responds, "It show you." "It shows you what?" "What to do." "No, that's not it. Tim, do you know?" "It tells you the problem." "No but you're close. What it tells you to do is to concentrate on only those problems above the line and none of those below it. Do you all understand?" No responses from the class. "OK, I'll get ready and you get ready and we'll all try to start together." She finishes her directions and tells the class to begin.

She comes to the back of the room and tells me that yesterday the test got so frustrating for the class that she had to end early. She says many of the children cannot read well enough to complete the items and they became very upset. She begins walking through the class talking to the students, telling them not to worry and just to do what they can. She speaks to me again, "I know talking to them during the test is not supposed to happen, but I don't like to see them so frustrated. Isn't this all a waste of time." She seems quite agitated. I note that one of the boys, David, has closed his book and is drawing circles on the cover.

At the end of the fifteen-minute test period, Mrs. Brown tells Craig to collect the papers. Ian begins to cry. He says he could not do the test and he did not answer a single question. He is crying quite loudly. Mrs. Brown goes over to him and puts her arm around him. She tells him it is OK and she knows he tried to do his best. Ian, still sobbing, says, "But I couldn't get even one." Mrs. Brown leaves him and comes to the front. "OK, we'll take a break and have recess." Ian is still sobbing. "I know how you feel Ian, we all felt that way yesterday. Just do the best you can." She continues, "By the way, boys and girls, we have some more tests to take this afternoon. How many of you think taking the test is fun?" Two hands go up. She looks at me and frowns. Lori calls out, "It's no fun 'cause I can't read the questions." Several other children voice their agreement with Lori, including Brad, Kim, and Donald. Mrs. Brown dismisses the class to the playground.

September 24

By the fourth week of school, a rather sketchy characterization of each of the four Administrative Transfer students in the first grade had emerged among the first-grade teachers. Gloria, they thought, was the most promising academically and "fit in" best; Donald they viewed as marginally capable, but they thought he could not settle down to complete his work; Joyce was viewed as shy and dependent, with rather low academic ability; and the child who was seen both behaviorally and academically as having the least chance of doing well at Brush was Jeff, the single A.T. student in Mrs. Wills's class. The observation on this day was in Mrs. Wills's first-grade room. Mrs. Wills had drawn four different shapes on the blackboard and under each printed the name of a color. She then told the students to draw these shapes on their papers with crayons, using the color indicated for each.

Jeff is out of his seat looking at the supply box brought by Kurt. A girl sitting next to Kurt says to Jeff, "You're not supposed to use anyone's things but your own." Jeff picks one of the crayons from the box, breaks it, and puts the pieces back. The girl gets up from her seat and goes to tell the teacher what happened. Mrs. Wills comes and quietly tells Jeff he should keep his hands off other people's supplies. She says Jeff has his own supplies and should use them.

Jeff is up out of his seat. He goes to the front blackboard and calls out to Don, "Don, this say black?" pointing to one of the words on the board. Don says yes. (The class had gone over this and the three other words on the board, but Jeff was not paying attention at the time. He was drawing on the sole of his tennis shoe with a pen.) He goes back to his chair, and pushes it far back so it is up against the desk of the student behind him. He watches her for a short while and then is up again and back at the board. He calls out to this girl, "Ellen, this say black?" She says yes and Jeff comes back to his chair. He now begins to draw on Ellen's paper, and she pushes his hand away, telling him in an irritated voice that he should be doing his own work. He stops drawing on her paper but does not turn around.

Mrs. Wills, who has organized a reading group on the right side of the room, has observed part of this exchange. She calls out in a quiet voice, "Excuse me. I believe it is now time for everyone to be working on their own papers." Jeff pushes his chair back to his own desk, but gets up again. He goes to the teacher and says "Teacher, teacher." She responds, "What?" "Watch me." He goes to the board and asks if the word at the bottom says "black." She says it does. Jeff goes to his seat and gets out several crayons. He starts playing with them by rolling them together across his desk. Soon he is writing on his desk with one of his crayons. Mrs.

Wills, who has come to her desk for a paper, sees Jeff and comes over to him. Again in a soft voice: "Jeff, we are not to write on our desks, only on the paper." With no other comment she goes back to her reading group. Jeff takes one of the crayons and begins to print his name on his paper.

As the observation drew to a close, Mrs. Wills told me that she was especially pleased I had chosen to observe on this day, because it was the first day in the school year Jeff had attempted to do the assignment. He had been able to write the "Je" of his name and had used the correct color in one of the two shapes he drew, but he had drawn both as circles although one was to be a triangle. Mrs. Wills also told me that Jeff's morning routine usually consisted of barely making it through the morning excercises before falling asleep until recess at 10:20; after recess, he again slept until lunch at 11:00. (I learned from the teacher later in the afternoon that Jeff had gone to sleep after the recess period on this day as well.)

September 25
Every fall Brush School held a "parent open house," so that the parents could come to their children's classrooms to see their work and meet with the teacher. This event had been scheduled for the following evening, September 26. The morning of the twenty-fifth was largely devoted to making papers especially for the parents. What follows is an observation in Mrs. Brown's class of the preparation of a newspaper "your mothers and fathers can take home to read."

Mrs. Brown tells the class they are going to make a newspaper. She says they should do a good job on their papers so the parents will have something "pretty to look at." She also says, "I don't want you to worry about a grade on this paper. I'm not even going to grade it."
She begins writing the heading for the paper on the board, "Our Newspaper," and below that is to go the name and date. She asks the class what they will draw on page 1. "It should be important because it's on the front page." One boy calls out, "A rainbow." Another says he will draw his bike. A girl says she will

draw a picture of her mother and father. This comment seems to please Mrs. Brown considerably. She exclaims, "Oh, that's wonderful. I am sure they'll be very happy." A boy calls out that he will draw the building where his father works. Mrs. Brown tells the class they can choose what they wish to put on the front page. "Just try your best to make it pretty."

She instructs the class to open their folded papers to page 2. "This will be our financial page. I know that's the page your father likes to read. But we don't put finances on our page, we will put our math instead. Mrs. Brown draws a square on the board and tells the class that will be page 2. She divides the square in quarters and writes in the first, "Two blue." She asks Debbie to read the square and she does. She then asks Donald what color he would like to use in the second square. He responds. "Red." "How many red things would you like to make?" He answers "three." Mrs. Brown writes "Three Red." She follows the same procedure with two other students.

When one of the two children chooses the color green, Donald calls out, "I got no green." Mrs. Brown tells him he can go to her desk and look in the crayon can to see if a green one is there. She winks at me as she says this. Donald finds one and comes back to his seat.

When all four squares are completed, Mrs. Brown asks Donald to stand: "Let's show them you know how to read now, Donald." She points to the first square and he correctly says "Two blue." He repeats correctly also his own square, "Three red." He knows none of the four words in the last two squares: "Six orange" and "Five green." Mrs. Brown helps him by suggesting the first sounds of each word. Mrs. Brown then tells the class they can begin work. "Remember, you don't have to worry about a grade on this one."

Often during the observational periods in the classrooms, I was able to have short and informal conversations with the teachers. Occasionally, I would initiate them and at other times the teachers would. I commented to Mrs. Brown that Donald was beginning to recognize some words. She responded that he was "beginning to pick up and do better." She went on to say that Donald was beginning to make friends in the room. At the first of the year Donald had few friends and almost no one to play with, she said, because the students believed he was taking their pencils and crayons. "I don't think he steals on purpose. But he's so desperate to have what everyone else has that when he sees something he wants, he just takes it." Mrs. Brown mentioned that on several occasions pencils belonging to other children have turned up in his desk. When she would ask him if they were his own, he would say no, that he had found them, and then he would give them back. "I think now, though, that he is over that. At least I hope so."

That Donald was still taking pencils became clear later in the morning, when I observed him doing so. The rest of the class had been dismissed for recess and Donald was the last student remaining in the room. He was at the pencil sharpener sharpening two of his own pencils. I was at this same time putting away my notebook and putting on my coat. By the time Donald had returned to his desk, he had a handful of pencils, perhaps five or six. I asked him if they were all his, and he said, "Yeah." He put them all in his drawer and went outside. I checked them after he left the room and on two of the pencils was imprinted "Trish Weller."

As I was about to leave the school building, I met the principal and we spoke briefly. Almost immediately he brought up the current controversy in the newspapers over the comments of the principal at Boise School. He said, "You really have to be careful what you say these days." He thought the principal at Boise was probably telling the truth in that there were black schools where white students would have an exceedingly hard time fitting in. "But even if it was true, you just can't make statements like that. You have to be very careful what you say. I know I don't want to talk to the press any more."

September 27

In Mrs. Daley's third-grade class were two A.T. students, Melvin and Duke. It was Duke whom Mrs. Daley had described as "definitely not third-grade material." Melvin, she thought, would make it at Brush, but with a struggle. The following is an observation of a mathematics lesson in which both Duke and Melvin participated. What is of interest here is the performance of both students on several occasions as well as the techniques Mrs. Daley used to order her class and move it toward the objectives she wanted, even when the class itself seemed confused about where she was going.

Mrs. Daley is in the front of the room with her arms folded. She says, "I'm waiting." Melvin is drawing lines across his paper and Duke is spinning his ruler on a pencil. The noise level decreases and the teacher begins the review of the math lesson from yesterday. Melvin stands, turns around, and tucks in his shirt. He sits back down.

Mrs. Daley is working with the concept of "expanded numerals." She writes 613 on the board and asks Melvin what the expanded numeral at the hundreds place is. Melvin has not been paying attention and does not know. She asks another student and the correct answer of 600 is given. The next expanded numeral is asked for and the correct answer of 10 is given by a girl. Duke had raised his hand this time. Another student gives the correct answer of 3 when the last of the three expanded numerals is asked for.

The teacher then writes 452 and the same exercise is repeated. Duke and Melvin both raise their hands on all three occasions, but are not among those called on. Mrs. Daley then asks who can give her all three parts of the expanded numeral. Melvin raises his hand and is called on. He responds, "400 plus 5." "No. Class, can anyone tell me what is wrong with that answer?" Several children say a 50 is missing. She says that is correct and asks Melvin if he can now give the entire answer correctly. He responds, "400 plus 50." Mrs. Daley: "Good, Melvin. You're correct so far. Can you remember the rest?" Melvin answers, "Plus 2." She exclaims, "Oh, that's wonderful. It makes me so happy to see people do their work correctly." During this exchange, Duke has been drawing on a sheet of paper. His picture looks to be a war scene.

Mrs. Daley then passes back the math papers from yesterday. When Melvin has his, he comes back to his row and tells the boy behind him, "See, I told you I'd get them all wrong." I ask to see his paper since I am close by, and he shows it to me. The paper has a star. Every problem was answered correctly. Melvin starts comparing his paper with others around him. The boy in front had three wrong (out of fifteen), and the boy behind him had a perfect paper. Duke missed twelve of the fifteen.

When all the papers are passed back, Mrs. Daley folds her arms. "I'm waiting." There is little response from the students, who are making a good deal of noise comparing scores. She repeats herself, "OK, I'm waiting." The students still do not follow

her lead and she writes on the board, "Minus 5 minutes on P.E."
When the students see this, the noise level drops immediately.
"It's a shame that we can't get quiet and get organized. If we lose
time now, we have to make it up somewhere. Isn't it a shame to
lose time?" When the noise subsides, she tells the class a number
of them have a "See me" written at the bottom of their paper. She
says they should come to her desk once everyone begins to work. I
hear Melvin say to the boy next to him that he is glad he does not
have a "See me" on his paper. The other boy responds, "I hate
'See me's'."

Mrs. Daley then gives the assignment for the period. It is in
their math books. She says she will work through the first few
problems with the class. At one time she asks Melvin what
number comes after 329. He answers, "340." She responds, "No
that's not it." Todd is called on and gives the correct answer. For
the remaining four problems Melvin continues to hold up his
hand. So does almost every other student except Duke. The students seem so eager to answer that they are straining out of their
seats, reaching toward the teacher with their arms outstretched to
gain her attention so she will call on them. A number of them are
calling out, "Mrs. Daley! Mrs. Daley!" Once she tells the class to
sit back in their seats. She also says, "I don't hear voices, I only see
hands."

For the final problem, Mrs. Daley asks for the expanded hun-
dreds-place numeral before 343. She calls on Duke, who makes
no response, though he had held up his hand. Five or six other
students are called on and all give an incorrect answer. She seems
to become frustrated and finally gives the answer to the class.
One of the five or six who gave the wrong answer was Melvin. He
offered 443. Mrs. Daley sees Tom looking in a book. She goes
over to him, takes the book away, and tells him to go stand on the
square (one of the blocks of tile in the upper left corner of the
room). He does so. She now tells the class to get to work on their
assignment. Melvin begins to work, but Duke puts his head down
on his desk.

An important dimension of the interaction between the students
and the teacher here is the students' strong urge to participate
and to perform. They are straining to get the teacher's attention
so that they can answer. They call out her name and wave their
hands. Likewise, they are keenly interested in how others are
doing. Note the difficulty the teacher had in settling the class

down after she had passed back the papers. The competitiveness of the class was apparent, not just to me but to the students as well. They all seemed to understand that their performance and grades were important, they all wanted to know where they stood in relation to their peers.

September 28

If there was one classroom qualitatively different from the others in this study, it was that of the fourth-grade teacher, Mrs. Hill. In no other room was the sense of self-discipline so apparent, were there such prolonged periods of concentration, was there the positive desire on the part of students not to interrupt one another while working; and nowhere else was the teacher's use of control mechanisms so subtle and noninterventionist. Throughout the year I observed in this room, my notes reflected the quiet, the intensity, and the sense of self motivation among the students. I often found myself thinking of them as much older than they actually were. I sensed the absence of many of the childlike qualities I saw among the third-graders just one door away. When I commented on this to the teacher, she seemed somewhat taken aback and said, "What do you expect. They are in fourth grade." If the competitiveness of the school was beginning to make itself manifest in the third grade, by the fourth competing with other students was a deadly serious business. It was as if the students were now fully aware that both teachers and parents expected them to excel. School became the arena where they had doggedly to begin the task of making their performance count.

As the students return to the room from the fire drill, there is very little talking. They immediately take their seats and begin work without any comment from the teacher. I note that there are three black children in the room. One black boy, Will, sits with a white boy in the rear of the room. One black girl sits with a white girl on the left side, and the third black student, Alex, sits by himself on the right side.

The black boy and white boy in the rear begin working together. Soon each has an arm on the shoulder of the other. The black girl, Diane, is also busy, though by herself. Alex is not working. He sits looking about the room. The room is absolutely silent within several minutes from when the class came through the door.

Mrs. Hill comes to where I am seated and tells me that I should pay particular attention to Will and the white boy, Eric, next to him. She says they are working extremely well together because the white boy is one of the most brilliant students she has ever had in a class. Eric, she mentions, had taken it on himself to help Will, and asked if he could sit by him. Eric and Will have been sitting together for about two weeks, and Will's performance has improved ever since. She says Eric is so far ahead of the remainder of the class the he has essentially become a private tutor for Will.

During this conversation, Diane had continued to work, and Alex had not. He had gone to the bathroom, sharpened his pencil, and made one tour around the room. I note that he has completed two, perhaps three of the problems. Others sitting nearby have completed twenty or twenty-five. Mrs. Hill makes no announcement that it is time for a language group, but instead goes quietly through the room tapping the shoulders of those she wants to come to the reading table. The children, almost without a sound, bring their chairs when they are selected. It is as if everyone is consciously making an effort not to disrupt the concentration of others.

For the next fifteen minutes Mrs. Hill gives the language group a lesson on the use of italics. The remainder of the class, including Diane and Will, continue to work without interruption. My notes on Alex during this time document a continual evasion. He does not work. In fact, he does no more problems on the sheet during the remainder of the morning. I learned something about Alex's background from the teacher when she came and spoke briefly with me while her language group was filling out an exercise in a workbook.

Mrs. Hill tells me she is glad I came to her room today because "things are running so smoothly." But she adds that she thinks I would have found it "much more interesting a week or so ago," when Alex first joined the class. She said that when Alex first arrived, his behavior was "totally uncontrollable. He was just wild. There were days we did not get a thing done because I had to constantly deal with his disruptions." I said if that was the case, there had been a profound transformation in the past two weeks. She smiled and responded, "We are beginning to see the emergence of internal self-control."

Mrs. Hill says the situation had become so intolerable that she called Alex's mother, who was extremely upset to hear about his behavior. She said the mother came to the school and met with her for more than two hours. "Ever since that phone call and meeting, things have been getting better. His mother seems interested in helping and I think it's beginning to pay off. He's not working yet, but at least he is quiet and not disturbing others."

Mrs. Hill lowers her voice yet further and continues to discuss Alex. She says that when he first came to the room, he did not have a single friend and he "turned off" both the white and black students. He was completely isolated, she added, until he began to calm down in the room. Now that he is progressing more rapidly, it appears that the boys in the class are beginning to include him in recess activities.

One incident she relates to me in some detail. On the second day Alex was in the class, one of the white boys, Jim, reported that his watch was taken while he was making papier-mache. Mrs. Hill says she asked him if he might have left it in his desk and he said no. Both he and she were looking for it in the room when one of the girls told her the watch was in Alex's desk. Mrs. Hill says she went to Alex's desk and found the watch there. She was particularly distressed about this incident because Jim's parents are the host parents for Alex. She says Jim told his parents that he did not want Alex any more at Brush School and that his parents should never have him over to their house.

October 1: "Cultural Awareness" and Teacher Training

I think it no overstatement to claim that one of the most murky and least understood aspects of the entire educational process is teacher education. In spite of reams of writing and countless research projects, there remains little agreement on *what* makes for the competent teacher or *how* one trains to achieve that competence (see Edgar 1974). Whether the education in question is a four-year college or university program, a summer teacher institute, or in-service courses during the school year, there is no clear agreement on what teachers should know and how they should organize their behavior in classrooms.

What follows is an observation of the first of several in-service classes for the teachers at Brush on the topic of "Cultural Awareness and Intergroup Relations." This series of classes was organized by three teachers who the previous summer had attended a two-week workshop sponsored by the Portland school system. The workshop's goal was to train teachers to set up in their own schools programs to facilitate and enhance the Administrative Transfer Program. These sessions at Brush merit attention, for they were the only exposure all but three of the teachers had to issues of "cultural awareness" and "intergroup relations" as the A.T. Program got under way. Further, the content of these classes suggests how the busing program at Brush was defined and what sorts of intergroup relations could be expected. For those teachers who had never taught a black child, the sessions offered a definition of what to anticipate and hints on how to respond. But it should be kept in mind that *these classes were initiated only after school had been in session for a month.* For that first month, there had been no assistance or assurance for the teachers. They had been left on their own during what I consider the most critical period of the entire school year.

I enter the library just as the principal is finishing the introduction of the panel moderator, a man who is an administrator in the city schools. I look for a seat and have to go to the far back corner. It appears that every teacher in the school is present. The moderator begins to discuss the history of the A.T. Program in Portland, saying it has grown as the result of the increased concern of the school system about racial isolation. He traces the year-by-year increases in the program since 1965. After a lengthy discourse on the history of the program, he asks rhetorically, "Now, what about the future? What are the goals of the Portland public schools?" He goes on to answer his own questions. "The first and foremost goal of the Portland public schools is the elimination of racial isolation in all the district schools. We define racial isolation as either an all-white or an all-black school. A second goal is to provide educational opportunity for all disadvantaged students, both black and white. Third, all the schools which are participating in the A.T. Program should continue to provide remedial skills to all those who need them, both black and white."

After nearly twenty minutes, he finishes and asks the four other panel members if they have comments. The first person, a black man, says he is most interested in seeing that black students develop a positive self-image and that parents become more aware of the resources available to them within the school system. On neither point does he elaborate. The second person introduced is a white female who tells the teachers her interest is in learning more about why some black children do not make it at their receiving school and return to their original school. She says the teachers should be aware that not all their students are going to make it. The third member of the panel, a black female, tells the teachers she thinks it very important for them to "come to understand the background of the black children." She says the children often come from families with high mobility, one-parent families, and those "who have no roots anywhere in the city."

The fourth member, a white male who is a high school counselor, begins by saying he agrees with the philosophical position of ending racial isolation, not only for the black students, but for the white students as well. In his view, the most important benefit of racial integration is the benefit to white children, because with contact with blacks, whites lose their racial stereotypes and their racism diminishes. He tells the teachers that their first priority is to treat the black children the way they treat all other children. The black children are not oddities to be stared at. "Integration is a two-way street. Black students can give and receive just as do the white students. And, finally, for you teachers, 'Ask not what you can do for your students, but what they can do for you.' "

For the next twenty-five minutes, there was a question and answer period between the panel members and the teachers. Questions were asked in a variety of areas: How is integration possible with such small numbers? (Answer: some is better than none.) Could after-school bus service be started so black children could stay for extracurricular activities? (Answer: it will begin in three weeks.) Do more black students want to join the A.T. Program? (Answer: the well is not drying up.) Can two-way busing be expected in the near future? (Answer: not unless whites ask for it.) And finally, do the panel members think the cultural differences of black children mean that they should be evaluated and treated with standards different from those of white children? This question provoked the longest and most intense discussion by the panel. The following is a summary of that exchange.

The first panel member to respond is the black woman. She answers that teachers should try to teach all children in exactly the same way. "The problem is that when people try to treat blacks differently, especially when they treat them extra-nice, they are setting them up as different. And let me tell you, I am no different than you are." The principal, seated in the audience, speaks up and tells the panel that some of his own teachers have had "hang-ups" about how to discipline the black students because they cannot keep them after school the way they do the white students. Because the black children have to catch their bus, he says, the teachers cannot use the same disciplinary techniques. The black woman responds that the school should expect the same behavior from black children as from whites and treat them the same. Further, she adds, if the teacher does discriminate between her black and white students, she is violating the professional code of ethics that teachers give equal treatment to their students.

The black male on the panel says that by judging black children by different standards the teachers are being patronizing to the black students. He says the first to know that he is being patronized is the black student, and, in response, the student will manipulate the teacher whenever he can. Instead, he says, teachers should give fair treatment to all students. The black woman adds that one of the greatest concerns of black parents in putting their children in a busing program is whether their children are being evaluated on the basis of a double standard. She says that she continually has to tell parents in the black community that this is not so. The black man says the teachers should expect some "testing" from the students, since "they are away from their home base and are trying to find the boundaries in a new situation." The teachers should be themselves, he adds, not only with the new A.T. students, but with all the students in their class.

The program was slated to end at 5:00 P.M. The principal's final remarks gave one more indication of his orientation towards the A.T. Program:

It nears five o'clock. The teachers start to shuffle papers and put on their coats. The moderator asks if there are more questions. The principal stands and says with it so near five, the teachers will have no more questions. He thanks the panel for coming and then begins a discourse of his own. He tells the panel that they were saying the very things he has been saying since the program began, that all A.T. students should be treated like everyone else. He adds that every teacher knows there are white students in the school, and he names four or five, who have caused so much trouble that without a doubt he would take the five A.T. students in place of these white students. He says the matter is not one of race. All children should be treated the same. "Just be glad," he tells the teachers, "you got the A.T. students you did as opposed to more white troublemakers." It is 5:02 and all the teachers are standing with their coats on. The principal again thanks the panel and the teachers start for the door.

October 4: The First Fight

The introduction of the element of race into Brush School had a variety of consequences, one of which was to heighten sensitivity to the activities of the students when they involved cross-racial interaction. Whereas a fight between two white boys could be dealt with, perhaps with a lecture from the principal and the excuse of "boys will be boys," a fight between a black student and a white student prompted a quite different response. On the afternoon of October 3, two white students fought with two black students. Because the fight happened after school, the principal was not able to deal with it until the following morning. That the fight would have to be dealt with was made almost a certainty when the father of one of the white students involved, a doctor, came to the school and, in the words of the principal, "made it damn clear he wanted me to get to the bottom of it." What follows is an account of how the principal, the four students, and eventually the entire third- and fourth-grade student body were drawn into the aftermath of the fight. The narrative is lengthy, but it shows how that fight engrossed the principal and several classrooms for nearly an entire morning.

When I enter Mrs. Hill's fourth-grade room, I immediately notice that Alex is seated by himself in a corner. Mrs. Hill comes to me and says that yesterday afternoon Alex was involved in a fight, but she does not know much about it. I ask her how she learned of it, and she says the father of one of the white boys came to the school after it happened.

The principal comes into the room and goes over to Alex. The teacher goes over as well. None of the children in the class are working on their papers; they are all watching the activity. The principal speaks first and tells Alex he has been lying, that his story does not hold up. He says Alex is "on his way out of the school" because none of the students can lie to the principal and get away with it. Alex is told that his story does not match with that of the other three boys. Alex speaks, but too softly for me to hear. The principal responds that he had just heard a story different from the one Alex told when he first got to school this morning. He tells Alex it will do him no good to lie because, he, the principal, can tell when people are lying. He asks, "Alex, do you want to get out of trouble?" Alex says, "Yeah." "OK, then tell me the truth. Now I want to hear what you have to say." Alex speaks again, but too softly to be heard. Mrs. Hill has continued to stand by the principal, and the class has continued to watch. Alex raises his voice, and I can hear him say the fight started when Henry fell down and Jon started to beat on him. The principal says this is the first he has heard of anyone falling down and asks why Alex had not told him this before. Alex says he forgot. Alex is told that if he is in another fight during the year, there will be no point in his coming back to the school. He can "pack his books and go home for good."

In the midst of this, the principal changes the subject and tells Alex he also had better quit chasing the girls. The principal says he cannot chase girls so why should Alex think he can. "Do you think you are better than me?" Alex says no. "Well, then, what gives you the right to do things that I can't do." Alex says he does not know. The principal tells Alex to stay put, and says he will be back.

I watched the principal go into another of the fourth-grade rooms. Soon he left that room and went into another. Mrs. Hill stood at the doorway and watched as well. She then went back to the front of the class and told them to continue work on their assignment. I sensed a tension and restlessness in the students that I had never observed before. The black aide came into the room momentarily. She had spoken to the teacher and was about ready to leave when she said to me, "He's really upset about that fight. Now he has the whole school uptight."

Shortly, the principal comes back and tells Alex he wants to see him in the hall. I follow. In the hall are one black boy, two white boys, and another fourth-grade teacher. One of the white boys, Joel, is crying. The principal asks Alex to give his version, and Alex says the fight began when Henry fell down and Jon laughed at him. He says Henry got mad and started after Jon. He says he and Joel never did get into the fight.

The principal says that from what he has heard, two things happened that were wrong. He asks each boy what was wrong. Alex says he should not have told Henry to fight. Jon says he should not have laughed. Henry says he should not have kicked Jon, and Joel says he did not do anything. The principal tells Joel to think some more, and then says to Henry that just because someone laughed at him, he did not have the right to kick that person. He continues, "Are any of you better than me?" All the boys say no, and he responds, "Well, if I can't hurt anyone who laughs at me, why should you be able to?" There is no response. The principal says Jon can be excused from the group because it is really not bad just to laugh and he himself does it "all day long." Besides, he says, Henry probably looked funny when he fell.

As Jon is about to leave, Mr. Norris sums up, "Now let me repeat what I said. If any of you four get in a fight for the rest of the year, that's nine months, I'm not going to ask if you were right or wrong. I'm just going to send you home. There will be no questions asked if you're in another fight." Each of the four is asked to repeat what the principal said. With some coaxing and repetition, the principal gets all four to say it. He dismisses the two white boys and then turns to Henry and Alex, "Do you two like it here?" Both say they do. "Well, you're going to have to be good if you want to stay. Do you understand?" Both boys say they do, and the principal dismisses them.

Mr. Norris begins moving from one fourth-grade room to another. As he passes me, he tells me to "stick around." I ask what is going to happen, and he says, "I'm getting all the classes together. You may not like it, though, when you hear what I have to say."

As Mr. Norris moves from room to room, he tells the teachers to take their classes to the room of Mrs. Miller, one of the third-grade teachers. Soon all the third- and fourth-grade students are out of their rooms and moving down the hall to Mrs. Miller's room.

The principal begins the meeting by saying that he has a problem and needs help. "We've got a problem with name calling, pushing, shoving, and running. But most of all, we've got a problem with some students trying to take over their classes from the teachers. I want you all to know that I'm not going to let that happen. The teachers are in charge here. They give the orders. They are the cops. No one else sets the rules but them."

He continues by saying he had talked to four boys earlier and had told them to quit playing cop, and that if they tried again, they would be on their way out. "We are really a great school, but we have to knock this off. We simply can't have more of this kind of behavior. You know me well enough to know I mean what I say. You have to follow the rules. I have to follow the rules, and none of you are any better than me. So we all have to follow the rules together. If you can't follow the rules, you're not going to have the freedom you have now. I will start making your teachers go with you every time you leave the classroom, but I know you don't want that. So we all have to shape up. And you all know if you can't behave here at school, I'm not going to let you go on field trips out into the world and have others see you misbehave. So if any of you are having problems, work them out or go see one of your six cops. And if you don't want to do that, you can come see the chief himself." He asks if there are any questions. There are none and the classes are dismissed. As the children and teachers start to file out, one of the teachers comments to me, "He has got to have this whole school just perfect."

October 5

In discussing what children should learn from the classroom experience, a fruitful distinction is frequently made between pedagogical outcomes (for example, reading, writing, spelling) and those more nebulously known as "social adjustment," "personal growth" or just "getting along with others." On the grade cards Brush students periodically received, the latter categories were subsumed under the rubric of "citizenship."

Citizenship was important at Brush. The value teachers placed on social and emotional development in their classrooms set the stage for what I think was one of the major concerns about the

A.T. students: that they would not "fit in" because their behavioral characteristics diverged from the school's norms. In short, whether they could succeed academically or not, there would be "problems" because of their actions. In this light, the assessments of Jeff and Donald given by their respective teachers are important, for each suggests improvement in their behavior, in terms of both what had been extinguished and what they had learned.

Mrs. Wills comes to the back of the room, where I am seated. I ask her how Jeff has been doing this week. She says he is staying awake much more frequently and is spending more time working at his desk. She also mentions he is not the behavioral problem he was. I ask what she had regarded as a problem and she responds that when he first came, he would crawl around the room on his hands and knees, steal pencils, push desks, and continually make trips back and forth to the bathroom. Now she is more firm with him, she says, and he is trying harder. "Every day when we have a reading lesson, he scoots his chair right up against me. Sometimes he is practically in my lap. I think he is developing a good relation with me, and it is showing up in his trying to do his work."
She says that last week Jeff was tested by the district psychologist. "Since he has been doing so poorly, I wanted to find out how much he has got to work with." The scores indicated that Jeff was, in her words, "very low." I ask whether she remembered any of the terminology used by the tester, and she responds that she thought the term "borderline mentally retarded" was used to describe Jeff. She says she wants to talk to the tester again to find out what that implies for the level of academic work he can do. "I know he's slow, because he's still having trouble recognizing "A" and "B," even after we have been working on them for three weeks. Besides, just looking at his papers suggests something, the way they are disorganized."

After the observational period in Mrs. Wills's room, I was on the playground talking with Mrs. Brown. In the course of the conversation, I asked about Donald. Her first comment: "Oh, he is fitting in very well. Some of those early problems I was having with him seem to have gone away." I asked what she thought those problems might have been attributed to, and she responded that most likely it was the "newness of the situation" and that Donald was "scared." She said he was fitting "nicely" into the classroom and was beginning to concentrate on his work. When he first came to the room, she noted, she was afraid and uncertain about how to treat him. But this is no longer the case, for she has decided he should be treated "like everyone else, which means now I am pretty firm with him." Her final comment: "But more than anything, I'm glad he has quit taking all those pencils. I don't like people stealing in my room."

October 8: More In-Service Training

For this, the second of the in-service training sessions, the three teachers in charge of the program had scheduled two films, one narrated by Robert Culp entitled *Black and White Uptight* and another called *Bill Cosby on Prejudice*. The meeting began twenty-five minutes late because the principal used that time to discuss a new teacher-evaluation form he wanted to use at the school. The teachers were upset at what they thought was a *fait accompli* and a violation of their contract, which says that any new evaluation forms have to be mutually agreed upon. Finally, the principal backed off to the extent of agreeing to a secret ballot the following day on whether the form would be used. (The proposal was soundly defeated.) After this upsetting and sometimes angry exchange of words, the teachers were shown the two films. There was no discussion of the first film when it ended, and the time between films was used up by the principal in trying to get approval of the wording for the ballot the following day. When the second film ended, the room was cleared in about three minutes.

October 9

As noted in the observations of September 25 and October 5, Mrs. Brown expressed concern over Donald's taking of other students' supplies. Though she had optimistically said that Donald had ceased such activities, the events of this morning, October 9, were to contribute to a change in her basic definition of Donald. Whereas previously she had described his stealing as "not really Donald," subsequently, she viewed him as a child "with sticky fingers" who constantly had to be watched. She came to view his stealing as an integral part of the "real Donald."

I enter Mrs. Brown's room and find a seat in the rear. She is at her desk, but almost immediately gets up and comes to me. "You should have been here earlier." I ask why, and she replies that Donald's mother had come to arrange the time of the conference (to be held in lieu of the first-quarter grade card). She says that while she and Donald's mother were talking, Bruce came up to them and said Donald had taken his money. Mrs. Brown says she defended Donald because once before in the morning Bruce had said Donald had taken something when in fact he had not. Donald's mother, however, asked Donald to come to her and give her all the money in his pockets. At first, Mrs. Brown says, he took out the fifteen cents his mother had given him. But when he was told to "dig deeper," he came up with Bruce's milk money. Mrs. Brown says Donald's mother became very upset and was on the verge of tears. She told Donald's mother not to worry because, she said, children at this age often take things, thinking that if they take something, it is theirs. Mrs. Brown tells me that nothing she said seemed to help, that Donald's mother remained upset and quickly left the room. I ask Mrs. Brown what Donald's mother was like, and she responds by saying she was young, attractive, friendly, and very interested in Donald's performance.

This incident came to play an important role for Mrs. Brown as the year progressed and Donald periodically was found with other students' supplies. Gradually, Mrs. Brown came to redefine Donald's mother's response this morning as one of indifference and apathy, and she then explained Donald's behavior as resulting from lack of "training in the home."

ITEM: During an observation of the morning recess period of the three first-grade rooms, the four black children, Donald, Jeff, Joyce, and Gloria, played only with one another. Their interaction with any of the fifty or sixty children on the playground was minimal. Donald had no interaction with any white children until his was the last class left outside. I mentioned this to Mrs. Brown, and she said that if there were more black children in the classrooms, they would not "need to cling together" on the playground.

October 11

Throughout the year I frequently asked the teachers how they thought "things were going with the A.T. students." I found this an informative (and informal) way of gauging the teachers' perceptions about the individual students in their respective classes, as well as their views of the program at the school. On this day, I asked that question of Mrs. Daley and received the first response I had had from a teacher indicating what she thought was a negative assessment of Brush by one of the black students.

In response to my question, Mrs. Daley begins talking about Duke. "Well, Duke is having real problems now, and I don't think he wants to stay here any more. The reading specialist who works with him in the afternoon says he doesn't cooperate at all any more with her, and he isn't doing much in here either. I think he is feeling sorry for himself because he can't keep up. He wants to do more than he can. The only program we have going for him now that seems to be working is when he tells a story to the aide and then she writes it down for him to copy. He will work hard on that, but that's about all. You know, I think he would leave if he could."

During the first six weeks of the A.T. Program, this comment was the sole indication I had that a teacher perceived any of the black students as being unhappy at the school. In response to my question "How are things going?" the teachers were consistently affirmative. Though no data were available, it can be posited that one of the reasons for their continued optimism about the A.T. Program was their own perceptions that the black students *wanted* to be there. Believing this, they may have been more inclined to accept and work with the students than if they had believed that the students disliked Brush and wanted instead to be in their neighborhood school.

October 12

In the observation of Mrs. Hill's room the day after the fight, there was one point that should not be overlooked: Alex was in a corner of the room isolated from the remainder of his class. *This phenomenon, the physical separation of the black students, was to reappear time and again during the year.* It is difficult to assess the effect of this isolation because there were various reasons for it: punishment, to diminish talking to other students, to allow concentration on work, or even personal choice by the student. During the year, all four of these explanations were offered by either the teacher or the student involved.

On this day in the observation of Mrs. Wills's class, Jeff was off by himself and as I was to learn in talking with him, he said he chose to remove himself so he could do his work.

When I enter Mrs. Wills's room, I look around and do not see Jeff. Thinking he is absent for the day, I am about to leave when the teacher points to the area behind the piano. I look and there is Jeff at his desk, his head down in his arms. He is at least seven or eight feet from the nearest desk. Between the piano and the bookshelf, he is out of sight.

Later in the morning, while Jeff still had his head down, I asked the teacher if she would mind if I talked to him when he awoke. She said that was fine with her. I waited from 10:25 until 10:40 before Jeff opened his eyes and lifted his head. He got up, went to the bathroom, and was back in his seat at 10:45. I went over to him.

I ask Jeff what he had drawn on his paper. He says it is his house. The object is a purple square with a circle in it. (His house is painted purple, incidentally.) He begins to quickly color in the circle with an orange crayon. He tells me those are the leaves on the tree in his back yard. I note he has spelled his name correctly. He shows me the back of the sheet, where there is an orange object. I ask what it is and he responds, "A boat." I ask if it is a special kind of boat, and he says it is sinking. I ask why and am told, " 'Cause the water deep." He takes the orange crayon and colors over the boat, presumably as if water were covering it. When he finishes, he says, "See water over the boat. Now it sink."

I ask Jeff if he likes Brush and he says he does. He adds he likes his teacher too. He volunteers that he asked to be put up in the corner because the boy next to him "kept messin with me." He says he told the teacher he wanted to do his work and she should move him to the corner. I ask if he wants to stay in the corner and he responds he does, so no one will "mess with me and keep me from doin' my work." Our conversation continues and I ask if he has any friends at Brush. He names two, Donald and Gloria, both first-grade A.T. students. I ask if he has any friends right here in his room and he names one girl and two boys. It is now time for the lunch period and Jeff goes to take his place in the line at the door.

October 15: And More In-service Training

The third in the series of "cultural awareness" programs was unusual in that it was the single program to which the parents of the A.T. students were specifically invited. Three black people attended this meeting: Diane's mother and grandmother and Gloria's mother.

I enter the library just as the principal is beginning to speak. The teachers are told to make sure all their conferences at the end of the first grading period are arranged. He says a special effort may be needed to make contact with the parents of the A.T. students, but his goal is that every parent in the school has a conference. That is his only announcement.

One of the teachers organizing these sessions tells the group that they are going to divide into five small groups and discuss reading material she will pass out. Later in the meeting, all the groups will come back together and share what they have learned from the material. The color of one's name tag determines which group one joins.

I join the green group with five teachers. We are given two pieces of material. The first is a section entitled, "How I Can Control Them" from a book called *The Teacher and Integration*. The second is a short excerpt entitled "Good Noise" from a book called *Intergroup Relations for the Classroom Teacher*. The first piece is essentially a refutation of the notion that "No noise is good noise." It says nothing about multicultural education or cultural awareness. The second piece summarizes itself with the statement, "Negro parents and children are not satisfied with leniency or with being overlooked. They want equality of interest, of treatment, and of opportunity to learn in the mixed school. Until there is no difference in the quality and quantity of what you do for white and Negro pupils, you will not have achieved integration in your classroom." The teachers in my group spend almost all the time on the first piece, talking about how much noise they feel they can tolerate in their classrooms.

After twenty-five minutes, the groups are called back together. Each is to report on what it found pertinent in the material it read. The first group says it concluded from its material that it is incorrect to stereotype either middle- or low-income students; another group decided that teachers should be flexible to use both homogeneous and heterogeneous class groupings; the third says that children with different cultural heritages should be able to respect their heritages and not have to hide them.

The fourth group's discussion on discipline generated the only audience participation of the afternoon. The question the group posed was: If a black child in the room was more disruptive than any other child, and the teacher, who refused to create a double standard, consequently had to give that child more attention and discipline than any other child, was the teacher then setting the stage for charges of persecution and racism?

The principal was the first to speak in response, and he began with his now familiar comment that black people want for their children what white people want for their children, and that everyone wants to be treated the same. He continued, citing examples of whites at the school who were disruptive and who needed much attention, but who were not receiving what he termed "special attention." Finally, he concluded with the following: "So what I am saying is that you don't put someone in the top spelling group just because you like them, and you don't keep someone out just because you don't like them. Everyone is to get equal treatment." The original question remained unanswered, for the meeting had run past its designated time, and teachers were beginning to put on their coats. The organizer made a special effort to thank the black parents who came. It is difficult to know why they were invited, given the proceedings.

October 18

Mrs. Evans's first-grade room was the only first-grade class with two A.T. students, Gloria and Joyce. In a number of conversations during the first weeks, Mrs. Evans described Gloria as self-assured and outgoing, and Joyce as reserved, withdrawn, and friendly only to Gloria. (see the comments on Day 10 in the previous chapter). Further, Mrs. Evans saw Gloria as a good student who completed her work and Joyce as "flighty" and "unable to concentrate" because of her "short attention span." The observation in the room and of Joyce in particular this day bears on these descriptions.

Joyce goes to the teacher and shows her she had copied all the letters the teacher printed on her paper. Mrs. Evans folds Joyce's paper and puts it in the basket. Joyce comes to the far side of the room and begins looking through a stack of orange folders for her own. I am seated nearby. While Joyce is looking through the folders a boy, Nathan, asks me why I have hair on my face. I tell him it is called a moustache. He then asks why I have so much hair on my head and I tell him I like to wear my hair long. He says, "You're weird." Joyce hears this comment and says to Nathan, "It's you who weird, boy." Nathan responds, "It's you. You old fool." Joyce retorts, "You the old fool." Joyce leaves and goes to the teacher's desk. As she leaves, Nathan mimics her with an exaggerated inflection, "You the old fool, boy."

Joyce comes back to her seat with a large sheet of green construction paper. She cuts out a circle and goes to show it to the teacher. Mrs. Evans says it is a nice circle but asks if Joyce has all her other work finished. Joyce says she does not. The teacher tells her that before she does more circles she should finish her work.

Joyce returns to her seat. She passes Nathan, who sticks out his tongue at her. Joyce reciprocates and says, "Back to you, boy." Joyce goes to show her circle to Gloria, and on the way back to her own seat, another boy, Tom, calls out to her, "Joyce, what are you doing?" She answers, "None of your business, boy." Tom replies, "None of your business, girl." He repeats it. Joyce says she is going to tell the teacher, who at this time is in the upper right corner of the room with a student reading group. When Joyce tells the teacher, Mrs. Evans leaves her group and comes to the back of the room. Joyce follows and when they reach Tom's desk, Mrs. Evans asks, "Joyce, who is it that makes you sad?" Joyce points to Tom and he is told by the teacher to go into the hall. Mrs. Evans follows. Joyce goes to get a sheet of white construction paper. The teacher and Tom return from the hall. He is very quiet, goes back to his seat, and the teacher returns to her reading group. Joyce is now gluing the green circle on the white construction paper.

In my estimation, Joyce comes through in this observation as anything but a quiet and withdrawn child. She was protective of her self-esteem, and mine! She did not follow directions from the teacher, but she had a project she was carrrying through on her own. Further, I sensed an independence in the child, perhaps defined by the teacher as being withdrawn and not wanting to interact with others. And what may exacerbate this interpretation is evident from the observation: that Joyce had no exchanges with anyone but Gloria and the teacher that were not antagonistic.

A final note: the teacher's actions in response to Joyce's complaint were in character. Throughout the year, she would, more likely than not, stop whatever she was doing, in this instance a reading lesson, to deal with the interpersonal relations of the children. She also spoke frequently in the class about "respecting the feelings" of other students and said that the pupils needed to help one another "feel OK." This same teacher, more than any other observed, touched the children. Both in the class and on the playground, she was continually hugging, patting, holding, or simply touching children, and girls more frequently than boys.

October 12: Reading Group Placement
On this day, I asked each of the five teachers participating in this study about the reading group position of the A.T. student(s) and whether that position had changed in the first eight weeks of school. *In all five rooms* (three first grade, one third grade, and one fourth grade), *the A.T. students were currently in the lowest reading group and had been in that group since the beginning of the year.*

While moving from room to room to speak with the teachers, I spoke only briefly with each, except for Mrs. Daley, who was on the playground with her class and had time to talk. I asked the standard question, "How are things going?"

Mrs. Daley says Melvin is doing "OK academically, but it is Duke who has the problems. He's so slow he doesn't belong in a third-grade room. You know, I just can't see what good it has done to bring him over here. He is so far behind he is all by himself. He is my lowest group of one." I asked how the two boys have been getting along socially. She says they are doing just "beautifully" and there are "no problems at all." "Melvin has been elected to a class office and has some special responsibilities in the class. Both of them seem to get along real well."

I ask about Duke specifically, and she says "Duke is such a sensitive child. He must know he is far behind everyone else. The longer he's here, the further behind he's becoming. I think it's now starting to show up, because he seems to be trying harder for attention. He's not malicious, but he's always doing things to get other students to pay attention to him. Yesterday, I heard one of the girls call him a class clown."

October 25

Several times during the year a teacher who had A.T. students would want to talk to me about some incident that had upset her. This day was one of those occasions with Mrs. Brown. From the time I entered the room I could tell she was upset. Her voice dropped in pitch and she was curt with the children. I took my seat at the rear of the room and began to observe. The assignment had just been given and the children were working on their own.

Mrs. Brown comes to the back of the room. She sits down beside me and asks, "Do you know what Donald did yesterday?" She seems upset. She tells me that while she was in the lunchroom yesterday at noon, Donald and Melvin (from the third grade) came into her room and went through her desk drawers. One of the other teachers saw them and chased them out on to the playground. She says when she checked later, she found $1.20 of lunch money missing from the desk. She adds that never before has she had to lock her drawer in her own room, but she has decided that from now on she will. She asks me what I suggest she should do, but before I can answer, she answers her own question by saying she thinks she will let it pass. She also says that in a way it's her own fault, for she knows that Donald "likes to steal" and so it was just a matter of time before he began taking from her as well as from the other students. She is up and about to go to one of the students who has her hands raised when she turns and says, "I've always tried to run an open classroom. But no more. Now things get locked up."

Later is this same observational period I was to learn from Mrs. Brown that a new first-grade A.T. student, Lou, had come to the school and was in Mrs. Evans's class. Her comments about Lou merit attention.

Mrs. Brown comes to the back and tells me, "Oh, I almost forgot. You have to go next door and talk with Mrs. Evans. She got a big one. You know, another A.T. student." She tells me the child is "very big" and that he belongs in kindergarten, but because of his size, he was placed in the first grade. She adds, "He can't do a thing." This last comment leads her into a further discussion of the A.T. Program. "I can't see what good integration does in these circumstances. What will the white children think when the blacks they see are so academically poor? And what about the black child's self-image? What is he going to think about himself when he compares his work with the work of the white students around him, and finds out he is at the bottom of his class? I just don't know what the heck they expect to accomplish with this. It doesn't make sense to bring these children here if they are not equipped to do well with the children that are already here."

These comments suggest that Mrs. Brown viewed the goal of the integration program as essentially the achievement of academic parity. For her the key benchmark was that of academic performance. The notion of the priority of academic parity fit well with the broader approach Brush School took to school integration. To wit: If all the black and white children were performing equally well, then the program would be successful. The racial assimilationist perspective would be realized, for there would be nothing to set the black children apart from the white children. What was setting them apart now and what must be overcome are their academic deficiencies, which continued to cause them to be seen as different. When the black class members could no longer be distinguished on the bases of scores or test performance, integration at Brush would have been achieved.

October 26

In response to Mrs. Brown's information, on this day I went to Mrs. Evans's room to observe the new A.T. student, Lou. This was his third day in the room. Though I concentrated on Lou's activities I also noted Joyce's behavior. It fitted much better Mrs.

Evans's previous description of her as "flighty" and "unable to concentrate" than it did the description of her as "withdrawn." Lou and Joyce absorbed much of the teacher's time and attention for both behaved in a manner starkly different from that of any of the other students in the room.

Lou follows Joyce as she leaves her seat and goes to the teacher. Joyce says she and her mother went to the store yesterday. The teacher responds, "That's nice." Joyce returns to her desk and Lou follows. Joyce sits down and Lou stands beside her. Tom comes over to Joyce and asks if she "lives downtown." Joyce says, "Nah, I live in a house." Tom goes back to his seat and Lou goes to the teacher. "I ain't got no pencil." The teacher gives him one, which he goes and sharpens. Joyce is up out of her seat walking around it and the desk behind her. The teacher says, "Joyce, will you please sit down?" Joyce goes instead to the teacher and asks what kind of paper she is supposed to be be using for the assignment. During this time, the class is doing a printing lesson. Joyce and Lou are the only two students not at work. Gloria is well into the lesson.

Since Lou got a pencil from the teacher, he has not gone back to his seat, but continues to wander about the room. The teacher says, "Lou, let's sit down and begin our work, shall we?" Lou ignores this comment and goes to the back of the room, where he starts looking at pictures on the wall. Mrs. Evans looks at me and shrugs her shoulders. Joyce has not begun. She is out of her seat, talking to the boy behind her.

Mrs. Evans observes Joyce, comes over to her, and takes her desk and pushes it across the room so it is now up against the teacher's desk. She tells Joyce to follow with her chair. As Joyce pushes her chair across, several of the children tell her to pick it up and carry it. When Joyce is settled in her new location, the teacher prints the lesson from the board on her paper and tells her to copy it. (the same as the teacher did in a previous observation, October 18).

Lou continues to roam through the room. He moves quickly from one place to another, looking first at another student's paper, then at something on the board, then moving to the water fountain, then to the supply table, then to the science table, then back to another student's desk. His motion has been perpetual. Occasionally he makes high-pitched screeching sounds as he moves. Mrs. Evans comes and takes Lou by the arm and guides him to his seat. She sits him down and begins to copy the lesson for him as she did for Joyce. He makes the screeching sound the entire time she is with him.

Mrs. Evans leaves Lou's desk and comes to me. She asks if I would like to see his file. "After what you've seen, I'm sure you are interested." I say I am and she brings it to me. She also brings the files on Joyce and Gloria. She says she is surprised to find them for she did not know they had come. She adds that these two files must have gotten to the school during one of the days last week when she was ill.

Mrs. Evans tells the class to put their materials away because they are going to the library. After several minutes of shuffling and of arranging the lines of boys and girls, the children are ready to leave, girls before the boys. "Let's all be good citizens and stop talking. We should be very quiet in the halls. If you all stay real quiet, I'll be so proud of you." The last two in the girls' line are Joyce and Gloria, and Lou is the last in the boys' line. Lou starts to lag behind as the group moves in the hall, and one of the other boys call out, "Lou, come on." Lou responds, "Forget you." Another boy tells Lou to "quit fooling around." Lou makes no response.

When the children are in the library, I return to Mrs. Evans's classroom to look at the files she had left for me. On the outside of Lou's folder is an index card with big red letters: "FIRST GRADE ON TRIAL BASIS." In the folder are comments from both the kindergarten teacher and his former first-grade teacher. They say essentially the same thing, that Lou "acts out," has a "poor self-image," and creates "disturbances" in the class. The most important piece of material, in my estimation, is a carbon of a letter from the principal at Lou's previous school to Lou's mother. In the letter, he says that Lou has "caused much concern and has been upsetting" to the teachers and their classrooms. He asks the mother whether she is at home during the day so Lou can be sent home on occasions when he "cannot be handled within the normal classroom routines." There is no reply from the mother in the file. The letter was dated four days before Lou was transferred to Brush. In the files of both Joyce and Gloria were forms filled out by their respective kindergarten teachers. On both were only positive comments, such as "friendly," "outgoing," and "interested in school."

October 29: And Still More In-Service Cultural Awareness

The session today was held in the sixth-grade room, and the program consisted of a presentation by a woman from the district office on the topic of "Classroom Behavior: How To Deal With Problems." When I entered the room, I counted twenty-three teachers, plus the principal and two aides. The material to be used by the woman in her lecture was on transparencies. The first of these she showed the group began "Unacceptable behavior leads to the treatment of . . ." and then there were two choices, "symptoms" or "causes." Examples of each were listed in the appropriate column. The lecturer stressed that teachers had the option of treating either, but implied that it was more effective to treat causes.

The second transparency listed three ways of dealing with behavior in the class: (1) permissively, (2) in an authoritarian manner, or (3) effectively. If one opted to use the third method, the lecturer stressed, one would have to be concerned with "the needs of children." The session continued in this vein, with more material on teacher effectiveness, accepting children, and how to be an "active listener." As the lecturer began to summarize her presentation, she stressed the need to "separate the child from his behavior." When the presentation was finished, the teachers were asked if they had any questions. There were none and the room was silent.

Papers were then passed to the teachers entitled "Listening for Feelings." The first of the two sheets consisted of a list of twelve statements by children and the second was a list of "feelings" to be matched to the statements. For example, the statement "This is the most stupid school I've ever gone to. None of the kids here like me and I don't like them" was to be matched to the following: "upset, insecure, not wanted and lonely." The teachers were asked to fill out the first sheet without reference to the second, and then check their answers.

The teachers then received five dittoed sheets stapled together. This was a story about "warm fuzzies." The moral of the story: when people stopped sharing "warm fuzzies" and instead gave "cold pricklies" to one another, the world would become a less humane place to be. The guest speaker read the story to the teachers, and when it was finished, the meeting disbanded with no further comments.

October 31

In contrast to other schools where I have observed, it was not standard practice at Brush for the classrooms to celebrate with a party most if not all of the holidays during the school year. As I learned was the case for all three first-grade teachers, they offered their students the choice of two holidays on which they would have parties. In Mrs. Brown's room, the choices were Christmas (called "Winter Holidays") and Valentine's Day; in Mrs. Evans's room, they were Christmas and Valentine's Day; and in Mrs. Wills's room, they were Thanksgiving and Christmas. Consequently, none of the first-grade rooms was celebrating Halloween today. It was school as usual.

Mrs. Brown and I were able to talk for perhaps five minutes on the playground during the morning recess period. Three points stand out from that conversation. First, with strong feeling she emphasized that the rising incidence of "broken homes" was affecting the performance of the children in her room. She estimated that five of the twenty-two children in the room were now living in single-parent families. This led in turn to point two: she was recommending that four of her students have extensive diagnostic testing. They were Pam, Craig, David, and Ian. She brought this up only incidentally as she said that of the four being sent for testing, three came from single-parent homes. I asked if Donald was to be tested, and she replied he was not because he was "normal." He needed only to "settle down and do his work."

The third point involved Lou, the new student in Mrs. Evans's class. Mrs. Brown asked if I had observed him yet and I responded I had. She commented, "Isn't he a mess?" Before I could respond, she continued, "What do you think the white children here think when they see someone like that. Here is a boy who can't do his work and does nothing but cause trouble. I don't see why he's here." I said that it would be unfortunate if the students tried to generalize from one person to a whole group, and that Lou's behavior might become less disruptive once he learned the class routine. Her comment: "Well, I sure hope so, because he's a bad example now, if this is what integration is all about."

CONCLUSIONS

Intuitively, we know that how teachers structure relations in their rooms has consequences for students. Their lead in defining the milieu where they and the students interact shapes the patterns and content of those interactions. And these student-teacher exchanges are critical to our understanding of the socialization processes in the class room. Furthermore, the influence of such processes on the child's life outside the classroom are of increasing concern to those dealing with the realities of inequality, poverty, racism, and segregation in American society.

Though one may argue that a teacher's aspirations and goals relate to individual style and are not applicable to any larger systemic analysis, Bowles (1972), Fuchs (1969), Henry (1963), and Ogbu (1974), among others, have all argued that such goals generally conform not only to school patterns and values, but to the larger social expectations about race and class differences as well. Failure to take into account the linkages between the classroom, the school, and the society has led to the inconclusiveness of much of the research on the relation of teaching styles to larger social conditions.

It is not my purpose here to portray teachers as either villains or saints in their relations with students. Rather, teachers should be viewed as *mediators* of the socialization processes at work in the school. It is by understanding the position of those persons with the role of "teacher" that we are able to see how this society impinges on the lives of children and shapes and influences their experiences. If schools exist to conserve the present social order, then the teachers through their own training are taught to preserve that order and thus become as enmeshed in it as do the children. As Corwin (1965:83) has noted: "Persons who expect the schools to eliminate the problems of racial prejudice or religious intolerance ignore the important fact that schools traditionally have been places where such attitudes were reinforced . . . The schools are a part of society, not apart from it; and as a result, the beliefs of those in control of society find their way into the classroom."

The implications of this argument are far from the facile misinterpretations of the Jencks et al. (1972) study, where Jencks was purported to have concluded that "schools make no difference." Nothing could be further from the truth. Schools have a profound influence and do make a difference, but in such a way as to sustain what is, not to change it. The difference schools make is that we see no difference. Linking this back directly to the life of children in classrooms, Leacock (1969:116) notes:

> Teachers define goals for children directly when they teach and set up rules for classroom behavior. Further, they establish goals for behavior indirectly when they praise, punish, or ignore different acts. The influence they exert on children is particularly strong, not only because the amount of time children spend with them is considerable, but also because their sanctions receive powerful reinforcement from a child's point of view due to the fact that they are applied before the watchful eyes of age-mates. This is not to suggest that children necessarily accept the attitudes and goals being presented. Some children internalize them deeply, some accept them casually, others actively rebel against them or casually ignore them. Whatever the response, "socialization" is taking place. In whatever part accepted or rejected, the normative expectations for behavior and attitudes presented in the classroom are being learned by children as crucial aspects of the world with which they must cope.

In sum, the formal academic instruction that a child gains in school is but one part of a total socialization experience. What some have termed the "hidden curriculum" or the "second curriculum" of schools is also critical. It is in this domain that the student learns the norms and values in the society govening such diverse concerns as patriotism, race relations, social-class differences, sex differences, proper interactional styles for children in relation to adults, and, of course, schooling.

The data presented in this chapter suggest that individual

black children had quite different experiences within the same school. Clearly, Donald and Gloria appeared to be doing well. They had friends, were spoken of in favorable terms by the teachers, and were able to maintain a level of performance within the range of that of the majority of the white children in their classes. Both in observing them and in the responses of the other children, I sensed that they were comfortable with their peers and with the status position they had achieved. Joyce appeared to be somewhat less well thought of in her class than was Gloria and also had fewer friends. She was, in large part, isolated from the white students in the room in terms of interaction, and she directed her attention almost exclusively to Gloria. Her teacher, Mrs. Evans, also appeared to think that Joyce was not able to perform as well as Gloria and that little could be expected from her. For the teacher, Joyce was not a "problem child," but she was a "problem" student.

The situation for Jeff and Lou was different. Both were negatively thought of by students in terms of friendships and perceptions of academic performance. While Jeff was accepted by his teacher, who essentially left him on his own because his performance level was far below that of the others in the room, Lou was becoming increasingly difficult for Mrs. Evans to interact with in any positive fashion. The teacher's frequent, if not exclusive, way of interacting with him was to control or discipline him. The teacher seemed to think that Lou had very little capability for academic work, and that the best to be hoped from him was as little disruption as possible during the day.

The same dichotomy emerges in an analysis of the situation of the black students in the third and fourth grades. In Mrs. Daley's room, Melvin had friends and was marginally able to keep up with the material. Mrs. Daley spoke of him in positive terms. Duke, however, she viewed as "definitely not third-grade material" and as the "class clown" because of what she believed to be his insecurity and frustration in being so far behind the other students. Mrs. Daley also appeared to believe that while Melvin could be counted on to participate and be an active member of the class, Duke would be able to do little and would have to be watched closely because of his antics.

In Mrs. Hill's fourth-grade room, Diane and Will were struggling to make it both academically and interpersonally, but I sensed that they would increasingly become involved with the other students, though their academic performance would remain weak. Alex, though, was in much the same situation as were Lou, Jeff, and Duke. He had few friends, was perceived as a "problem" by the teacher, and demonstrated little in the way of academic competency. After the fight, Alex had been pegged by the teachers and principal alike as a "troublemaker" who would have to be watched.

For all four of the boys in this position, the school was increasingly to play a custodial function, demanding little besides conformity and expecting little besides obedience. Academics had been written off. What the teachers hoped for was to get through the day with as little disturbance as possible. As the following chapters will detail, these four boys in particular came to be very real isolates within the school and within their classrooms in particular. The seating arrangements began to reflect the teachers' view of these children as problems; they were frequently physically separated by some distance from others in the room, perhaps with the hope they would then have fewer opportunities for interaction, but surely with the hope that with them "out of the way" the class could get down to the serious tasks of learning and schooling. For those black children who were "making it" within the norms operant at Brush School, it became increasingly receptive to them; for those who were not making it, the school increasingly came to resemble a warehouse where they were to be stored and ignored.

5.

Class, Status, and Power:
The Dynamics
of Classroom Socialization

With the early weeks of school now behind them, the teachers and pupils were settled into the routines that would carry them through the remainder of the year. The structure of the activities within the classroom, the hierarchical arrangement of ability groupings, and the friendships and interpersonal frictions all helped to provide a logic and patterned stability to the events of the school day. Going to school for both the teachers and pupils was not a venture into the unknown. School was predictable.

This chapter further elaborates the nature of that stability. Of particular importance is the focus on the means and methods of socialization. Schools are a place where something is supposed to happen to children. That schools are compulsory is an effort to make sure that what happens there is not left to chance. That schools are to shape the lives of children is precisely what is intended.

November 12
In an informal conversation with Mrs. Hill, a fourth-grade teacher, she related the following:
1. Will, one of the A.T. students, had been absent from the class for the past seven days. She said that after ten consecutive days of absence, he would be taken off the class roster if no con-

tact had been made with the parents to explain the reason for the absence. Several phone calls to the home received no answer.

2. With Will out of the room, she had tried moving Alex next to Eric, the white student at the rear of the room who had been helping Will. Apparently, this had not worked out, and Alex was back by himself in one corner of the room.

3. For the first time in some days, she was pleased with Alex's behavior. The class had attended a showing of Indian art at the city museum and she had anticipated that Alex would be "his typical self." However, Alex had been no problem, and she said that he was interested in the exhibits. Her comment: "I kept waiting for him to break loose, but it never came." She said she was so surprised at his behavior she told him so.

November 13: Progress and Problems in the First Grade

Of the first-grade teachers, Mrs. Brown appeared to be the most seriously committed to a content approach in her class (see Brophy and Good 1974:121). The emphasis was on mastery of material and academic performance, less on socioemotional development. (As she occasionally told the class, "You are here to work, not to play around.") The following account of a brief lesson on counting well represents her approach, though perhaps here she is a bit more intense than usual.

Mrs. Brown tells the class, "I want all of you to listen so you can get stars on your papers." Her voice is loud and domineering. "Just let me catch one of you not listening and you'll catch the dickens." Mrs. Brown calls on Donald to count to ten. He does well up through eight and then falters. Several other students call out "nine" and he repeats it. He falters again and the others say "ten." He repeats that.

Mrs. Brown says that now she will call on one student at a time for only one number, and begins to go through the room pointing at students who have their hands raised. Answers come rapidly, with little or no time for hesitation. At about number seventeen or eighteen, the students just start calling out. She tells them to wait their turn. She sees David staring out the window, "David, quit looking out the window. I want you to look right here at me." Her voice is loud. As she moves through the room, she says "good" to those who offer a correct response and nothing to those who do not. At one point, she is snapping her fingers to indicate the rapidity with which she wants a response. She is now in the twenties, continuing this quick-answer emphasis. Almost immediately she is at thirty and the lesson ends. The time lapse was two to three minutes. She now turns immediately to a printing lesson the class is to have with the word "quick."

Clearly, a premium was placed on the students' ability to give quick answers. There was no reward for the student who could not play this exchange game. The style was more than simply one of using interrogatives as a teaching technique. The emphasis was on the students' being able to answer immediately. No attempt was made to work through the numbers in such a way that students like Donald would be able to follow. The exchange was essentially one among those "in the know." All others were relegated to the role of spectator.

Later in the morning, while the students were on the playground, Mrs. Brown asked me for my impressions of the class. Among other items I mentioned was that the students appeared to be building rather cohesive groups in the class based on placement in their reading group. She responded that she had thought about "mixing up" all the students in different groups, but had decided against it because of the "penalty that would put on the fast readers." She said there was such a diversity of ability in the room that there was "no way" to teach except by forming small groups of students with comparable performance levels.

As she elaborated on the spread of student abilities in the class, she added that she also had to deal with so many problem students that it was best to keep the classroom organization "as simple as possible." I asked her who she thought were her problem students, and she said that just the previous evening she had taken the time to list the fourteen students in the class who she thought fitted the category. This is a summary of her comments:

Donald's problems were two: not being able to concentrate on his work and stealing. *Tina* chased every man who came into the room ("There's not a man who comes into the room that she does not want to run up to and kiss"). *Tim* came from a broken home and his mother was spending little or no time with him. *Brad* was repeating the grade and did not seem to "catch on." *Peter* was also a repeat and "talked all the time." *Bruce* was not able to concentrate on his work and wandered around the room. *Trish* was much too young and should have been in kindergarten. *Sue* was from a divorced home and had just gotten a new father; with the new marriage, Sue began sucking her thumb and saying she did not want to go home. *David* was having "severe emotional disturbances," to the point where he was under the care of a psychiatrist. *Ian* could not slow down long enough to concentrate and never completed his work. *Mat* talked so frequently to anyone who would listen that he never completed his assignments. *Pam* never seem to understand the directions being given, and as a consequence, ended her days with incorrect and incomplete work. *Dawn* had a speech problem and could not enunciate the words so that others could understand what she was saying. And, finally, *Janice* was also repeating the grade and having as much difficulty with her reading this year as last.

This list gives a critically important insight into Mrs. Brown's conceptualization of "problem students." She gave an equal number of instances of academic and socioemotional problems. Stealing and not reading, thumb sucking and misunderstood directions, chasing men and not completing work — all were problems Mrs. Brown believed she faced in her room. Thus, it is clear that her concerns reached beyond the pedagogical. Her values and attitudes about behavior and social relations manifested themselves in her definition of the situation in her room, and it should be noted that her perceptions cut across all groups in the class, black or white, male or female, high achiever or low achiever. Perhaps, in this context, the notion of a "hidden" curriculum as something simply tangential to the schooling process needs to be redefined to emphasize its coequal existence with the academic.

November 20
As noted at the end of the last chapter, Jeff was one of the A.T. students increasingly isolated from his classmates. As time went on, he continued to be physically separated from others on many occasions, and he also began increasingly to "tune out" what was

occurring in the room and engage in activities independent of others. I observed one such instance during what was for other students in the room an interesting and involved lesson.

On the board is a four-line story that the children are to copy on their paper. It reads as follows: "Some animals live above ground, some live below. Some animals like the weather hot, others like the ice and snow." Four girls are each asked to read one line of the story, and all read their line quite well. Mrs. Wills goes back to the first line and begins to discuss with the children the kinds of animals that fit the description. The children are so anxious to offer their ideas of the appropriate animals that they are waving their hands and calling out to the teacher to recognize them.

I note that in the midst of this Jeff has taken out a library book from his desk and begun thumbing through it. He is humming to himself as he turns the pages. Mrs. Wills is now on the second line, and the children are so anxious to answer they are out of their seats with their hands waving. Jeff pays no attention to all the activity around him and goes on working through his book. Mrs. Wills is allowing many, if not all, of the children who have their hand raised to name an animal. Jeff puts down his book and starts trying to cut his pink eraser with scissors. He gives up trying to cut through it and starts chewing on it instead. It finally breaks. Mrs. Wills has just completed the fourth line of the story, again with many students offering names. She now tells the students to print the story on their paper and then draw an example of each of the four kinds of animals. Jeff is now drawing with a pencil on one corner of his desk.

It is important to stress that there was nothing necessarily "wrong" or inappropriate about Jeff's behavior. To the contrary, Mrs. Wills frequently allowed the students to pursue something of individual interest when the class had moved to another topic or activity. Further, it is erroneous to assume that throughout the day all students are actively engaged in class-related efforts. More probably, there is a continual process of "tuning in" and "tuning out." But in Jeff's case, "tuning out" had become quite frequent, and it had begun to hinder his ability to complete his desk work, for he often missed discussions bearing on the assignments.

November 21: Teacher Talk

During the time the first- and second-grade teachers were together having lunch in the lounge, they were working on a form passed out by the principal. The form asked them to name the students in their respective rooms who they believed were in need of social services. As their discussion evolved, it became apparent that the majority of students they were mentioning to each other were A.T. students. Mrs. Evans said she was not sure what could help Lou. She commented that he was "nearly impossible to control" and did not care "the slightest" about participating in the class. Rather, his major interest was to "roam about the room trying to disturb others." The "nicest times" in her room, she added, were when Lou decided to leave and wander through the school and out into the neighborhood. (On several occasions during class hours, I had seen him as far as a block away from the building.) Mrs. Evans made no comment on either Joyce or Gloria.

Mrs. Wills picked up where Mrs. Evans ended and said that earlier in the fall she had been afraid Jeff was going to turn out like Lou, but instead he was "slowly beginning to catch on and try." Jeff was also staying awake more frequently in the room, and she thought that was an indication of his growing interest. Mrs. Evans asked how she got Jeff to stay awake since, if she could do the opposite, she could put Lou to sleep. "It would be perfect if he did nothing but sleep." Mrs. Evans added that she hoped Lou would be absent soon so she could determine what effect he was having on the room. She thought that opportunity would arise today, but Lou arrived later in the morning by cab. The reason for the cab was that the bus driver had refused to let Lou on the bus.

Mrs Brown told the group that Donald "has been coming along well." "He is capable of doing the work," she added, but he "can't settle down and concentrate." Mrs. Evans said the same of Gloria, that she was a capable student, but was having difficulty in completing her work.

At this point I asked the teachers if any knew how the individual A.T. students had been chosen to come to Brush. Mrs. Brown suggested that the students had been chosen at random, but Mrs. Evans said she had heard that the sending school had chosen only those students who it thought "would do well in this environment." She continued by saying she did not believe this, however, because Lou was far from being a student who would do well at Brush. In fact, she added, she suspected Lou had been sent to Brush precisely because he was not fitting in at his previous school. Mrs. Brown then told the other teachers about the letter in Lou's folder, from his previous principal to Lou's mother asking if she would make arrangements to have him at home when he became too disruptive in the school. Mrs. Evans said she suspected Lou was here because no solution had been worked out. Mrs. Brown added, "That's a heck of a way to integrate schools, isn't it?"

November 26

As I passed by the rest room near Mrs. Evans's room, Lou opened the door slightly and said, "Hi." He asked if I was going to his room. I answered his greeting and then said I was going there to observe. I asked if he was coming and he responded, "No, I got things to do." He closed the door. When I entered Mrs. Evans's room, she asked me if I had seen Lou. I told her he was in the bathroom, and she responded, "Just as well."

I took a seat at the rear of the room and began looking around for Joyce and Gloria. Gloria was in her usual place, but Joyce was now separated from the remainder of the class by six or eight feet. Her desk was in the far upper-right corner of the room. Fred calls out to the teacher that Lou is peeking into the room. Mrs. Evans: "I know he is, but we are not paying any attention to Lou right now." Lou closes the door and does not come in.

Shortly, Mrs. Evans dismisses the class for recess. Lou appears on the playground and comes to the area where the children are playing. He grabs one of the balls and starts to run. Several of the other students catch him and try to get the ball back. Mrs. Evans breaks up the group, takes Lou firmly by the arm, and marches him back into the room. She tells him to go over to his seat, but he walks back out the door. Mrs. Evans seems almost on the verge of tears as she sits at her seat and begins writing out a long note, I learn, to the principal. When she finishes, she calls the office on the intercom and tells the secretary Lou has left the room, she doesn't know where he is, and she is not going to take the time to find out because she has twenty more students to look after. When she puts down the receiver, she looks at me and says, "That child is completely out of control. He can make it for a little while in the morning, but every afternoon turns out like this." She then asks the class to come in from the playground.

After the children have put their coats away and are in their seats, Mrs. Evans tells them they should be "on the lookout" for the two students they think are the best behaved in the room. She tells them that in four days the class will again select their two "citizens of the month." (This is an event which will take place throughout the year.) A large bulletin board in the rear of the room has in capital letters: CITIZENS OF THE MONTH. Below both the months of September and October are pictures of the winners. Several of the children begin calling out, "I know who I'm going to vote for." Mrs. Evans answers them, "Oh no, we're not going to have any politicking now. You should all wait and look real carefully at each other for the next four days before you decide. Watch each other's behavior very closely before you vote." She adds, "Remember, when you vote, it is not necessary that you vote for the very best two readers, but for the ones who have been the very best, and work the hardest."

A hidden curriculum, indeed!

November 30

ITEM: For the first time in any of the five classrooms there was a picture that included black people. In her room Mrs. Brown had put up a poster from the American Dental Association entitled "Have a Happy, Healthy Smile." In the picture were two white children and two black children. At the bottom were the lines "Clean Your Teeth, Visit Your Dentist, and Choose Foods Wisely."

ITEM: Mrs. Brown told me she had decided to request special testing for Pam and David, two of the five students in her lowest reading group. Both were having "severe difficulties" with their reading, and she thought testing might indicate whether they needed specialized instruction. I asked about the other three students in the bottom group, and she commented on each in turn: Donald would not need testing because he had the capacity but just "could not settle down" to do his work; Trish was so immature she really wasn't ready to read; and Tim was living in such an "unsettled home situation" that he could not be expected to do his work.

ITEM: For the first time Mrs. Brown spoke of the possibility of having a student repeat first grade. Her comment came in conjunction with the discussion above on the low reading group. The student she mentioned was Trish. "She is so young and tiny, I think it would do her good to stay with me for another year."

December 4

One salient characteristic of the A.T. children was that among their peers there was the same diversity in behavior as among the white students. The black students could no more be categorized as an aggregate than their classmates. There seemingly was a comparable spread of behavioral patterns between these categories of students. Consequently, it is erroneous to attribute success or failure in the classroom to some behavioral pattern supposedly "racial" in its origins. Rather, what appeared to be at the base of assessments by teachers like Mrs. Evans was that *any* student who behaved in a way deemed inappropriate would be in academic difficulty.

This attitude was in evidence when I observed Joyce during a printing lesson in Mrs. Evans's room. Several times the teacher told me to watch Joyce closely if I wanted to understand why she was falling further and further behind the class.

Joyce is at the front board drawing with chalk. The teacher asks her to come back to her seat. She does, but does not begin the assignment. She puts her head down on her desk. Then she gets up and goes to the back of the room, where she takes a drink. She comes back to her seat, takes a piece of paper, and goes to ask the teacher on what line she is to begin printing her name. The teacher takes out a red pencil and marks it for her. Joyce is told to go to her seat and begin work. She goes back to her seat, begins printing the heading "Dear Santa." She completes the first six letters and is again up out of her seat. She goes to Gloria and shows her the Band-Aid on her arm. She comes and shows it to me and then goes back to the front board to work on the same picture she was drawing before. She comes over to me and tells me it is a picture of a girl.

Mrs. Evans ends the "silent reading group" going on in another part of the room. She tells the class to take out their math books. The other students do, but Joyce takes out a white barbie doll she had in her desk and begins braiding its hair. She never does take out a math book during the lesson.

Interestingly, not once during the study did a teacher indicate that the lack of academic performance by an A.T. student was due to anything other than behavioral or situational factors. The genetic hypothesis was never raised. It is perhaps a measure of their professionalism that the teachers in this study looked to environmental explanations for success or failure. It is also true that holding such a view allows teachers to believe that in fact they can have an impact on students. To think otherwise requires a very different justification to continue teaching.

During this particular observational period, there was one significant interchange involving the teacher and Gloria. It came during the show and tell period.

Gloria and two other girls are the last ones with their hands still up for show and tell. The other two girls are called and Gloria is the last child in the class, among those who had their hands up, to come to the front for show and tell. When Gloria reaches the front, Mrs. Evans says to Mary, the student selected to choose the order of appearance, "Mary, what is it I told you to say when Gloria comes to the front?" Mary calls out to the class, "Quiet, she has a low voice." Mrs. Evans adds, "Yes, that is correct. We all need to be quiet because Gloria speaks so softly." Gloria tells the class, "I have a hurt on my arm," and points to her Band-Aid. Sean calls out, "I bet it's broken." Gloria does not respond to Sean and continues, "The other day I got me a cricket in my neck, and it still here. It hurt so bad I stayed home for four days." Mrs. Evans answers, "Yes, I know you did, and I appreciate you bringing me a note telling me why you were absent. Thank you, honey."

When the children had been dismissed to the playground, I asked Mrs. Evans about Lou's absence today. Her first comment: "Happily, I don't know where he is." She went on to tell me she thought Lou was staying out of school these past five days so he could look for another school to attend. The principal, she said, had sent home to Lou's mother a very strongly worded note informing her of Lou's behavior. (Before the principal had sent the note, he had tried to get the kindergarten teacher to take Lou in the afternoon, but she had refused.) Mrs. Evans said she thought that Lou's staying at a school until he got to be unbearable and then looking for another was a pattern he had followed before coming to Brush.

After hearing this from Mrs. Evans, I went to the office to check with the principal to see if Lou was, in fact, in the process of withdrawing from the school. The principal and his secretary were together in the outer office. I asked about Lou and the secretary spoke up first, "Oh, I've heard that rumor, but I think it's just wishful thinking on the part of Mrs. Evans." The principal said nothing had yet come across his desk that would indicate Lou was leaving. He added, "But I bet a lot of people here wish he would."

December 6

The same classroom behavioral characteristics as those described above for Joyce were observed for Jeff. During the time between 9:32 and 10:20, when the class went onto the playground for morning recess, Jeff was the only student in the room who was not at work on his assignment. He was playing with his bottle of glue, looking through a book, drawing on a piece of paper, and watching others. But he himself did none of the assignment. At one point, Kurt called out, "Mrs. Wills, Jeff isn't doing his work." She shrugged her shoulders and said, "You just be sure you get your own work done." No comment was made to Jeff.

During the time the class was on the playground, I asked Mrs. Wills my perennial question. "How are things going?" Her response was unanticipated:

Mrs. Wills begins by saying that yesterday morning she and Jeff had had their first "run-in." I asked what had happened and she said she had confronted Jeff with the fact that he had three bottles of glue and twelve pencils on his desk. She had asked him where he got them, but he insisted they were all his own. However, only one of the three bottles was his; the other two were marked as belonging to other students. She then took the bottles and pencils and passed them out to those who recognized their own. Jeff, while this was going on, she said, left the room in tears and did not show up again until it was lunch time. She says, "I really felt bad about him leaving, but I didn't want him to get started stealing like Donald." She continues by saying that during the noon recess, Jeff was telling others in the class that he hated Mrs. Wills and did not want to be in her class. "I didn't find out about this from him, but others in the room came and told me." I asked what happened when he did come back, and she replied there was no problem. He had stayed awake all afternoon and tried to do one of the assignments. She added, "By today, I think it is all forgotten."

Among the implications of this statement, two are especially important. First, Mrs. Wills clearly considered that Jeff was not a "problem"—was doing acceptable work—if he "stayed awake" and "tried to do one of the assignments." Second, Mrs. Wills's mention of Donald in her discussion of Jeff's stealing shows that Donald's reputation as a "stealer" was not confined to his own room; in fact, it was widespread among the teachers of the lower grades.

December 10

As mentioned earlier (November 13), Mrs. Brown had listed Donald as one of the fourteen students in her room who she thought had "problems": in Donald's case, stealing and not being able to concentrate on his class work. As for the latter, Mrs. Brown did not think that he was incapable of doing his assignments, but rather that he never "settled down." On this day, she was working persistently to change that.

Mrs. Brown is at her desk sorting papers. When she is finished, she comes to the back of the room where I am seated and points to one of Donald's papers she has tacked on the wall. "This is one of the first of his I've been able to put up. But now he's starting to produce. I'm watching him like a hawk. He's got to stay in his seat to do his work."

Mrs. Brown goes on to say she was "almost cruel" to Donald one day last week when she found him wandering through the room while he had work to complete. She says she put him in his seat and told him he would "be sorry" if he got up before it was completed. While we are talking, Donald gets up out of his seat and goes over to Tim. Mrs. Brown walks over to Donald, tells him to get back to his seat and not to get up again until the work is completed. She comes back to me and says she has been thinking of not promoting Donald to second grade if he does not begin to do his work. But now that she is pushing him, he may make it. "I'm just going to have to stay with him to make sure that he gets it done."

Mrs. Brown adds that Donald is not now one of her major problems in the class. "You know, I've got many white children in this room that are in worse shape than he is. Take, for example, Janice," and she points to her. "There is a child who had been in second grade and had to be sent back. She's the daughter of a big lawyer in town, and both of the parents are just torn up about her. I go through the material with her time and again and she is still lost."

Donald gets out of his seat as we are talking, and the teacher goes over to him immediately. She tells him to get back in his seat. Donald looks at her with a pained expression and tells her he erased his paper so hard it tore. Mrs. Brown looks at the tear, says that it's not a bad one and that he can continue to work on that sheet. She goes to her desk with Donald and patches the tear with a piece of tape. Then she tells him to go back to his seat and not to get up until the page is completed. Mrs. Brown calls for a new reading group, and as she passes, she tells me, "I'm going to get it out of him because I know he can do it."

Later in the morning, when the class had been dismissed for lunch and Mrs. Brown and I were left in the room, she began talking about herself as a teacher. She said I probably looked on her as an "old-fashioned teacher who was too strict with the children." She continued that though she guessed she was strict, she thought strictness was acceptable so long as she did not "traumatize" the children. I asked what she thought would traumatize them, and she responded that trauma would occur when a child developed a deep dislike or hatred for others and self-hatred as well. She said that as far as she could tell, none of the children in the room disliked her, though they all knew that if they "got out of line," she would speak to them. She thought not playing favorites was the best way of letting the children know she was fair. Finally: "It's OK to be firm with them, so long as no one thinks they're being picked on."

December 11

Two of the four boys listed at the end of the last chapter as increasingly less involved in the class and more peripheral to both academic and social life in the room, Alex and Lou, had been absent for several days, Alex for fifteen, and Lou for nine. As I was to learn in several days when he returned, Alex had "gone South" to visit his grandmother while his mother "took care of some business." Lou, however, did not return. I spoke with Mrs. Evans on this day, and she said that the request for a transfer of his papers to a new school had come through. She commented that she had been expecting that "all along" and added, "You know, he left us in such a bad way. The last afternoon he was here, he went around telling everyone how he hated them and hoped they would all die. He was saying over and over how he wanted to go back to his first school. I told him if he really meant what he was saying, he should be sure to tell his mother so she could do something about it."

December 12

The isolation of Jeff from the life of his classroom took on an added and qualitatively different dimension on this day. Mrs. Wills decided that Jeff should no longer participate in one of the three reading groups in the room, since, as she put it, "He is so far behind that there is nothing to be gained by having him sit there and not be able to do anything." Instead, Jeff was to have individual tutoring from the teacher and from the eighth-grade student who helped in the room one hour each day. During the time his reading group was involved in their lesson, I recorded Jeff's activities.

Before Mrs. Wills begins the group, she goes over to Jeff's seat and tells him he can begin work on a Christmas card to take home to his mother. She tells him to select a piece of construction paper and an old Christmas card from which to cut out a design.

Mrs. Wills points to the felt pens on her desk and says he can use them to write the message she has printed on the board: "Merry Christmas and Happy New Year." She goes back to the reading group, and Jeff begins work on cutting out part of a Christmas card.

Jeff was to work on the card during the twenty minutes the remainder of his group was reading. Later in the morning, he received fifteen minutes of tutoring from the eighth-grade student on his arithmetic lesson. This was his only formal instruction during the two hours of the observation.

December 13

Both Duke and Melvin were observed receiving individual assistance from the teacher. During the time the class was involved in a show and tell period, Mrs. Daley brought them individually to her desk for work on their assignment. Each received, perhaps, ten minutes of help. When Melvin, the second to work with her, left for his seat, Mrs. Daley turned to me and said, "Today is just one of those days. Sometimes they get it and sometimes they don't. And when they don't, you have to work with them alone."

A short while later, Melvin came back to her to show what he had completed. Mrs. Daley was positive in her comment and Melvin seemed to enjoy the attention. He was smiling when he went back to his seat. As Melvin returned, Mrs. Daley told the class to "clear their desks" for a writing lesson. Melvin was chosen to pass out the paper. As he began, he stopped at each desk and repeated the teacher's directive by saying, "Clear your desk," attempting to imitate the teacher's tone. He seemed pleased with himself and would not put the paper down until the student had cleared his desk. Mrs. Daley finally told Melvin he was taking much too long to pass the papers.

December 17

ITEM: Mrs. Brown was asking students in the class what they wanted for Christmas, and she got such responses as electric train, horse, watch, walkie-talkie, trip to Hawaii, and tape recorder. When she came to Donald, he said he wanted Tim as a present so they could be brothers. Mrs. Brown responded, "Donald, you're just being silly. Now I want you to sit there quietly until you can think up something serious." A little later Donald raised his hand, and when called on, said he wanted a dump truck. Mrs. Brown smiled and said, "Now, that's much better."

ITEM: Mrs. Brown told to me that she was going to call Donald's mother because she did not think Donald should continue to receive a free lunch when he had money in his pocket for spending. "It irritates me as a taxpayer that they think they should get something for nothing." (As I was to learn later, Mrs. Brown did call over the Christmas vacation. When school resumed in January, Donald began to bring his lunch. Besides telling me she had called, Mrs. Brown made no further mention of this situation.

ITEM: When observing the class on the playground during noon recess, I asked Mrs. Brown, the teacher assigned as noon playground monitor, whether Donald and Tim were becoming good friends. I commented that they had been playing together this entire noontime and seemed to get along quite well. Her comment in response: "Yeah, they are getting to be friends, but it's no good for Donald. Tim is such a troublemaker that when he and Donald get together, Donald quits doing his work. Tim has been a real problem, and now just when I am starting to get Donald to settle down, here he has to go and get chummy with Tim."

December 18

As has been noted, Mrs. Brown, Mrs. Daley, and Mrs. Hill had all mentioned the possibility that they would be retaining one of the A.T. students in their rooms for another year. On this date, Mrs. Evans made similar comments on Joyce. Mrs. Evans said that yesterday she called Joyce's mother to ask permission to give Joyce a series of psychological tests to try to find out why Joyce is not concentrating in class. The mother agreed and said Joyce was in the same position now that she, the mother, had been in years earlier—not concentrating and waking up too late to realize school was important. Mrs. Evans said she told the mother that at Joyce's current level of performance, she would not be able to pass her on to second grade. The mother was also told that when the test scores were available, she, the teacher, and the principal would have a meeting to plan for Joyce "and impress on Joyce that school is important."

With the addition of Joyce to the list, four teachers at the end of the fifteenth week had decided that retention was a distinct possibility for at least four A.T. students. (If one added Mrs. Wills, who seemed from the way she took Jeff out of the reading group to assess his performance as low, one could conclude that all teachers in the study had notions of retention, involving five of their nine A.T. children—Donald, Joyce, Duke, Alex, and Jeff.)

ITEM: On the back board under the heading "Citizens of the Month," a picture of Gloria was tacked up, indicating she was one of the two students selected by the class for the month of December. When Mrs. Evans saw me looking at the board, she came over and commented, "Isn't it nice Gloria won. She's such a darling little girl."

December 20: A Christmas Party

On this the last day of school before the Chrismas break, there was to be an afternoon party in Mrs. Hill's room. Several of the mothers had come with punch, cookies, doughnuts, candy, and nuts. During the time the mothers were preparing a table in the back of the room, Mrs. Hill had organized the class for a spelling bee, with the boys against the girls, each group lined up along one of the side walls. One boy and one girl would come to the front together, where the teacher would give a word they were then to spell on the board. Anyone who got help from other students had to drop out of the game.

Any student who spelled a word correctly was able to go to the back of the line and wait another turn. Those who spelled incorrectly had to sit down. Diane, an A.T. student, was the third girl in line, and when it was her turn, she incorrectly spelled "symbols" as "simbols." She was the first girl to have to go to her seat.

Alex, who had just returned yesterday to the room, had the word "Asia" and he misspelled it as "aysa." He was the third boy to have to go to his seat. When he sat, I discovered that *he was sitting all by himself in a corner, at least seven or eight feet from the closest desk.* As the game drew to a close, there remained three boys (two from the top reading group and one from the second) and one girl (top reading group). Mrs. Hill called the game a tie and told everyone to have a seat, because the treats were ready.

Mrs. Hill tells everyone to come and file past the table in the rear. Most of the boys immediately scramble to get to the back, with Alex in the midst of them. Will, one of the other A.T. students, does not. There is much jostling among those at the back, and the teacher threatens to call them all back to their seats if they don't "act more orderly." The boys quiet down only slightly, but the teacher says nothing else. As the boys pass the table (they all do so before the girls), Alex goes and sits with a group of boys. Will is sitting by himself. When Diane goes to her seat, she is also by herself. Neither of them is talking to anyone, though in general, the students are gay and enjoying themselves. Mrs. Hill puts "I'm Dreaming of a White Christmas" on the record player.

Alex has taken his ice cream and spread some of it on the top side of his lip, as if he were wearing a moustache. He begins walking through the room, showing it to everyone. One of the first students to copy Alex is Diane. In total, perhaps five or six other students do the same. Mrs. Hill comes over to Alex, and says in a sarcastic voice, "Alex, I think that's just silly." Alex ignores her comment and puts more ice cream on his lip. He continues to walk through the room and others keep laughing at him. At one time, he seemed to have the whole room looking at him, including the mothers, who were sitting in the rear.

A short while later, when the party was over and the students gone, Mrs. Hill began talking about Alex. She said that moving Alex into the corner was "so much better for him." I asked why and was told, "Well, you know, he was so frustrated because he could only do second-grade work. And when he was with the rest of the class, everyone could see what he was not able to do. I know it was hard for him when he compared himself to everyone else. But now that he is by himself, he won't have to worry about what others are doing because he won't have the constant reminders." Her final comment: "You just watch. He's going to be so much easier to handle from now on."

As I left, the decorations began coming down.

January 7: The First Day Back

In a discussion of a high-status school in Berkeley, California, that was in the process of integration, Metz (1971) described the teachers as stressing "academic material above all else." Much the same characterization would apply, I believe, to the teachers at Brush. For example, on the first morning of school after the Christmas vacation, Mrs. Evans had her class involved in a lesson within ten minutes after the first bell. There was no time spent on asking children what they received as presents or where they might have traveled; instead, the assignment was on the board when they entered, and as soon as coats were off and paper distributed, the focus was on the lesson.

In Mrs. Evans's class, an important change had been wrought over the vacation: *The teacher had rearranged the chairs and desks so that both Joyce and Gloria were separated from the rest of the class.* One was in the upper right corner and the other in the upper left corner of the room. Neither child made any comment about their new location; they, like everyone else, simply took their seats where they found them. No other students were separated in such a manner.

As had been first noted in an observation in late September, Joyce and Paul, another member of the low reading group, interacted in such a way that there was frequently bickering and antagonism between them.

When the students are told to begin the writing assignment, Joyce leaves her desk and goes to the front board. She stands about six inches away, looking at the words. Paul calls out, "Joyce, what are you doing?" She answers, "I'm looking." Paul calls out, "Teacher!" Mrs. Evans looks up from her desk and says, "Joyce." Joyce responds, "I'm looking." She then leaves and returns to her seat. Almost as soon as she does so, Paul begins reading out loud what is on the board. Joyce says, "Stop it, Paul." Paul continues. Joyce leaves her desk and goes to stand by the teacher. Shortly, she goes back to her seat for her paper, which she takes to the teacher. As she passes Paul, he says, "Baby." Joyce sticks out her tongue.

Later, during the time the children were working on their papers, Mrs. Evans passed through the room checking on the progress of each child. When she came to Gloria's desk, she said, "Gloria, I just know you can do it. Now try hard." Mrs. Evans then told Gloria to move her desk over to where she would be between Liza and Jessica, because "I want you to be inspired to do your work by sitting next to such good writers." Thus Gloria was brought back into the group for a dose of inspiration; Joyce was not.

January 8

During the month of December, it became apparent that Donald and Tim were building a friendship, much to Mrs. Brown's displeasure. During this morning, Donald came to the defense of Tim when he was in an argument with the teacher, the sum of which was a major disruption of the class.

Tim is out of his seat. As he walks past Mat, he pushes him out of his seat. Both Mat and his chair fall. Mrs. Brown sees this and says, "Tim, why did you do that?" Tim responds, "Because he was doing things." Mat calls out, "I was not." Mrs. Brown says to Tim, "Do you want me to push you like you pushed Mat?" Tim answers, "Do you want to fight?" Mrs. Brown is angry. She answers in a loud and angry voice, "What? What did you say to me? What did you say?" Tim makes no answer and Mrs. Brown tells him to go to his seat "without another word out of you." Now Donald calls out, "Quit picking on my friend." She turns to him, "Little man, either you get quiet or you will find yourself in the office."

The students, all of whom have been watching this exchange, slowly turn back to their work. Mrs. Brown comes to where I am seated and says, "I just don't know how I'm going to get through to Tim. Nothing I do seems to work with him. And besides, I can get no help from the home. You know, his mother was the only one who did not come for a conference. I tried several times to get hold of her, but there was never any answer. I think she is out a lot. She's divorced, you know."

January 10

Mrs. Wills had decided in the weeks before Christmas that Jeff would no longer be a part of any of the reading groups in the room. During the first part of the observation this morning, Jeff sat at his seat and colored while all the other students were in one of the three reading groups, of which one was taught by the teacher, one by the teacher's aide, and one by the eighth-grade classroom helper.

When Jeff finishes the paper he is coloring, he starts back with it to the teacher's desk. Mrs. Wills sees him and asks him to come over to where she is with one of the reading groups. Jeff comes over and shows the picture. "Oh, you've drawn your house. Can you tell me the names of the colors you used?" Jeff shrugs his shoulders and says nothing. Mrs. Wills points to one of the colors and Jeff says correctly that it is pink. Now the members of the reading group with Mrs. Wills stand and crowd around the teacher and Jeff to watch as she points to various colors for Jeff to identify. Mrs. Wills points to all the colors on the page, and by the end most of the children in the group are calling them out, Jeff included. When this is finished, Mrs. Wills says, "Thank you, Jeff, now you may put it on my desk." Jeff does so. A few moments later, the reading group disbands, and Mrs. Wills asks Phil to work with Jeff on a math lesson. She tears a page out of a workbook and tells Phil that he and Jeff should work through all the problems on one side. (When I was able to see the page, it contained all one-digit addition problems.)

Mrs. Wills comes and tells me, "Phil is so patient. He would spend all morning working with Jeff if I let him. I don't know if it is helping, but both of them seem to enjoy doing it."

During the fifty minutes of the observation, the help from Phil was all Jeff received in the way of formal (informal?) instructional assistance.

January 14: Further Perceptions of Problems

The frequent interaction of Donald and Tim continued to be of concern to Mrs. Brown. On this occasion she told me that in the early part of the morning she had first seated them on opposite sides of the room and then put them next to each other, trying in each instance to find out which would lead to the least disruption and talking on their part. She said she had read in one of her educational psychology books the previous evening that separation was the most effective technique, but when she tried it, both boys either called out across the room to each other or else got out of their seats. After the morning recess she placed them together in the left rear part of the room, with the idea that if they were together and at the back of the class, they would cause less interference for others, even if they themselves continued to talk.

In Mrs. Brown's room, seemingly more so than in the other first-grade rooms, the reading groups were an important factor in peer selections and rejections. One of the manifestations of this was that the friendships in the room tended to be among those of the same reading group, with Donald and Tim but one example. What follows is one of the few instances observed during the year when a student from the high reading group asked Donald if he would like to share a game. The situation unfolded as follows:

As the students are about to prepare to go to the lunchroom, Mrs. Brown tells them she thinks they will have to come back to the room when they are finished eating because it's raining. As Mrs. Brown is talking, Donald and Tim are together at Donald's desk with Donald showing Tim a key chain.

Mrs. Brown asks which of the children have brought "inside games" to use when they return to the room. Five children, including Donald, hold up their hands. Mrs. Brown asks them one by one what game they brought. When she comes to Donald, he says he has no game but will play with Tim and his game. Tim is asked if he has a game and he says he took it home last Friday. Mrs. Brown tells Donald he will either have to color at his seat or listen to the record player. Brad calls out, "Mrs. Brown, Donald can play with me because Tom says he doesn't want to play." She responds, "What game is it you brought?" Brad answers, "The Harlem Globe Trotters." "Oh, that's wonderful," she answers, "I bet Donald will really want to play that game. I know I wish I could."

When the children were sent to the lunchroom, I went to visit the principal. As invariably happened, the conversation soon turned to the A.T. Program at Brush. Though I did not take notes at the time, the following are parts of my summary of that conversation:

Mr. Norris said that the only problems Brush School was having with its desegregation effort were academic problems. He said that of the thirty or so black students in the A.T. Program, he estimated only four or five would score in the normal intelligence range on IQ tests. The remainder were all below normal, with some scoring close to the borderline of the classification "educable mentally retarded." He also mentioned that a number of the students would be repeating their grade again next year. He began listing students from the first grade on up. Both Jeff and Joyce were listed, as were Duke and Alex. When he mentioned Alex, he elaborated a bit by saying that he and Mrs. Hill disagreed on where Alex should score. As a result of this disagreement, he was going to ask for individual testing of Alex and "then we will see who is right. I bet he is in the range of 75 to 80 and no higher."

He went no further in listing students who would be repeating the grade and instead began talking about IQ tests. He said he used to believe such tests were free of cultural influences, but now he believes they are measures of environment rather than innate ability. All one would have to do is to look at the scores at Brush year after year, he said. The parents at the school were described as spending hours and hours with their children getting them ready to go to school and compete academically. He mentioned that the students at Brush think it would be "no big deal" to go to a museum or concert, because they are exposed to such events as a regular part of their life. In addition, when the parents are not exposing the children to cultural activities themselves, they are paying someone to do it for them. I was told there were probably "not many" other schools in the city with as many children taking music and dancing lessons as there were at Brush.

He related the performance of the white children to that of the black children by saying that the busing program in Portland would never "really make it" as long as the black children remained so far behind the white children in performance and exposure to cultural activities. In his opinion, putting black and white children together was not enough, because "what the white kids have got is not going to rub off on the blacks quick enough to help."

I asked if he thought there had been any improvement in the performance of the black children during the course of the year.

He was quite emphatic in his response. He said yes, he was sure there had been improvement because now, when he goes onto the playground, there are so many fewer fights involving the A.T. students and they chase the white girls less and less. He added, "Now if I catch them doing it, all I have to do is ask them once to quit and they will."

I think this conversation with the principal was extremely important for understanding his perceptions and values. One, he obviously believed tests were useful and accurate, and though he spoke of environmental influences, he did not conclude that they were necessarily unfair to the black students. Two, he also had been developing firm notions about their success or failure, as indicated by his talk of who might or might not be promoted in June. Three, he thought the integration process had been improving because the black male students were involved in less fighting and less chasing of white girls. Four, he discussed white students in terms of academic performance and parental encouragement; the black students he discussed in terms of behavioral conformity. Finally, he felt that the integration process at Brush would advance greatly when the white students' characteristics began to "rub off" on the black students. *This statement clearly buttresses the view put forth at the beginning of this book—that the dominant motif of the integration program at Brush was the assumption that success would be measured by how well the black children assimilated the characteristics of the white children.*

January 17

During the morning recess period, I was on the playground with Mrs. Wills. I asked about Jeff's absence, and she said he might not be returning. As it turned out, Jeff's older brother, Henry, had for two days early in the week come on the bus, but then skipped school. When his mother learned of this (a friend apparently saw him in downtown Portland), she decided to take both Jeff and Henry out of Brush School and put them back in their neighborhood school, where she felt she could keep a closer watch on them. Mrs. Wills said she had not seen Jeff for two days and could only assume that he was being transferred. Twice during the course of the conversation, she said she hoped he would be coming back to Brush. "He's just getting a start. It would be a shame to put him back where he would be submerged in the hundred and one problems those schools have."

I went to the school office to find out whether Jeff had really transferred. The principal was not in, and I talked to the secretary. She said that what had precipitated Henry's first disappearance was that he had been in a fight with another fourth-grade boy, and when he was sent to the office, he instead left the school. The secretary said the principal spent nearly two hours looking through the school and neighborhood for him, but to no avail. When he was unable to locate Henry, he called the mother to inform her of the situation. She called back that afternoon at four o'clock to let the principal know Henry had finally come home. The next day Henry had come on the bus, but had never gone to his room. Yesterday (the sixteenth) the transfer forms had been mailed, on the mother's request, for her to complete and return to the school.

The principal soon came into the office, and I asked if Jeff and Henry were leaving. His response: "Maybe, maybe not." When asked to elaborate, he said he had decided not to recommend transfer when the forms came back to him for forwarding to the district office. His comment: "I know Henry is a pain in the butt, but I want him and Jeff to stay here where they have a chance. Of course, they are problems, but we are supposed to be able to deal with problems. They will be lost in a black school. Besides, we've got white students here who make Henry look like an angel. I would gladly keep him before any of my real hell-raisers."

I said I could understand why the mother would want to have Henry transferred, but wondered what would prompt her to take Jeff out as well. The principal said he suspected the mother was still upset over the stealing incident. Two days ago, he said, Jeff had been caught stealing from a store about three blocks from the school. He had gone there during the lunch break and been caught filling his pockets with candy bars. The store had called the school, and he, in turn, had called Jeff's mother. He added, "I can see why she would want them both back home. In one week she had one of them fighting and skipping school and the other caught for stealing. What a mess to be in. But I still want them to stay. I know we can do them some good."

I discovered another element in this situation when I returned to Mrs. Wills' room to tell her what I had learned from the principal. (She had asked me to share with her any new information I got about Jeff's status.) In the course of our conversation, I mentioned the stealing incident. She replied, "I don't think I have ever seen a child cry as hard as he did." I asked what had prompted the crying, and was told that when the principal had been called by the store, he had brought Jeff to the office and spanked him. "I had to go along as a witness, and when it was over he cried all the way back to the room. Like I said, I don't think I have ever seen a child cry as hard as he did when he got that spanking."

Jeff had not returned to the school since this episode.

January 22: The Imperative of Scheduling

Of the three first-grade rooms, Mrs. Brown's was the one that most closely adhered to a schedule of activities and events. Throughout the day, Mrs. Brown strove to keep the organization and movement of the class in line with her time scheme. Her approach was consonant with her belief that schooling is primarily a process of instilling content in children and that this is best achieved by systematic instruction. For her, children were empty vessels that had to be filled, and the filling was a serious endeavor to be approached methodically and conscientiously.

During the observation in her room on this date, Mrs. Brown found herself, from her own point of view, "behind" before class had even begun. Her time before class had been taken up in a meeting with the principal, and she had not been able to organize as she had wished before the children came into the room. I entered when the children did, and she commented, "You would have to come on a day when I'm not ready." As the morning began, her apparent anxiety transformed itself into brusque comments to the children — "Let's get quiet; we're wasting time" — "Enough of that. I want all of you quiet."

When the organization period of the morning was over (counting lunch money, saying the pledge, having someone take the money and attendance count to the office, and so on), Mrs. Brown was ready to begin her first lesson. But from what follows, it should be apparent that the lesson never got started. The imperative to "get to work" ultimately meant the work never did begin.

Mrs. Brown comes to the front and says it is time for the math lesson. She starts to pass out a dittoed sheet with single-digit addition problems. Sue comes to the front and tells the teacher that she forgot to put the thermometer outside on the windowsill. Mrs. Brown tells her to go back to her seat and that she can do it later "when there is time." Sue responds, "But you said I was supposed to do it in the morning." Mrs. Brown, impatiently: "Go back to your seat." "But I forgot to do the thermometer." Mrs. Brown now takes Sue by the arm and starts to lead her back to her seat. Sue struggles, but Mrs. Brown gets to her seat and says, "Now, will you sit down. We are not even talking about thermometers now." Sue begins to cry. "Sue, be quiet, I don't want to hear you crying." Sue continues to weep. Mrs. Brown walks briskly over to the shelf where the thermometer is. She brings it back and sets it down firmly on Sue's desk. "Here it is. I know you are getting nothing from the lesson, so go and put it in the window." She looks at me and sighs as she goes back to the front of the room. Sue gets up and opens the door to set out the thermometer. She is still crying. Mrs. Brown asks the class to look at the first problem, but almost all the children are watching Sue. Mrs. Brown senses this and says to Sue, "Sue, do you know why I rushed you?" Sue, still sobbing, makes no response. "Well, I'm trying to teach the boys and girls this lesson, and if I had stopped to take care of your thermometer, I would've forgotten what I was trying to teach. We have to stay with our lesson. Sue, are we still friends?" Sue nods yes as she tries to wipe away the tears with the sleeve of her sweater. Mrs. Brown seems exasperated as she looks through the room and sees the children unprepared to work on the lesson. "OK, let's put the papers away. Why don't we instead begin to think of something we could color for Valentine's Day."

Episodes such as this were infrequent, but nonetheless present, in the classroom at Brush School. The frustrations, anxieties, and anger of the teachers manifested themselves in their interactions with the children. But there were also times when the teachers displayed concern and affection for the children. The fact that classrooms were occasionally scenes of emotion is not to be condemned. What is critical is the way in which the children saw adults handling their own emotions, as well as the way in which adults responded to the emotions of the children. In such circumstances the socialization process is central, for children learn through interaction and observation appropriate and inappropriate ways of expressing themselves and judging their own behavior.

One other aspect of the interaction between Mrs. Brown and Sue bears mention. The realities of classrooms are such that learning situations are tenuous and fragile. Interruptions of all sorts are constantly impinging on the class and disrupting the flow of activities — external interruptions, such as announcements over the P.A. system, a student coming in with a note for the teacher to sign, a parent coming with lunch money, or a student aide arriving with new supplies, and internal interruptions, such as Sue's insistence on fulfilling her responsibility as the thermometer monitor for the week, Donald's and Tim's conversations, or David's habit of falling out of his chair. Thus, the opportunity for an uninterrupted span of time when teacher and students can work together is not to be taken for granted. It is important to know more about how teachers handle such interruptions and which teaching styles are more tolerant of them.

January 25

ITEM: In Mrs. Hill's room, Diane is now seated by herself in the back corner of the room. There is no other student within six feet of her desk.

ITEM: There is a substitute teacher in Mrs. Hill's room today. When she was ready to begin the English lesson, she called out, "Alex, do you do English with the rest of us?" Alex said nothing, but a boy seated nearby called out, "He has special work in English and math." The substitute replied, "Well, I see he has the workbook. I'm sure he can do the work or he would not have it. You can follow along with the rest of us." Alex closed the book and put it in his desk. The substitute angrily told him to go and sit in the corner and that he would have no recess with the class.

ITEM: During one of the reading lessons, the group at the reading table was discussing batting averages of important baseball players. The story they had read was about Lou Gehrig. When the students were asked by the substitute if anyone knew the average of Henry Aaron, Alex called out from his place in the back of the room, "He's black like me." One of the boys at the table responded, "But I bet he isn't dumb like you." Alex stuck out his tongue at the boy.

January 28

During today's observation, one short exchange between Mrs. Brown and Peter revealed a further aspect of her content-oriented approach. If the goal is to "fill up" children with information, then one judges one's own success and that of the students as well by the evidence they give of how "full" they have become. But all judgments about "fullness" are conditional, both those by the teacher and those by the students themselves. Assessment is continual; there are no absolute pronouncements. Mrs. Brown said to Peter: "You know you're on trial just like everyone else. If you don't perform, I'm going to put you down a group." In first grade, then, one can observe the early stages of the rise of the meritocracy. Earlier I noted that the fourth-grade class was a good example of the "school is for real" syndrome, where work and the pursuit of achievement were focal concerns. By the time Mrs. Brown's first graders get to fourth grade, they will be ready, for they have been well socialized to accept that definition of schooling as paramount.

Later in the morning, Mrs. Brown began discussing with me Donald's latest stealing episode.

Mrs. Brown says that this morning when she was taking lunch money, Donald brought her a meal ticket he said he bought for ten cents. "Dumb me. I believe everything he tells me. I just put it in the envelope along with all the others." Apparently, Tina came up to her very soon after Donald had given her the ticket, and said that her own lunch ticket was missing. "I knew immediately where it was. I looked in the envelope and found her ticket with her name on it." She said she then talked to Donald and told him he was beyond the stage of taking things from others in the room. She did not say whether Donald said anything in response. Finally, she said, "You know, I still can't figure out why Donald steals. I think it really must be part of his makeup. Why else would he keep doing it?"

This discussion concerning Donald then moved into other areas. Mrs. Brown mentioned that Donald's mother had written a note to the principal requesting that Donald be reinstated in the free lunch program. But she would not put Donald on the program, Mrs. Brown said, until she had explicit directions from the principal to do so. "It just burns me up to see people wanting something for nothing. We have to stop shelling out all this money to people who don't need it." She also commented that Donald and Tim were still sitting together. Apparently, she was still working on how to seat them so as to minimize the disturbance to others in the room. Yesterday, they got in trouble because they went all around the playground during the noon period taking lunch boxes and hiding them behind a fence. "That made a lot of people mad at them. But those two, they just thought it was a big joke."

ITEM: I met Jeff on the playground during the lunch period. I asked him if he was staying at Brush, and he responded, "Yeah, we couldn't get no transfer."

ITEM: As I was leaving the school, I passed the bathroom that Jeff was about to enter. Kurt was inside and I could hear him call out, "Jeff you're not supposed to be here. I'm going to tell Mrs. Wills." Jeff responded, "I didn't know you was here." Kurt: "Too bad, I'm going to tell on you." Jeff: "OK, go ahead and tell. But I'm going to tell on you too. I'm gonna tell the teacher you didn't even use the bathroom." "Yes I did, and now I'm going to tell on you." "So," retorts Jeff as he pushes his way past Kurt and goes into the bathroom. Kurt walks down the hall to his classroom.

Much could be written about the formidable power of the school as an institution to mold six-year-olds so that they see it not only as an obligation, but as a positive goal to create difficulty for others by pointing out their infractions of institutional rules. In the episode above, a situation that could have been passed over with little or no comment stimulated Kurt to attack Jeff's behavior and retaliate by passing information to the teacher. The function of squealing or tattling in school is a potent one (see Henry 1963). Not only does it force others to conform, but it allows for the expression of power and hostility when one has knowledge that is damaging to another. In the exchange above, Jeff tried, seemingly unsuccessfully, to neutralize that power by threatening to squeal on Kurt's behavior as well. But Kurt had the upper hand and was not intimidated. Finally, Jeff recognized that he was the loser in the interaction; thus his "So" as he went into the bathroom.

What this exchange makes clear is that before the school year was half completed, Kurt had so accepted the norms and regulations of the school that he saw his situation with Jeff not as one where they could talk together out of the sight and sound of adults, but as one where a fellow classmate was a violator of institutional norms who had to be reported. Erving Goffman (1961) has written that, given the massive and monolithic nature of the institutions in which we must spend so much of our lives, it is in the cracks that we find our personal identities and private spaces. For Kurt and Jeff, the bathroom could not be a private space for even three minutes. Effective socialization to school regulations, however valid (or mindless) they might be, ensures that the school will remain a public space where those who deviate from its code of behavior are subject to penalties.

February 1: Report Cards at the Half-Year Mark
The students at Brush School had all received their report cards on the Monday of this week (January twenty-eighth). On Friday, the first of February, the cards had been returned by all students in both Mrs. Brown's and Mrs. Wills's rooms. I asked to see them and both teachers shared them with me. I did not ask Mrs. Evans for her cards because I had heard her say that several had not yet been returned. As things turned out, I never did see the cards from her room or from any other class in the school.

Apparently, Mrs. Brown had mentioned to the principal that I had seen her cards, and he questioned me about it. He asked why I would want to see all the cards if I was only interested in the A.T. students. I replied that I was interested in how they were graded in comparison with others in the room. I added that if he thought it improper for me to look at the cards, I would no longer do so. He seemed relieved at the suggestion and apologetically said that as far as he was concerned there was no problem. It was only that he did not know if any of the parents would be upset by my seeing the cards. Thus, what follows is the only data from report cards gained during the study.

In light of the various episodes of interaction in Mrs. Brown's and Mrs. Wills's classrooms presented so far, it is instructive to examine their grades by reading group. In Mrs. Brown's room the hierarchy of reading groups became both apparent and important early in the year, and the students responded in terms of it as they created friendships and alliances. In Mrs. Wills's room, reading group placement was less important; the hierarchy did not appear to influence friendship selections and she did not emphasize it by listing the groups on the board. (Hers was the only one of the three first-grade rooms *not* to list reading groups on the board.) Additionally, it is interesting to compare the grading practices of Mrs. Brown and Mrs. Wills because they had widely divergent teaching approaches and notions of classroom organization.

Table 1 summarizes the grading for the two rooms, based on their internal division into reading groups. The grade of C represents commendation; S represents satisfactory performance; and N means there is a need for improvement. Each child received twenty-three marks, divided into five areas: Habits and Attitudes (six); Social Studies and Science (four); Language Arts (eight); Music, Art, Physical Education (three); and Arithmetic (two).

Several items in the table are especially important. First, for all intents and purposes Mrs. Wills ignored the grade N, and Mrs. Brown made only slight use of it. On the two occasions when Mrs. Wills did assign an N grade, she also marked "Is a good listener," one of the items in the Language Arts section. Mrs. Brown re-

TABLE 1. Distribution of Report Card Grades by Reading Group

Reading Groups	Mrs. Brown Grades				Mrs. Wills Grades			
	C	S	N		C	S	N	
(1)	50% (58)	50% (57)	0%	n = 5	9% (17)	91% (189)	0% (1)	n = 9
(2)	24% (31)	74% (81)	2% (3)	n = 5	8% (9)	92% (128)	0% (1)	n = 6
(3)	25% (16)	75% (53)	0%	n = 3	8% (5)	92% (64)	0%	n = 3
(4)	12% (10)	87% (80)	1% (2)	n = 4	0%	100% (23)	0%	n = 1[a]
(5)	5% (5)	85% (98)	10% (12)	n = 5	7% (31)	93% (404)	0% (2)	n = 19
	24% (120)	73% (368)	3% (17)	n = 22				

[a]Though Jeff was essentially isolated from all reading group activity in the classroom, he is here placed as a reading group of one for reasons of inclusion and comparison.

served the N almost exclusively for those students in her lower reading groups. The lowest reading group, which included less than one fourth of the class, received nearly three fourths of the N grades.

Second, much the reverse situation prevailed with the grade of C. Here Mrs. Brown gave nearly twelve times as many grades of C to her top group as to her bottom. Mrs. Wills gave more than three times as many to her top group as to the bottom one.

Third, the data suggest that Mrs. Brown was more discriminating in her grading. Whereas Mrs. Wills overwhelmingly gave only one grade — 93 percent of the class got S — Mrs. Brown made use of all three. Perhaps this could have been anticipated, given her teaching style. She was clearly sophisticated and sensitive in her clinical evaluations of her children's reading performances, and this carried over into how she organized her reading groups. Her perceptions of gradations in levels of performance led her to create reading groups with as few as three members. Likewise, with her strong emphasis on competency in academic subjects, she was sensitive to how well the students were performing the tasks she assigned. While Mrs. Wills provided a generalized assessment of her class by giving 90 percent of the students S grades, Mrs. Brown thought it important to measure the difference in performance more precisely and to indicate them in the grades she gave.

Mrs. Wills and Mrs. Brown represent two quite different types of teachers: (1) a teacher who does not make much use of means to differentiate her students, with the result that the students themselves do not do so; and (2) a teacher who makes clear distinctions in assessing the reading competencies of students and organizes the class around these distinctions, with the result that her students also perceive such gradations and respond accordingly. The first type combines less clinical evaluation with less internal class differentiation, and the second, more clinical evaluation with more within-class differentiation. I would think it desirable to have the teacher do more clinical evaluation, so as to understand the skill levels of the students, but to have the students make fewer differentiations on the basis of these levels. The question, though, is whether teachers can create distinctions among the students without the students doing the same in emulation.

Let me be more explicit. I believe one can draw a distinction between clear academic feedback to a child and a classroom social structure that is largely based on reading ability groups. Many educators have assumed that one cannot provide clear feedback to students without also creating the familiar ranked, competitive structure of present-day classrooms. But surely it is possible to accomplish the first without the second. The work of Cohen (1973, 1975) and her associates supports this view. Thus, while it is probably true that it is better for the student to receive clear feedback on his reading competence and for the teacher to make highly technical decisions on reading grouping, it is not desirable to make reading ability the dominating principle of social organization in the classroom. Further, while it may be desirable to receive clear feedback about one's own ranking in reading skills, it is of no conceivable use to know everyone else's ranking.

POSTSCRIPT: BLACK PERCEPTIONS
AND WHITE POWER

Heretofore, I have only intermittently presented data on the parents, both black and white. Yet, as suggested in Chapter 2, the parents at Brush School strongly influenced how many decisions were made, activities carried out, and policies established. Two quite different, but subtly related sets of data follow: (1) the findings from a survey of the parents of the nine black children in the five classrooms central to this study, and (2) a long description of a meeting of the white host parents as they planned for the A.T. Program. Both shed light on the parents' perceptions of the integration process. But they also show a difference between black and white parents. Given their lack of access and participation, black parents had little to share but their perceptions. But white parents could translate their perceptions into action and influence. It is instructive to observe a group of parents in interaction with both the principal and the teachers.

Black Perceptions

By the first week in December, an interview had been completed with one or both parents of the nine black children focused upon in this study. Each of the interviews lasted approximately forty-five minutes, the shortest being thirty-five minutes and the longest an hour and a half. All of the respondents were mothers except for Joyce's father. The interviews were all conducted in the children's homes, and had been arranged in advance by telephone, except in the one instance where the family had no phone.

The parents' responses totaled thirty-five pages of data, here summarized in Tables 2 and 3. Table 2 shows how the parents felt after their children had participated in the integration pro-

TABLE 2. Summary of A.T. Parent Responses, December 1973

Question	Agree/ Yes	Disagree/ No	Don't Know
1. Does your child like to go to Brush School?	8	1	0
2. Has going to Brush School helped your child?	5	1	3
3. Do you feel your child needs special academic help?	6	1	2
4. Have you seen any specific benefits for your child in attending Brush School?	3	2	4
5. Do you have any positive comments on the program?	3	0	6
6. Do you have any negative comments on the program?	2	5	2
7. If you had to do it again, would you sign your child up for the A.T. Program?	7	1	1
8. Do you want your child taught black studies?	6	0	3
9. Do you think the teachers care about your child?	8		1

gram for thirteen or fourteen weeks. In sum, these responses show an essentially positive assessment of the program and the idea of integrated education (Q. #7) and a neutral to positive assessment of Brush School in particular (Q. #1, 2, 5, and 9). Likewise, the parents' assessment of their children's perceptions was extremely positive (Q. #1). The parents were somewhat hesitant to pass judgment on the program at Brush at this time (Q. #4 and 5). The key questions, in my estimation, are #2, #7, and #9. They indicate that the parents thought that the children would benefit from the program, that they as parents were not mistaken in signing up their children, and that the teachers at Brush were concerned about their children. These factors, taken together, may be sufficient to keep the parents in the A.T. Program, even if they could not see specific positive outcomes for their children.

These interviews also provided the first systematic information about the parents' background, presented in Table 3. The data in Table 3 are somewhat sketchy, because I questioned the parents cautiously so as not to arouse suspicion or anxiety that I had ulterior motives in interviewing them (cf. Rist 1973). I asked no questions about income or specific occupational categories. What emerges from the information I did get is that most of these parents had high school degrees and most were working. Only three of the families were on welfare (Jeff, Duke, and Alex). The A.T. parents as a group had a higher percent of employment and more education than the parents of children in the black sending schools averaged. For example, at one of the schools sending children to Brush, the percentage of children from families receiving welfare was above 65, and the median grade completion of the parents was below 10.5 years. Among the A.T. group, only a third of the families were on welfare, and the group included more families with an equal or higher educational attainment.

There are also differences between the A.T. parents and the white parents at Brush School: the A.T. parents ranged from the poor to working to middle class; the parents of the white students were generally all clustered in the upper-middle class, with an income average above $13,000, and a median grade completion above 12.5. Thus, while the A.T. parents ranked higher in socio-

TABLE 3. A.T. Parent Characteristics

Criteria	Number	
Education		
Mother: Some high school	8	(*N* = 9)
Completed high school	6	
Some college	2	
Completed college	0	
Father: Some high school	5	(*N* = 5)
Completed high school	4	
Some college	2	
Completed college	2	(Donald and Melvin)
Employment		
Mother employed	6	
Father employed	5	
Both parents employed	4	
Family on Welfare	3	
Family Size		
One child	2	(Donald and Joyce)
Two to four	6	
Five or more	1	(Jeff)

economic criteria than the average for other parents in their original schools, they were below the average of the white parents at Brush. These findings are the first clear indication of the class differences between the white and black children at Brush School.

White Power

On January 29, a meeting was held in the home of one of the host parents to discuss and plan for the A.T. Program. In attendance were twenty-seven host parents, nine teachers, the principal, and me. Everyone was white, and there were thirty-two women and six males. This meeting was perhaps the best example during the entire year of white parents and teachers discussing the A.T. Program. It is particularly important because it gives a strong indication of the amount of influence exerted by the parents at Brush School. This meeting was arranged, organized, and chaired by parents. Furthermore, the agenda was set by parents. The principal and teachers participated, but they did not have greater status or authority than did the parents. Represented among the parents were the professions of lawyer, doctor, college professor, and television station executive. This was a group of competent and professional people who were systematically dealing with an issue affecting their children and their school. One could envision these people dealing in the same manner with a proposed zoning change, the possibility of street widening, increases in public transportation. The school was but one of the institutions that affected their neighborhood, and all such institutions had to be systematically observed and monitored.

When the participants had arrived, the men in coats and ties, the women in long dresses or pant suits, the host and hostess served wine and cheese. After a few minutes of informal conversation, the host asked everyone to be seated.

The host passed out a dittoed sheet entitled "Agenda for the Administrative Transfer Host Parents, Teachers, and Others Concerned." His comment as he did this: "I suggest we follow this agenda if there are no objections." There were none. He began with point one—introductions. All present were asked to identify themselves and say what relation they had to the A.T. Program.

The second item on the agenda was "Activity Bus." The host said this item was included for discussion because many of the parents didn't know when the activity bus would start operating, and thus could not plan ahead for after-school activity involving the A.T. students. The principal began a long and elaborate explanation of the activity bus and why he had been hesitant to schedule it. ("What if some night the child misses it and is left standing in front of a dark school at 5:30 and no one there to help him? You know, I'm responsible for those students until they get on that bus to go home.") The discussion on the activity bus went on for some thirty minutes, as parents expressed their frustrations at not being able to plan for after-school activities. The principal countered their comments with more discussion of his difficulties with the bus and the problems it could generate. One of the parents, seemingly irritated with this conversation, called out, "I don't think we should change the bus schedule [running the activity bus would require rerouting] just so some parents can feel like they are doing good." There was an awkward silence.

The principal broke it by saying that he could think of something positive that would come from having the bus. If it were initiated, the teachers would be able to keep the A.T. students after school for punishment the same way they did the white children, who live in the neighborhood. He was asked if there had been any discipline problems so far that would have merited keeping an A.T. student after school. He answered, "No, we don't have discipline problems here, just academic ones." The host spoke up and said, "Isn't the real issue whether we can set this up so that the A.T. children can stay after school to play in our backyards and be friends with our own children?" Another father added, "Exactly. It may be desegregation to let them play together at school, but it is integration to let them play together at someone's home." The issue was shortly resolved when the principal said he would begin scheduling an activity bus each Wednesday from now until the spring recess. If it worked until then, he would keep it for the remainder of the year.

The next item on the agenda was "Spring Hike." The host said that one of the school parents, a biologist, had volunteered to lead a hike for the host parents, their children, the A.T. children, and their parents. It was said that the hike would be an informal setting in which parents and children could all get to know one another better. The host asked if there was a volunteer to organize the hike and make the necessary arrangements. No one volunteered. He asked again and still no response. Finally, he said, "Well, I guess interest will express itself as the time comes near." (Note: the hike never occurred.)

The fourth item on the agenda was "Suggestions for Helping the Low Achievers." The host called on Mrs. Miller, the third-grade teacher serving as coordinator of the A.T. Program at Brush. She began by saying that the new reading program, Distar, was about to begin at the school for those children having reading difficulties, and if any host parents wished to volunteer their time, this would be another way to get involved in the A.T. Program. (Note: this was but the first of many times when the term "low achievers" or "students with academic problems" was equated with "A.T. students.") One of the parents asked if the Distar program was to be exclusively for the A.T. students. The answer was no. The parent then continued, "Well, if there are white children in the program as well, does it mean that they are low achievers?" The principal was quick to answer, "Oh no. It could only mean they are having problems with their reading." Again Mrs. Miller mentioned the need for volunteers, and the matter was dropped.

The fifth item was "Next Year's Plans." The host said he thought it important to match the host parents better to the individual black student. He said that this year, there were host parents whose own children were not in the same room as the A.T. student with whom they were working. He suggested that next year the host parents come from the same room as the A.T. student. The principal responded by saying he would be able to do that more easily next year because he would then have a better idea of who and how many A.T. students there would be.

The principal was asked whether next year he would continue the policy of distributing the A.T. students through a variety of rooms, or try to concentrate all from one grade in the same room. He said he would continue the present policy because, in his words, "I've decided to treat the A.T. students like everyone else. If I start tampering with the class assignments, it would result in them getting individualized attention on the basis that they are different. And I'm not going to treat them as different."

The host said the agenda items had all been covered, and he wondered now if the principal would "take a few minutes to tell us your assessment of how the program is going." The principal began by saying that at Brush there were no racial problems, just academic ones. Only one fourth of the A.T. students, he said, were performing at grade level. The other three fourths were below grade level. He added that he was also having some "behavioral problems" but that they were diminishing. "Why, even Henry and Jeff are doing better. Henry isn't fighting and Jeff isn't stealing like they used to." One of the teachers spoke up: "I still watch Jeff. Why, he's like a vacuum cleaner. He'll pick up everything in sight." People started laughing. The principal interjected, "But seriously, the problems are not just with the A.T. students. Some of the white students also cause problems. I don't want any of you to think stealing is something special to blacks." I heard from across the room in a soft voice, "Yes, it is." Others must have heard it also, for again there was an awkward silence.

One of the teachers spoke up: "Regardless of the problems we may have here at Brush, they are nothing like what some of the other schools are having. Why, I've heard of teachers being beaten up and the children having their money taken away from them every day. I just hope we never get any more A.T. students then we have right now. Around thirty is a good number. You get any more than that and you get nothing but trouble. We can handle the ones we've got now, but that's about all." The principal added, "Well, don't worry about getting any more. There just isn't any more room."

At this time, the host said the formal part of the meeting had been completed, and he invited the group to stay, have more wine, and talk informally. Almost everyone did.

6.

The Patterns Persist

It may well be argued that in the three previous chapters not enough emphasis has been placed on race *per se*. Instead, it could be argued, what has been presented is a general analysis of the schooling process at Brush, with the integration program considered as only one facet of that process. That argument may be correct, yet for the wrong reason.

I have not deliberately played down the realities of race at Brush; rather I have portrayed them as they seemed to appear to those involved. The Administrative Transfer Program did force some new considerations on the part of the principal and the teachers, but it did not fundamentally alter the way they perceived either their activities or their goals. I think much the same can be said for the white students. Thus, a study of integration at Brush, if it is to portray accurately what happened, must have superimposed upon it a study of the culture of the school. The experiences of the black children and their reception by the white teachers, students, and principal were merely one set of threads in the weaving of a whole fabric.

And, of course, when one opts for an integration program based on racial assimilation, the goal is, finally, racial unawareness. If, from the vantage point of the whites, the few black students had become "just like us," then there was little or no reason to make something special of an individual's skin color. Lack of emphasis on race *per se* could therefore be anticipated in many episodes of interaction and activity at Brush. It would be a sign of the failure of the program if the racial consciousness of the students, both black and white, had been raised. If the black students were progressively less and less identified as "black," this may well have been the result of their gradual acceptance in the school as they became increasingly "invisible" in racial terms to the whites. (Indeed, though I have no way of knowing for sure, it is plausible that the black students would have been less "visible" had I not been observing how the integration program was proceeding.)

As will be more fully argued in the following pages, the pursuit of racial assimilation, the overwhelming dominance of the achievement ethos, the persistent evaluations of students' words and deeds, and the internal stratification based on perceived competence, all led to a situation where it was more the academic performance of the black children than their skin color that defined their experiences at Brush. The black students at Brush overwhelmingly found themselves in the bottom half, with all that implied in a school where perceptions of low achievement frequently translated themselves into perceptions of low worth.

February 4

My sense of Jeff's isolation from others in his room became more pervasive with each visit. Today, I entered the room and then turned to leave because I did not see Jeff. I asked the teacher, Mrs. Wills, if he was sick, and she said, no, he was over on the floor in the corner. He was lying face down, seemingly asleep. When I walked over to him, he looked up and smiled. He told me he was working on one of his puzzles, which was near by.

Mrs. Wills calls out, "Blue Group, it's time for your reading lesson." Three girls go over to where the teacher is seated on the right side of the room. Jeff does not make any move toward joining the group, though it is his reading group. He stays on the floor.

I found this interesting, for it indicated how separated Jeff had become from his reading group. When it was called, he moved not a muscle. The group no longer had significance for him, and he no longer considered himself a member. He belonged nowhere.

Later in the morning, when Mrs. Wills had dismissed her class for recess, she came to me and began talking about Jeff. Her first comment: "I had an experience this morning I thought you'd want to know about." She said that a mother of a second-grade student had called the school to complain that Jeff was intimidating her son in the bathroom and beating him on the playground. Mrs. Wills said she had no reason to doubt the woman's word and so had assumed that Jeff had in fact been doing these things. During the day, she said, she had planned to deal with any problems in the bathroom by requiring another student to accompany Jeff there. And when Jeff was on the playground, she herself would keep a "close watch on what he does." One final comment before she left for the playground: "You know, Jeff does wander some. When he goes to the bathroom, it sometimes takes him ten or fifteen minutes to return. I just figured he was staying out of trouble. I won't be able to assume that from now on since I know better."

February 7

In Mrs. Hill's fourth-grade class, a noticeable difference had gradually developed between the experiences of the two black children, Diane and Alex. Like Jeff, Alex for some time had been gradually left behind in terms of academic performance. And like Jeff, he was becoming a nonmember of the class, uninvolved in most of their activities. He filled his time in the room with much random behavior and small games he made up while others were working on assignments. And since the best part of the day in Mrs. Hill's room was devoted to academic endeavors, Alex had to find things to do to cover most of the time he was in the room. On this date, I recorded a number of his activities while other students were working.

Alex begins making faces at one of the boys four rows away. The other boy smiles, but makes no faces in return. When the boy goes back to his work, Alex takes out three pencils and starts tapping them on his desk. Soon he is making designs, mostly differently shaped triangles.

Alex is tapping out a tune with his pencil. Mrs. Hill does not leave her reading group, nor does she tell him to stop. Instead, she writes a note to him, and another student takes it over to his desk. He looks at the note and puts down his pencils.

Alex is again looking at the boy across the room. He calls out his name rather loudly, and the boy looks up. Alex gives him a big grin and the boy smiles, but sees the teacher watching and goes back to his work. Alex cannot see the teacher because his back is to her and calls out to the boy again. The teacher now says, firmly, "Alex, let's get busy."

Juxtaposed to these observations of Alex are those of Diane. Although she was still in the least advanced reading group, she appeared to be involved with her lessons and with some of the other students in the room.

Diane has a workbook out and is working on a lesson. Soon, she is talking softly with Mary, sitting next to her. I see her point to one of the problems. They talk for a short time, and then Diane erases and puts down a new figure on her own sheet. Shortly they begin talking again, and Mary glances periodically at Diane's paper. Diane asks a question. Mary answers and Diane goes back to her own paper.

Diane seems to be having a problem with one part of the assignment. She asks Mary, who shrugs her shoulders. Diane gets up and goes to the teacher. The teacher works with her briefly and she then goes back to her seat. She apparently tells Mary what the teacher had said.

During this observational period, there was only one interaction involving both Diane and Alex. It was instigated by Alex.

Alex is standing between Diane and Mary, talking to Diane. Suddenly, he leaves and goes to say something to the teacher, but so softly that I cannot hear him. The teacher nods and begins walking toward Diane. Alex is walking next to her. She tells Alex to go to his own desk, but he stays beside her. Finally, the teacher has to take Alex by the arm and lead him to his desk, where she tells him to stay. Now the teacher goes to Diane, leans down, and begins talking softly to her. She has her hand on Diane's shoulder and soon leaves for the back of the room, a candy bar in her hand. She puts the candy in her desk and then comes to where I am seated: "Did you see all that?" I say that I did, and Mrs. Hill says, "That was Alex trying to get Diane in trouble." I asked how, and she says there is a rule that students cannot have candy in their desk. Alex had come and told her about Diane's candy bar.

The teacher asks me if I saw Alex with a group of boys a few minutes earlier. I say I did, and she explains that Jon was selecting people to be in a play his reading group was going to perform for the class. She says Jon chose Alex to be in the play. So far as she knows, she says, Jon is the only student who has asked Alex to come over to his home after school to play. I ask the teacher what she thinks prompted Jon to include Alex in the play. She replies, "Jon told me he was going to ask Alex because Alex was doing well lately."

February 10

ITEM: The children in Mrs. Evans's room were to complete the following sentence. "I am me when I am . . ." A number of possible answers had been written on the board: swimming, skiing, sleeping, riding my bike, and so on. Gloria had chosen to complete her sentence with "I am me when I am running." She had also drawn a stick figure of herself with a brown crayon. Joyce had used none of the options from the board, but instead had written: "I am me when I am getting whippings." She had drawn on her paper a picture of a house.

ITEM: Mrs. Evans had continued to use the voting by the students for the "good citizen of the month" as a means of achieving conformity in the room (cf. the observation on November 26). Her comment on this day: "Children, you are being awfully noisy today. Don't forget that today is the day we're going to vote for the good citizen of the month, and if your name doesn't stay on the board under the list of good citizens, we won't be able to vote for you." Since October, Mrs. Evans had been keeping a list on a side board, under the heading, "Good Citizens," of the names of those students she thought were behaving "nicely" in the room. The students were supposed to vote for somebody on this list. Gloria's name had been on the list each month. Joyce had never been listed, and during the short time Lou was in the room, he had not been listed.

ITEM: The bickering and antagonism between Joyce and Paul was apparent again during this observation.

Paul calls out in a loud voice to Joyce, who is now standing in front of the board, "Joyce, get out of the way and get back to work." Joyce says, "I ain't got no work, I finished." "Sure you are, sure you are," retorts Paul. "Forgit you." Paul sticks out his tongue and then says, "Quit bothering me. Quit bothering me." Joyce also sticks out her tongue but says nothing further.

And again later in the morning:

Paul is counting out loud as he works on his arithmetic lesson. Joyce turns around and says to him. "Paul, you just stop talking to me." Paul answers, "Mind your own business. I'm not talking to you." Joyce: "Teacher, teacher!" in a loud voice. Mrs. Evans does not respond, so Joyce goes up to the teacher and says something to her. Shortly, the teacher comes over to Paul and asks him to count more softly so he won't disturb others. He gets a hurt look on his face, but says nothing.

ITEM: Mrs. Evans brings me Tina's picture and her sentence, which says, "I am me when I am fair." Mrs. Evans comments, "You can always tell when a child is from a good home."

February 12: Lincoln's Birthday and Jeff's Exclusion

As has been previously suggested, the socialization function performed by schools is critical to an understanding of their role in American society. It is in this institution that children learn much about what are believed to be important aspects of our cultural and political life. This socialization process springs into sharp relief on national holidays, when fundamental tenets of the national ideology are espoused. In a very small way, the lesson on Lincoln gives a sense of how, from the first grade on, this ideology is transmitted.

Mrs. Wills tells the class to come and sit on the floor in the front of the room, so she can read them a story. The children quickly come up and gather around her. She has brought her chair to the front. The story she reads is a short narrative of the life of Lincoln. The book says: "Lincoln believed all men who were slaves should be free. But not everyone agreed with him and soon there was war." The story ended with his assassination. The last line: "Abraham Lincoln was a great American." Mrs. Wills says, "The reason we want to know about Abraham Lincoln is that today is his birthday." Kurt calls out, "Are we going to have a party?" "No, that's on Valentine's Day; today we're just happy he was alive."

The teacher goes to the front board and says it's time for the writing lesson. "Who wants to start the story?" Jeff raises his hand and is called on. "Jeff?" Jeff answers, "I forgot." Anne is called on and she answers, "He was a President." "But what about when he was young? We want the story to have unity. Liza, do you have a suggestion?" "He had to walk nine miles to school." "Yes, but where did he live?" Kurt answers, "In a log cabin." "Yes, good, Kurt." Mrs. Wills writes on the board the first line of the story, "He lived in a log cabin." Continuing, she says, "OK, Liza, now we can add your suggestion," and she writes on the board, "He walked nine miles to school."

Mrs. Wills turns and faces the class. "Children, it's important for your story to have unity, to make sense. It's important to start at the beginning, have a middle, and then an ending. You don't start at the end of the story by saying he died, then he was President, then he walked to school, and then he lived in a log cabin. You turn that around so you can see how things happened to him during his life. Every story should have a beginning and an end. You don't start at the end and go back to the beginning."

Jeff is working on a sheet of blue construction paper. He began drawing on it almost immediately after he first raised his hand. Mrs. Wills asks if anyone has anything else to add to the story. Chris calls out, "He cut down the cherry tree too." "No, that was George Washington. We'll talk about him in a few days when it's his birthday." Kurt calls out, "Will we have a party then?" Mrs. Wills makes no response.

She now sings a song about Lincoln for the children. She asks them to sing it with her, but few, if any, do. The words of the song have to do with his beard and stovepipe hat. Then Mrs. Wills tells the children to begin writing a story. (Note: Though there was much emphasis on the unity and sequence of the story, on the board were only the two lines noted earlier.)

ITEM: Later in the morning, when it was time for the arithmetic lesson, Mrs. Wills told the class she had decided to split them into two groups, one to be taught by herself and the other by the teacher's aide. She called the names of the children to be in the two groups, omitting Jeff. Jeff said, "You forgot me." She responded, "Oh no, Jeff. I've got something special for you today." As it turned out, he was given a sheet out of a workbook while the rest of the class was receiving instruction. *Jeff now had no group membership in the room. He had sat alone while the class was receiving reading group lessons and he would now do the same during the arithmetic lesson.*

February 19

ITEM: Mrs. Brown had organized the morning show and tell periods so that each day the children would focus on a different topic. Monday was the day to "tell"; Tuesday was the day to show books or newspaper clippings; Wednesday was for showing items related to science. Today, Wedensday, Tina was showing something for science. It was in a bag and the students were to guess what it was (a mushroom). During the time Tina was in the front, Donald was at his seat calling out, "I got something to show, I got something to show." When he was finally called on to come to the front, he pulled out a newspaper clipping. Mrs. Brown said today was not the day for newspapers, but since it was the first time Donald had brought a clipping, he could show it. When he was done (it was a picture of football players) Mrs. Brown said she was "so pleased" with Donald and tacked the clipping on the board.

ITEM: Mrs. Brown was about to pass back the arithmetic papers: "OK, let's see who won." She counted out in one place all the perfect papers done by the boys (four) and in another all those done by the girls (three). Then she went to the board and added four to the number under the column for boys and three for the girls. The scores were eight and five, respectively. She later told me she was keeping score between the boys and girls to impress on the children the need to do careful work. "I thought if they were competing with one another, they'd be more interested."

ITEM: Mrs. Brown had put Tim and Donald across the room from each other. She told me, "You know, their relationship has changed. They used to get along, but now they're always picking on each other. They're really very antagonistic toward each other. I don't know if it's jealousy, or competition, or what, but they sure don't get along any more."

Later in the morning, Tim came back from the bathroom and told Mrs. Brown, "Donald has been running in the halls and he said a bad word in the bathroom." Mrs. Brown began walking toward the hall when Donald came in. "Donald, have you been running in the halls?" Donald said loudly, "No, but Tim was." Mrs. Brown then said very softly, "Did you say a bad word?" Donald, indignantly: "No." "Well, I sure hope you didn't." Tim added, "Yes, he did." Donald said, "Boy, shut up."

February 22: Reading for Awareness

During the fall, the teachers had gone to the in-service cultural awareness class organized with the intent of informing them of the multicultural dimension integration would bring to their school. There had been a list of books that the teachers were to read, but the books had never arrived. Thus the last session of the class, which was to be a discussion of the reading material, was indefinitely postponed. On this date, a note was placed in the morning bulletin circulated to all rooms that the books had arrived and could be checked out from the teachers lounge. They were: *Black Americans, Racism in American Education, Black on Black, Crisis in Black and White, Black Rage, Negroes' Self-Concept, Out of the House of Bondage, What Black Politicians Are Saying*, and, finally, *The Black Experience in America*.

February 27

ITEM: The previous evening there had been an open house in Mrs. Daley's room, as well as in the other third- and fourth-grade classes. On one of the boards in her room, Mrs. Daley had printed the schedule the class followed each day:

Organization	9:00-9:15
Mathematics	9:15-9:45
English	9:45-10:30

P.E.	10:30-10:50
Reading	10:50-11:20
Lunch	11:20-12:00
Sharing Time	12:00-12:30
Science	12:30-1:15
P.E.	1:15-1:30
Music	1:30-2:00
Social Studies	2:00-2:30
Organization	2:30-2:45

It is interesting to reflect, in light of a schedule like this, on the continual lament of teachers that so many children have a "short attention span." When each instructional period is less than thirty minutes, it may well be that children showing a "short attention span" are displaying a situational response to the fracturing of their school day rather than a deep-seated cognitive attribute. It may well be that such an instructional approach generates through a self-fulfilling prophecy the very attribute the teachers thought to exist in the first place. I know of no research indicating that thirty minutes or less is the maximum time most children can concentrate on a particular task.

Rather than justify the fragmentation of the school day on the basis of assumed limitations in the children, it would be well to acknowledge that this approach to instructional organization arises from pedagogical and bureaucratic assumptions about schools. The pedagogical belief is that schooling is a continual process of giving small doses. The child is an empty vessel filled over time with prescribed quantities of information; an information overload, that is, longer class periods, would short circuit the system. Bureaucratic justification comes from the belief that the reduction of activities to small, quantifiable periods of time allows for greater efficiency and higher productivity. The same rationale that governs the production schedule of a factory or the time schedules in a large organization governs the school as well. This is one of the major reasons that so many writers have drawn the analogy between schools and factories.

ITEM: I had seen Duke and Melvin on the playground during the noon period. But when I went into the room to observe, I waited twenty minutes and still they had not yet appeared. I asked Mrs. Daley what had happened to them, and she said that four days each week, immediately after lunch, they were given remedial reading instruction. She mentioned the sharing period "wasn't important" and they "wouldn't miss much by being gone."

ITEM: Mrs. Daley mentioned that she had called and talked to Melvin's grandmother because "Melvin was not doing his work like I knew he could." I said I had met the grandmother on a visit to his home. Mrs. Daley said, "I bet she's still pretty young, isn't she?" I said no, she was not. "Oh, that surprises me." I asked why and she responded, "Well, you know these people start reproducing earlier than we white people do. I saw in the newspaper once where a colored woman was a grandmother at thirty-three. She had had her first child at seventeen, and her daughter had a child when she was sixteen." I sensed that Mrs. Daley felt somewhat uneasy almost as soon as she finished the sentence, and so she immediately changed the subject.

March 4

Much emphasis has been placed on the quality of the teaching a child receives as a key determinant of academic performance. But the issue has yet another dimension. One must account not only for quality of teaching, but also for *quantity* of time actually spent with the child in instruction. The following lesson was the sum total of the reading instruction the lowest reading group in Mrs. Daley's room received this day. It was less than half that received by the other two groups. It was also when she was with this group that she tolerated the most interruption by other students.

Mrs. Daley calls out, "Melvin, Duke, and Andy, it's time for reading. Bring your chairs over here." The three boys bring over their chairs and the lesson begins. They had been told to read a story at their seats and be prepared to discuss it in the group. Her first question to them: "OK, who can tell me what it was about?" All three boys start to speak at once, and the teacher tells them she can only hear one person at a time. She calls on Melvin, who begins to explain. A girl comes from her seat to ask the teacher if she can use the record player. While Melvin continues to talk, the teacher says yes, if she uses headphones. The teacher says to Melvin, "Good job." Two other girls now come up to the teacher and want to talk to her. She first turns to the three boys and tells them to read the next story quietly to themselves, then starts answering the girls' questions. A boy comes up with a question on his mathematics. Melvin and Andy have finished their reading, Duke has not. Melvin stands up and looks around the room, and the teacher tells him to sit down. Duke finishes, and Mrs. Daley begins asking them questions about what they read. Andy answers the first question correctly. She begins to ask one of Melvin, but in the middle of it, she stops and says in a loud voice, "Melvin, whatever it is you've got in your mouth, go and spit it out right now." Melvin gets up and walks to the back of the room and spits his gum in the waste basket. When he returns, Mrs. Daley repeats the question. Melvin cannot answer it and she tells him to reread the section. He does, and in the meanwhile, a girl comes with a question on her mathematics. Mrs. Daley answers her. Now Melvin is finished and answers the question correctly. Mrs. Daley says, "Good, now you all can go back to your seats and get to work in your workbooks." She then calls for the highest reading group.

The length of the lesson for Melvin and Duke's group: eight minutes.

March 5

ITEM: Mrs. Brown told me that she was in the midst of a "reorganization" of her lowest reading group. That group — Donald, Trish, David, and Pam — was "so far behind" that it was necessary to work out a new schedule for them. Their new program would be "geared to their progress ability" and they would no longer be trying to stay close to the other three reading groups in the room. I asked why she had not included Tim in that group, and she responded, "Why, didn't you know? Since he was put on drugs, he has shot up a whole reading group. It's hard to believe what has happened to him."

ITEM: Mrs. Brown gave some rather lengthy comments on Donald.

I ask about Donald and she says she doesn't know what she's going to do with him because he won't stay in his seat. She also says she's "never had a child quite like him." I ask her to elaborate and she says that she could understand it if he was constantly moving because he couldn't do the work, but she can't understand why he won't concentrate when he has the ability to do the class assignments.

She rather abruptly changes the topic and asks, "Do you know what else he did today? He destroyed some property." She seems irritated as she tells of Donald using a sharp piece of metal to gouge out a piece of wood from his desk top and to make two deep scratches in one of his books. "I can't understand what makes a child do that. He's too young to be angry at the world."

ITEM: As Mrs. Brown and I were talking in the back of the room, Tim exploded in a rage at Bruce.

Tim starts screaming at Bruce to leave him alone. He also starts beating him on the back. Mrs. Brown immediately goes over to Tim and tells him to leave the room. Tim runs out and slams the door as he goes. Mrs. Brown goes after him into the hall and tells him to come back and close the door properly. As he comes back into the room, he flings the door open so forcefully it slams against the wall. Then he falls on the floor and screams that he hates Bruce. Mrs. Brown tries to pick him up, but he struggles with her and runs back into the hall. She goes after him and tells him he can stay out there until he learns to behave himself. She closes the door and glances at me with a frustrated look. I ask if she thinks the new drug he is on could have that effect, because in the past six months, I never before had seen such behavior from Tim. "I guess so," she responds, "but the person he sits next to could cause anyone to have problems."

ITEM: Once in a while, an exchange between a teacher and a student took on a bizarre, uninterpretable dimension. One of these strange episodes occurred today, in the midst of a science lesson where the teacher was trying to teach the children that when it rains there aren't any shadows. She had opened a book showing on the right-hand page a picture of a large tree in a field during a rainstorm and on the left a picture of the same tree bathed in sunlight.

Mrs. Brown holds up the book and asks Donald about the picture on the right. "Donald, what do you think this is?" "I think it some mud." Mrs. Brown makes no response to this, but continues: "On this side are the shadows. Do you see the shadows, Donald?" Donald answers, "Yeah." "You do? I don't," says Mrs. Brown. Donald responds, "You don't, but we do." Mrs. Brown seemingly ignores this exchange, for she continues with the lesson, asking the class if they think it's possible to have shadows during the night.

March 8

While the remainder of the class had been divided into two groups for an arithmetic lesson, Jeff had been given another sheet from a workbook. The page consisted of twenty problems, all involving the numeral eight ($X + 4 = 8$, $8 - 1 = X$, $3 + X = 8$, and so on). When he had completed the sheet, he put it in the teacher's desk basket. I was seated next to the desk and observed that of the twenty problems, he had done one correctly ($7 + 1 = X$).

Later in the morning, Mrs. Wills came to me and said, "Did you see this?" referring to Jeff's paper. I said I had and she went on, "I'm not sure what we're going to do with him." She said the testing on Jeff indicated he had problems with visual-motor coordination, and that the reading specialist suggested he work on jigsaw puzzles to improve his hand-eye coordination. She added, "That's one reason I don't mind if he spends a lot of time with the puzzles. Besides, what else is he going to do when he can't do the work?"

March 11

ITEM: Donald greeted me as soon as I stepped into Mrs. Brown's classroom: "Hi, Dr. Rist. Guess what I got?" I said, "Let me guess." Donald calls out, "I got new glasses. I didn't used to see the clock, but now I do."

ITEM: The following is an account of a reading lesson for the lowest reading group in Mrs. Brown's room. The book used by the children was *Pig Can Jig*.

After the three students are in the circle, Mrs. Brown tells them to sit neatly. "Show Dr. Rist you know what it means to be neat."

They are told to open their books to page 57 and Donald is called on first to begin reading the list of twenty words on that page. Before he can begin, Mrs. Brown says to him, "I sure like your trousers." Donald reads the list of twenty with only one error. Mrs. Brown: "That's wonderful. Why you are so smart?"

Mrs. Brown then asks questions about the words in the list. Donald is asked to find a word that means "to bite somebody." He chooses "bit." David is to find the word that names an animal. He chooses "cat." Trish is to find one that means "to turn on a light." She makes no response, and Donald calls out "lit." "That's good, Donald, but you should wait your turn." Mrs. Brown pats herself on the head. "What is this word?" Donald seems confused and says "You mean 'head'?" "No, what is this word?" David calls out "hand." "No, you're both just guessing. Those words aren't even on the list. Look at your list." Donald calls out "pat." "Wonderful, Donald." "Now, what word means you eat too much?" Davids answers "fat." "And what if I have a stick in my hand?" Donald answers "bat." "Oh, Donald. You're getting to be such a good reader."

Mrs. Brown tells the group to turn the page. Donald calls out, "Can I read first?" "No, it's David's turn. OK, David, let's go." David reads the first three words and then gets stuck. The teacher wants him to sound out the next word. She asks him what the first letter is (n) and he says he doesn't know it. Donald blurts out, "He don't even know his letters but I know." Mrs. Brown ignores Donald and says to David, "I guess we better spend some more time on you learning the alphabet." Donald is nearly out of his seat in his eagerness to give the answer. "OK, Donald, you read. Donald begins and soon Mrs. Browns interrupts, "Don't point to each word." He reads the paragraph well. Trish is called on to read. She reads the next paragraph, but needs considerable help from the teacher. Donald has his hand up waving it and asking the teacher if he can read next. "OK, OK, Donald, you can finish the page." He does so and reads it well. When he is finished, Mrs. Brown exclaims loudly and in an exaggerated tone, "Oh Donald, you're so good. I can't really believe that was you reading." Donald responds, "I don't think I'll read any more. I'm so good."

In this lesson, Donald clearly dominated both other students and the exchanges with the teacher. When Trish could not answer the first question put to her, Donald broke in and answered it. When David could not recognize the letter *n*, Donald again broke in. Related to Donald's acsendancy in the group is how Mrs. Brown tolerated his interruptions and rewarded his performances. He was the only one of the three she praised for reading. He was also the only one she gave extra attention to — "I sure like your trousers." With his final comment, Donald indicated that he clearly perceived he was at the top of the group. And being on top, he was ready to retire.

March 13

During a noon recess, I spoke with Mrs. Miller, the third-grade teacher working as the school coordinator for the A.T. Program. During the course of our conversation, I learned that she, the principal, the president of the PTA, and one host parent had the previous week met with five of the mothers of the A.T. students in one of their homes. I mentioned I would have been interested in attending the meeting, and she commented, "We wanted to keep the number of whites small. If too many of us had gone, we would have overwhelmed them." I asked whether the meeting was beneficial and was told it was, though the black parents "did not offer much. We went looking for ways to improve the program, and what we heard was that they were generally satisfied. In fact, no one criticized anything we were doing." She continued, "Maybe if more parents had come, we would have heard some gripes. But we knew we could never expect a perfect attendance, so we were glad to have those who did come."

I also asked her if she knew to what extent the white parents were making use of the activity bus (which the principal had scheduled after the meeting at the home of a host parent) to invite the A.T. students to their homes in the late afternoon. She said it was not being used much at all, except by the teachers in the fourth grade who were keeping some of the A.T. students after school for discipline reasons and then sending them home on the bus. She said only two white mothers, to her knowledge, had made use of it so they could invite the A.T. students to their homes.

Later in our conversation, I commented that some of the children's descriptions of their spring vacation plans indicated that their families were quite affluent. She responded that wealth had not affected the children, because it was just a "taken-for-granted" part of their life-style. "They just think everyone gets to do what they do. They don't know any different."

March 14

During the noon period in the teachers' lounge, Mrs. Evans began talking about a conference she had had the previous afternoon with Joyce's mother. Mrs. Evans mentioned she had said Joyce would have to repeat the first grade. The mother responded by asking whether there was an ungraded class Joyce could join. When she was told there was not, Mrs. Evans said it was her own impression that Joyce's mother would not let Joyce come back to Brush next year. Mrs. Evans added, "You know, Joyce is all by herself. She hardly knows her alphabet, let alone whole words. I give her special work every day, and she does practically none of it. At the rate she's going, it would be cruel to put her in second grade." One of the second-grade teachers added, "I hope you keep her back if she's that bad. I've got enough problems without having to teach the alphabet to second graders."

ITEM: New reading group assignments have been given to some of the students in Mrs. Evans's room. Paul, who had been with Joyce and Gloria in the lowest group, has been moved up one level. *The bottom group [called red] now consists of only Joyce and Gloria.* On a side board, Mrs. Evans has listed the four groups, using the appropriate color of chalk to match the name of each of the groups (red, blue, orange, and purple).

March 15: The Last Minutes before Vacation

By late in the afternoon on Friday, academic work had ceased in Mrs. Brown's room. She was trying to organize a large stack of student papers, and the students themselves were talking and moving freely around the room.

About ten minutes before dismissal, Mrs. Brown walks to the front. She has the papers with her and begins calling the students by name to come get them. She tells the class they should be sure to take the papers home with them today. When she is finished, she says, "I want you all to think about the kind of week we've had." Ian calls out, "It's been a good week." "Why?" she asks. "Because we've all been quiet." "I'm glad you have, but what's even more important?" Mary says, "We all got our work done." Mat calls out, "The boys won." Mrs. Brown continues, "The most important thing is, how many of you feel you have improved this week?" All the hands in the room go up. "Oh, that's wonderful. Every week we should try and do better."

Craig comes up to the front and tells the teacher she forgot to grade one of his papers. "I didn't forget. You didn't do what I instructed you to, so I'm not going to spend my time grading what wasn't done right." Craig goes back to his seat. Mrs. Brown looks at row one, and says, "You all look like you have clean desks. You're free to pass." The children in the first row get up, but so does everyone else. The organization in the room has just ended. Children are all over the room, getting coats, talking to one another, running out the door, or picking up papers they've dropped. A number of the children kiss the teacher goodbye.

March 25: The First Day Back

I visited all three first-grade rooms on this day. In each, the teacher mentioned the difficulty she was having in getting the children to "settle down and get to work." As Mrs. Brown said, "They are sure off to a rough start. Everyone had such a good vacation all they want to do is talk, talk, talk."

Mrs. Brown told me she had thought a good deal over the vacation about what to do with Donald. She said he was the best reader in the low group, and that she would like to do with him what she had done with Tim, move him up a reading group. But, she added, "I'm not sure I can, if you know what I mean." I said I didn't, and she elaborated: "Well, you know I've put Tim up a whole reading group. But the only way I would do that was that his mother assured me she would work with him every night. I'm just not sure I would get that kind of cooperation from Donald's mother." I asked if she had called Donald's mother to ask, and Mrs. Brown said she hadn't.

ITEM: As a way of getting some indication of the varying levels of reading in the first-grade rooms, I noted the complete story each of the four groups in Mrs. Brown's room was working on the first day back after vacation. The four groups, from the top one down, were reading stories of 620, 490, 79, and 72 words, respectively. Some idea of the complexity of the stories is indicated in the following excerpts. The most advanced reading group was reading a story entitled "The Whale Who Likes Lemonade":

"I have a taste for lemonade, but I don't have any lemonade. Could you tell me where I could get some?" "Swim that way," said the crab, pointing south with a claw. "Go five miles past the Green Mountain, and there you will find your lemonade. The whale swam five miles past the Green Mountain and soon had reached Africa.

The second most advanced group was reading "The Wagonmaster":

"Why have we come?" Kit asked his father. "This western land is empty." "It is empty," said his father, "But it is a land where a man can plant crops. It is a free land where a man can be someone if he wants to be." But it was a bad land to travel in. There was wind and thunder. There was dust when it was dry, and mud when it was wet. And there were drums in the land.

The third group was reading "If I Had a Ship." This is the entire story:

If I had a ship, I would run and I would skip to the bank. To the pond I would dash. On a fresh wind song I would sing and I would sing and I would go on the pond in a flash. From my ship I would fish, I would wish for a dish, and a fresh, flat fish I could fry. I have not a ship for a west wind trip, so I wish I could fly.

Donald's reading group, the least advanced, was reading the story "Rags." In its entirety it is as follows:

Rags was Jim's pet. Kit was Dot's pet cat. Rags and Kit had not yet met. "Let's get Rags and Kit," said Dot. Jim and Dot ran to Rag's mat. Jim said, "Rags is not at his mat." "Yip, yip, yip," said a pet. "It's Rags, it's Rags," said Jim. Kim and Dot ran to Kit's mat. At the mat was Kit. At the mat was Rags. Rags and Kit had met.

March 26

Before school began this morning, I went to see the principal. In the outer office was one of the A.T. students from the second grade. I greeted her and asked how she was. Before she answered, the principal said, "I bet she's sad today." I asked why and he said, "Didn't you know? Joyce has left the school. Her family moved over the vacation and now they live only a half a block away from another school. So the mother decided to take her out of here and put her in that one nearby."

Later in the morning when I saw Mrs. Evans, I told her I had heard about Joyce leaving the school. She responded, "Isn't that sad? I will surely miss her, and I know Gloria will too."

March 29: The Classroom as Public Space

The architecture of American schools reflects a set of dominant assumptions about how the schooling process is to be conducted. Since children are to be segregated by age, buildings are designed with many self-contained rooms, each isolated from the others. Since there is a difference in status between teachers and children, there are special rooms set aside for teachers and not for children. Since children are to be scrutinized and supervised by adults, classrooms are designed so that all children are in constant view.

On this day, my observation in Mrs. Hill's room suggested the problems this situation poses for the children, who do not always want to be "onstage" and in sight of a teacher. *Classrooms at Brush School had no spaces for children who wanted to be alone.* The children were continually in public space. What follows is an account of Diane's attempt to keep some distance from the teacher, ending, finally, in her total withdrawal from the classroom. Mrs. Hill, meanwhile, believing that children should not separate themselves, worked to keep Diane involved in the lesson.

Mrs. Hill is in the front of the room. She tells the class to get out their science books. Almost as soon as she says this, Diane turns completely around in her seat so she is facing the student behind her. Mrs. Hill begins talking about the lesson and as she scans the room, notes Diane. "Diane, will you please turn around? It's time for our lesson." Diane does so and opens her book.

The lesson is on the difference between how light and dark materials absorb sunlight. As Mrs. Hill continues, Diane turns sideways at her desk so she is facing out the window. Mrs. Hill is asking questions of different students, and comes to Diane. She asks Diane if she would wear light or dark clothes in the summer if she wanted to be cool. Diane makes no response, and as Mrs. Hill is about to go to another person, she says, "Diane, please face the front and work with us on the lesson." Diane turns around.

At the end of the discussion of the lesson, Mrs. Hill assigns a number of problems in a workbook. The other students begin to work, but Diane is now nearly three quarters turned at her desk. She stays like this momentarily, and then turns completely around to face the student behind her. As Mrs. Hill walks through the room, checking the students' progress, she comes to Diane and asks "What's the matter? We should all be doing our work." Diane gets up and says she has to go to the bathroom. "Are you sure you do?" asks Mrs. Hill. "Yeah," she answers as she walks out of the room. (Note: She does not return until eight minutes later, when the recess period begins.)

April 1: Training for Cultural Awareness—The Finale

After a hiatus of nearly five months, the in-service training program for the teachers was to have its final session. The books for the class had arrived several weeks previously and all the teachers had had an opportunity to check out one or more before this meeting.

The meeting itself took place in the auditorium. When I arrived, the teacher in charge of the program had just introduced a man from the district office who was serving as a "resource person" for the discussion of the reading material. She asked for a show of hands from those teachers who had been able to read at least one of the books. All raised their hands. The group was then divided into small subgroups, so that each person could share with a few others what he thought most important in the book he had read. These "buzz groups" were to last for approximately thirty minutes, and then the whole group was to reassemble.

I sat in one of the groups, and there the discussion focused on two themes, sex and violence. Two of the teachers had read *Black Rage*, and both commented on the number of times reference was made to sexual behavior as a basis for conflicts between white people and black people. This topic was discussed for some minutes, but no clear conclusions were reached. The final comment of one of the teachers: "I don't think it's all that important." No further explanation was given, and I was not sure what the "it" referred to. Then the group started to discuss violence, and one of the teachers commented, "You know, this is where I get turned off. All this violence that the blacks want to do doesn't make any sense to me. I'm not going to be helping anybody who is out there looting and burning places." The other three teachers spoke in agreement. The final comment of a sixth-grade teacher before the larger group was called back: "You know, I didn't like all this reading one bit. All it tried to do was to make me feel guilty, and I don't feel guilty about anything. What happened a hundred years ago isn't my problem. It's what we do now that counts, and I have enough problems just getting through the day."

When the large group was reassembled, the resource person from the district office passed out two sets of papers: "Evaluation Checklist" and "Checklist for Teachers." The former was a list of nine questions with multiple-choice answers. These questions were apparently meant to assess the effectiveness of the workshop. Two examples: "Have you made individual growth in working with all staff members?" (answers: not at all, somewhat, neutral, a great deal); and "Are you receptive to criticism in keeping with the needs of the group?" The "Checklist for Teachers" was a twenty-six item checklist taken from an article in *Integrated Education* entitled "Teachers, Free of Prejudice?" The items were essentially meant to help teachers determine whether they were using nondiscriminatory material and practicing nondiscriminatory behavior in their rooms. The teachers were told to answer both checklists on their own and use them as they saw fit. The group was then dismissed.

When I left the meeting, I went into the lounge for a soft drink. Soon afterward, the teacher coordinating the in-service program came in. Her first comment: "Boy, am I glad that's over!" I said she sounded tired, and she said she was, but that was not the reason for her feelings about the program. She mentioned she had gotten several "nasty comments" and "dirty looks" from other teachers whenever she brought up the program, and she was tired of having to deal with a group of teachers who were all "walking around with chips on their shoulders." "You know," she continued, "ever since I started this program last fall, I've heard nothing but how the teachers here didn't need a program like this because they all know how to deal with kids." Because of their attitude, she had on several occasions thought seriously of letting the program drop, but then she decided that it was precisely because of their attitudes that they needed it. Her final comment: "I'm glad it's over, even though I'm not sure it was worth it."

April 2: Teachers' Comments

Mrs. Brown asked me if I was going to be doing any writing from my study at Brush. I said I anticipated I would, and she said, "Well, I hope you don't just focus on Donald, because, you know, there are some others in the room with bigger problems than he has. You look at Tim and Sue. They both come from broken homes and they both are having really severe problems. Donald can't sit still, but that's a far cry from being messed up."

And:

While the children were on the playground, I asked Mrs. Evans how Gloria has been doing since Joyce left. "Oh, quite well. I think she's starting to come out more and play with the other children. You know, as long as Joyce was here she was always clinging to Gloria and complaining if Gloria started to play with anyone else. Gloria stayed with her because she is so good-hearted. The maturity gap between Joyce and the rest of the class began to show up recently, and I realized that Gloria was the only one who would play with Joyce."

She added that a new boy had come to the room today, and she knew he had come from a school where there were many more black children. Consequently, she put this new boy next to Gloria in hopes that he would more easily make friends with her. (Note: "more easily" than whom she did not say.)

Mrs. Evans made one last comment about Gloria and Joyce. She said that Joyce wanted to play "very immature games," like running and tag, and that only Gloria would play with her. But now that Joyce was gone, Gloria was starting to play "more sophisticated games" with the other girls. I asked for examples of these games and was told "dress-up" and "Chinese checkers."

April 4: Parent as Teacher

As has been suggested, the classroom circumstances in which effective learning can occur are fragile and episodic. To organize a group of students for instruction and have that instruction proceed so that both the students and the teacher gain some satisfaction from the experience appears, from my observations at Brush School, to be a relatively rare occurrence. (And this is in a school that prides itself on its academic standards.) The same seemed true for the group of mothers who volunteered several days a week to teach the Distar reading program in the first-grade rooms. I observed their lessons on a number of occasions. Only infrequently did their sessions seem to satisfy them. More often than not, the result was closer to the following:

Mrs. Wills tells the Blue Group to go out in the hall for the Distar class. Jeff asks if he can go along and the teacher says yes. When the five students have all pushed their chairs into the hall, John asks the volunteer, "Hey, Mother, have you got any boy or girl here?" She answers, "Yes, but they are older than you boys and girls."

The lesson begins, an attempt to teach the sounds for *A* and *M*. During the lesson, Jeff continually blurts out his answers without being called on. The teacher asks him to wait until she gives the signal for answers, but to no avail. Jeff persists. But Jeff's participation soon ends, as he gets up to follow Paul from Mrs. Evans's class to the bathroom. As soon as he gets up, so does Gina, who says she must go to the bathroom. Then Cynthia gets up also, but the teacher says she must wait. Jeff now walks back slowly to the group, pretending he is blind. He gropes his way down the hall, stumbling into things as he comes. He takes a very long time and the others in the group watch him. When he sits down, he falls out of his chair. He gets back up and almost immediately wants to go back to the bathroom. The teacher says, "Jeff, do you want to stay and learn, or do you want to go back to your room?" Jeff sits back down and, for a second time, falls out of his chair. The teacher says, "Now, Jeff, let's sit up and learn." Cynthia takes her chair and pushes it into the chair next to her, hitting Pat's hand. Pat screams and hits Cynthia several times on the arm. He is sobbing. The teacher, in a frustrated voice, says, "OK, that's all for today. Let's quietly put our chairs back in the room." Jeff and Cynthia start pushing their chairs down the hall in a race to the door. Cynthia stumbles and falls face forward over her chair. She begins to scream almost hysterically. The teacher picks her up and carries her into the room. Jeff continues to push his chair to the door.

Mrs. Brown comes out of her room to ask what has happened. I explain and she comments, "Well, they ought to know by now that they have to pick up their chairs when they move them." She goes back into her room. I bring Cynthia's chair into Mrs. Wills's room. The mother who taught the lesson turns to me as she is leaving and says, "What a fiasco!" The students from the Blue Group only slowly go back to their seats and begin to take out their work. After several minutes, Mrs. Wills call out, "I like the way the Blue Group is getting to work; thank you." In reality they were not, nor did her pseudo-praise make them get down to work any faster.

April 12

ITEM: I watched Mrs. Brown give Donald some twenty minutes of individualized instruction. She later told me she wanted to move him up a reading group, but he first had to finish another book. Thus the extra reading periods. She said she would be calling Donald's mother this evening to ask if she would begin giving him the extra help he would need if he was to "make it" in the higher reading group. She said it was critical to work closely with Donald because he seemed to be ready to "take off." She said that he was developing very rapidly and it was important to make use of this spurt, because these spurts "come and go." Besides his increased proficiency in reading, he was also doing more difficult work in mathematics. So she moved him out of the group doing special "watered-down" assignments and had him do the regular class work. Her final comment: "You know, last fall I couldn't see any good reason why he should be bused over here. He wasn't doing his work and he was causing nothing but trouble with all his stealing. But now, he's changing so fast and doing so well, I would be real sorry to see him go back to one of those ghetto schools where there is all that stealing and no one does the lessons. *For the first time, I think he's really got a chance to make it"* (emphasis added).

April 16

ITEM: Since the class had returned from the spring holiday, Mrs. Wills had each day been posting what she called "The Paper of the Day" on the front board. From the papers done the previous day, one was selected and put on the board in the late afternoon after class had been dismissed. Thus, each morning when the students came, there was a new paper. On this day, Jeff had his paper on the board for the first time. It was posted because he had correctly answered ten arithmetic problems. As a reward, the person whose paper was selected got to put the weather symbol on the calendar.

April 19: Becoming Test-Wise

It would be neither new nor startling to note that there has been considerable controversy in American schools over the use of testing as a means of evaluating and sorting students. Though the arguments have been many, both pro and con, there is one aspect of special interest here. It has been argued that just as the test, as an instrument of evaluation, is inevitably culturally related (as opposed to culturally "free"), so also the taking of tests is an activity that is culturally related. In short, *test scores may be as much a result of what one knows how to do well as what one knows*. Thus, those who are good test takers would achieve higher results than students with comparable knowledge who had not mastered the test-taking skills.

At Brush School, there was considerable emphasis on the mastery of test-taking skills. The students were frequently tested in the classroom, and occasionally they were given standardized tests so they could learn how in the future to take what one teacher called "the tests that count." During two weeks in April, the principal had arranged for all students in the first four grades who were reading at grade level or above to have a series of special tests, ostensibly to measure as precisely as possible their reading level. Frequently during observations, the classes would be less than half complete because some students were away taking one battery of tests or another.

It should be stressed that this testing was not being done at the behest of the district office or of the superintendent's office. It was done locally and at the discretion of the principal. The outcome, besides whatever additional information the tests gave the teachers about the reading performances of a select number of students, was to give the students practice and experience in taking standardized tests. For students from a middle-class neighborhood, there would be years and years of such tests to come, with the culmination being the S.A.T., the G.R.E., the Miller's Analogy, the entrance exams for medical, dental, or law school.

Toward the end of the testing period at the school, I met the teacher who had been released from her regular assignment to give the tests. We were able to talk for some minutes in the lounge.

I asked her how she had been and she replied, "Fine, except I'm totally worn out from all this darn testing." I asked why it was being done. "Oh, you know. It's what the principal wants done every year to give himself and the teachers a big ego trip. Once they find out how many students they have that are ahead of grade level, they start bragging to each other and the parents about how good their students are. Besides, I know he wants to keep his brightest kids warmed up on how to take tests. They're the ones that put the school cumulative way up in the citywide testing."

Without my asking, she went on to say that when this testing had been completed, the principal wanted her to test every A.T. student at the school. This she had done. I asked how it went. Her reply: "You can forget it. None of them were interested and many times they couldn't even read the instructions. The only way I got them even to sit still was to bribe them with candy bars. Every time they finished a test, they got some more candy. But what some of them did was just to race through marking the first answer in every row. *You know, they sure were not test serious like the white kids* [emphasis added]. Why, those white kids were just waiting for me to spring another test on them. The black kids couldn't care less. That's why I went broke buying candy bars."

April 23: Private versus Public Lives of Teachers

In the social-service institutions of American society, the dominant motif of the interaction between those providing services and those being served is the "staff-client" relationship. In writing of mental institutions, Goffman (1961) has noted that in this relationship, there is a vast discrepancy between the amount of private information the staff member has about the client and the amount the client has about the staff member. The same holds true for schools. *Teachers know more about the lives and private thoughts of the children than the children know about their teachers' lives.* This advantage of maintaining one's privacy has been one of the prerogatives of "professionalism." In general, teachers can share as much or as little of their private life as they desire. They are under no pressure to do so in the way in which children must do so each day.

What follows is an account of one of the very few instances during the entire school year where the private life of the teacher was brought into the public space of the classroom. By chance, this episode came to involve Melvin as well.

When I entered Mrs. Daley's room for an observation, she was not present. Many of the students were out of their seats talking to one another.

Mrs. Daley entered almost immediately and told all the students to take their seats. She was accompanied by a young woman who was carrying a child. She tells the class to be quiet and when she reaches the front, she smiles and says, "Boys and girls, this is a special day. I want you all to meet my daughter and my grandson. Isn't he a cute baby?" Several of the children ask his name, and she responds, "Melvin." A number of students turn and look at Melvin and say, "Ah, Melvin, now you're a baby." Mrs. Daley adds, "Yes, that's right. Now we've got two Melvins in the room." Melvin smiles at this. Andy calls out, "But they aren't the same. One Melvin is black and one Melvin is white." Mrs. Daley seems somewhat embarrassed by this and says, "So they are, so they are."

The children in the room are then allowed, row by row, to come to the front to look at baby Melvin. Mrs. Daley stands by her daughter and talks to the baby as the children come up. When all the children have passed by, the daughter and baby leave. Mrs. Daley says to the class, "Isn't this a nice day? But now we have to get to work."

April 29: White Racism

A situation that arose on this day pointed up one of the possible tensions in the division between client and staff: the *assumption* by the staff that their official position on integration was shared by the clients. At Brush, the teachers and principal apparently assumed that their assumptions about the integration program, based on the goal of racial assimilation, were shared by the white students. The staff apparently never tried to find out what the white students believed or how they were going to approach the integration program. In short, the staff, seemed to take it for granted that the students would imitate them. As a result, *there was never a deliberate attempt to deal with whatever racism the white children might have had.* For to do so would jeopardize the "color blindness" that was the cornerstone of the program. Racism can only occur if race is an issue. And at Brush, race, according to the official orthodoxy, was not an issue.

One result of this attitude is that the staff, so far as I observed, never made any effort to ensure that black students were not harassed or taunted. As a result, incidents like the following were intermittently observed.

I arrived at the school approximately ten minutes before the first bell. As I walked onto the playground, I saw Jeff and Donald together by the jungle gym. I walked toward them, and as I got closer, I could hear one of a group of fourth graders who were at the top of the jungle gym yelling to Donald, "Hey, shithead. I bet you eat shit." Another boy was yelling at Jeff, "Hey, nigger boy, hey, nigger boy." When I reached the boys, I asked the group to get down and apologize.

As the group came down, Donald and Jeff started after one of the boys, who was saying softly under his breath, "Nigger, nigger, nigger." The older boy was able to keep ahead of the two first graders and taunted them as he kept about five steps ahead. Finally, the others in the group left when I asked them to go to their own part of the playground. The boy taunting Jeff and Donald also left. They then both came over to me. Donald was in tears. I told them, "I'm sorry for what those boys said to you. It wasn't a nice thing to do." Donald said, "You know what else they called me? They said I'm a pisshead." Jeff added, "That's what they call me too." I told both boys that name calling was bad and the older boys should be ashamed of themselves. Also I told them both that it made no difference what the other boys said. They were OK and I knew that other children and their teachers liked them. I told them I liked them too.

April 30: The Invisibility of Students

Throughout the year, I had informal conversations with teachers in their own classrooms. Often these conversations occurred when the students were working on an assignment or were involved in activities that did not require the teacher's participation. I found these talks tremendously informative and did nothing to convey to the teacher that I did not enjoy them or that they were disrupting my observation. The only shortcoming, and it was a critical one, was that infrequently parts or all of these talks could be overheard by the students. This happened today when I was chatting with Mrs. Hill in her room. The conversation mainly involved Alex. It had no more than begun when he came over to where we were standing and stayed with us the entire time we talked. *Mrs. Hill continued as if he were not there.*

Alex walks over and stands listening to us. Mrs. Hill continues, "He just won't do his work. He spends more time trying to manipulate me so he won't have to do his work than he does actually working. I wish I could get him to settle down, but now he's so far behind that I think it's too late." I ask if Alex has joined one of the Distar groups, and she says, "Oh, no. He's too far behind, and too old besides, to pick up the basics now." I think it best to end the conversation, and so say I should be leaving. As I start to put away my notebook, Mrs. Hill comes over and says, "The real problem is that he just can't do any fourth-grade work. He sits all day (still away from the remainder of the class) knowing what he's doing is far behind what everyone else is doing." I note as she says this that Alex has followed her over to me and is standing beside her as she speaks. Her final comment: "I guess the only thing he's really good at is P.E. He has no problem when he's on the playground."

May 6

ITEM: The students in Mrs. Evans's room are standing in line waiting to go back into the room. A new student in the group calls out to no one in particular, "I wish I wasn't a teenie-weenie first grader. I want to go back to the second grade." After the students have come into the room, I ask Mrs. Evans about that comment and she says that the student, Brian, had been sent back to first grade because he could not do second-grade work. Apparently, the child had been in six different schools in the past two years and his parents had requested that he go to the first grade to pick up material he had missed. Mrs. Evans comments, "Academically, I guess he did need to come back to first grade. But socially, he's been a disaster. Why, he even compares to Lou in causing trouble." When Brian took his seat, he was in the back of the room, far removed from any other students. (Gloria was also removed from the group, and her desk was up against that of the teacher.)

ITEM: Mrs. Evans had written on the board, "I would like to be a — — because — — —." The students were to fill in the two blanks and then draw a picture of what they wanted to be. At the time of the observation, six papers had been completed, including Gloria's. She wrote, "I would like to be a secretary because I could help the boss." The two other girls also chose traditional female roles—those of teacher and nurse. All three of the boys who had completed papers said they wanted to become baseball players.

ITEM: The citywide testing of the students each spring had been completed and Mrs. Evans had the scores for her students. Gloria scored at or above grade level on each of the four subsections of the test except the one on "word knowledge." I said I was pleased that Gloria was doing well, and Mrs. Evans replied, "Oh yes, she's quite a smart little girl. You know yesterday she made a card for me that said, 'I love you. Love is delightful.' Isn't that creative?"

ITEM: Mrs. Evans summed up the test scores of her students by saying that they ranged from those who scored as high as the various tests would measure (generally grade 4.0) to those who "barely hit the bottom line" (grade 1.0).

May 7: A Problem Student

In Mrs. Daley's room, much of the attention to date has focused on the activities and performances of Melvin and Duke. But it would be well to note that there were also white students whose behavior and academic achievement were of intense concern to Mrs. Daley. One such student was Mark, who was not in her estimation performing well and whose grades reflected that evaluation. Mark's parents, however, disputed her assessment of his work, and there were frequent conferences throughout the year between teacher and parents to discuss the situation.

In the classroom, Mark had gradually moved to the periphery of activities and seemingly had few friends. He was often alone on the playground. Though he was a quiet student, he occasionally became a target for others.

Melvin calls to Mark, who is sitting clear across the room from him, "Mark, I see you got some gum. You know you not supposed to have it now. Teacher, teacher, Mark got some gum!" Melvin gets up out of his seat when he gets no response from Mrs. Daley and begins following her through the room. Finally she stops, turns to Melvin, and says, "Young man, what are you doing here? Get back in that seat and get busy." She points a finger at Melvin's desk, motioning him to return. As Melvin walks back, he calls out again, "Mark, you better throw out that gum." Mark makes no response.

Later in the morning Mrs. Daley said to me, "Why don't you watch Mark for awhile? I just can't figure him out." For the next twenty minutes I did so intensively, and the only thing Mark did was sit at his desk working in his workbook. His major muscle activity was to yawn and stretch his arms. He did nothing out of the ordinary.

Still later, Mrs. Daley brings me a math sheet Mark had done yesterday. "Look at this. This is all he accomplished the entire day. And taking all day, he still could only get ten or fifteen right." She continues, "I can't figure it out. I don't know if he has a behavioral problem or a learning problem, but something is definitely wrong. And all hell is going to break loose when his parents learn I'm going to recommend he be retained in third grade next year."

Mrs. Daley leaves and comes back almost immediately. "Look at this." She hands me Mark's report card from the last grading period. On the back in the space for teacher's comments, Mrs. Daley wrote that Mark was not concentrating and thus not performing as well as he should. The mother wrote a reply saying she thought the lack of concentration was a lack of maturity. The note continued that Mark "tries hard" but it is obvious his best is "not good enough for the system." "I know he's not lazy, because he's terribly afraid of failure, and fear motivates him to work."

Mrs. Daley, when I finished reading: "Sounds like a cop-out to me. I just can't figure Mark out. He reads up a storm, but he is so disorganized and sloppy with his work, I wonder if there is not an emotional problem. You know, he got a stepfather about three years ago, but I don't know if that's it or not." It is obvious from the tone of her voice that she is anxious and worried about Mark.

ITEM: Mrs. Daley mentioned that Melvin was going to be passed to the fourth grade. "I know he can do it. If he gets a strong fourth-grade teacher, he'll have no problem." For Duke, another year in third grade. "I have to retain him. He simply isn't doing his work. I've tried to have conferences with his mother, but she doesn't respond. There's just no cooperation from his home."

May 10: Target Students
Two days earlier, Mrs. Miller had sent to all teachers a form on which they were to list the students in their room who they thought would need special assistance the next academic year. The areas specified on the memo were "reading deficiencies,"

"math deficiencies," and "social deficiencies." A number of the A.T. students were included, but others were not. The comments were as follows:

Jeff—"He is now learning the letters of the alphabet. He is not in a first-grade math book. He tries on his worksheet and writes his numbers for practice. There has been good improvement shown in his social behavior."

Melvin—"Melvin is socially well adjusted, but he has a short attention span at times."

Duke—"He has a difficult time with English, and he has some trouble with multiplication. He has a tendency toward pouting when he is really upset."

Alex—"Alex seems to be a reluctant learner. Whenever possible, he will avoid his work. He often refuses to work in a one-to-one relationship. Alex is an A.T. student."

May 15: Peer Tutoring

Though all three first-grade teachers had commented at one time or another on the wide disparity in performance levels among their students, seldom if ever were those with advanced performance levels called on to help others. Instead, students tended to work by themselves or in reading groups; peer tutoring was not part of the pedagogical structure of the classes. In one instance where it was observed, it did not go well:

Mrs. Brown tells Paul to help Donald with his math problems. Paul moves over by Donald as Donald begins working. He watches as Donald writes an answer. Paul says it is wrong, erases it, and tells Donald to try again. Donald tries again. Paul says it is also wrong and erases it. Paul now puts in the correct answer.

A moment later, Donald calls out in a loud voice, "God, Paul, I'm going to tell." He jabs Paul with a pencil. Mrs. Brown sees this and says in a firm voice to Donald, "Donald, Paul is trying to help you." Donald responds, "I did it because Paul keeps telling me to act right." "Do you want Paul to help you any more?" she asks. "Yeah, if he will act right." Mrs. Brown: "But are you acting right is the question." Paul: "No." Mrs. Brown: "Well turn around and get busy on that page, Donald."

Paul is apparently checking another answer of Donald's and says it's wrong. Donald now seems really frustrated and says to Paul, "How do you know it's wrong?" "Because," says Paul. "I'm going to tell," answers Donald. Paul: "I'm saying it's wrong." Donald: "Look, you've marked up my whole page." Paul: "I'm not going to help you any more." He gets up to leave. Mrs. Brown calls out, "Paul, are you still helping Donald?" Donald interrupts, "I don't want him to help. All he does is mark everything wrong." Paul: "Not everything, just four of them." Donald: "See." Donald is on the verge of tears. He gets up, hits Paul, and tells the teacher he's going to the bathroom. Mrs. Brown says, "Thank you, Paul. I know you tried."

May 21:

ITEM: Mrs. Evans had placed a display on one of the bulletin boards entitled "Books to the Moon." The display showed a rocket ship on its way to the moon with stages of the rocket falling away periodically. Each of the stages represented 10 books read since the Christmas vacation. If a student read 100 books, he arrived on the moon. The location of the students on this chart suggests the *quantity* of reading done in the room in the past five months. One boy had reached the moon with a total of 107 books. (Mrs. Evans said he was reading at the fifth-grade level.) Two children (boy and girl) had read more than 80 books and two other boys had read more than 90. There were also seven children who had read less than 10 books. Gloria had read 11 books and was now in her second stage.

ITEM: Mrs. Evans was the only first-grade teacher who used television as a part of her classroom activities. Four or five afternoons each week, she would turn on "Electric Company." During that time the lights in the room were turned off, and the children could watch the T.V., color, or work on a project. Most watched the program. Mrs. Evans said she thought the children enjoyed it and that it was of benefit to them. I asked why and was told her room was the only one of the three first-grade rooms where there were no students in Distar—because, she said, the students were receiving such beneficial assistance from the program that they did not need the additional help of Distar.

June 3: The Last Week

On this day the last week of school began. And by the last day, one of my dominant impressions was that the teachers continued with academic content up to the final few hours. There was no slacking off in the work; the established patterns persisted and the routine was maintained. Indeed, Mrs. Brown said that this week she would have to do some "double time" to accomplish all she wanted to have done by Friday. On this first day, the major part of the observation was in Mrs. Wills's classroom.

Mrs. Wills has to leave her reading group to come and talk to four girls sitting at one of the tables. She says to them, "Is there something wrong here?" There is no response and she tells them to get back to their papers. As the teacher passes Jeff, sitting at the same table, on her way back to the reading group, he calls out, "They not working." She responds, "I can tell." Judy, one of the four girls, calls over to Jeff, "Tattletale!" Jeff reaches across and tries to jab her with the eraser end of his pencil. She calls out, "Quit it, Jeff."

Judy gets up from her seat and starts toward the teacher. Jeff calls out, "Teacher, Judy's out of her seat." Judy turns and comes back. As she passes Jeff, she says, "Mind your own business." Jeff smiles. When she sits, she says, "Now see, tattletale, I'm back." Jeff says, "Shut up." Judy seems to be getting very angry at Jeff. She starts talking to herself under her breath, and Jeff retorts periodically, "Oh, shut up." This ends when Mrs. Wills disbands her reading group and the students start moving through the room to find their seats.

All the students are shortly dismissed to go on the playground. I stand with Mrs. Wills and watch. I say to her that it seemed Jeff and Judy were after each other this morning. "I know," she answers. "But I think Judy is so good for him. She is one of the only students who takes time to talk to him. And, you know, Jeff needs to have the feeling that people will listen to him."

I asked if she has finally decided whether to pass or retain Jeff next year and she said she has. "There's no doubt that he needs another year. In fact, I hope I can keep him, because I think I work well with him." While Jeff was on the playground, he spent the entire time playing with four girls on a jungle gym. I asked Mrs. Wills if she thought that was typical of Jeff and she said it was, unless Donald was available. "Then," she added, "you couldn't split them apart if you tried."

June 4

I had planned an observation in Mrs. Brown's room, but when I arrived I was told, "Donald's not here any more." I asked why and Mrs. Brown said he had left on the past Friday to go to Mississippi to visit his grandmother. Donald's mother had called the school on Friday to inform the principal and Mrs. Brown. She also asked for materials to work with Donald during the summer. Mrs. Brown added, "I sure hope she does, because I've decided to pass him on to second grade and if he doesn't work this summer, he'll be behind everyone else. And if that happens, he could become a holy terror." I asked what finally tipped Mrs. Brown in favor of passing him and she said, "Oh, I guess it really wasn't me. You know, his mother said she wanted him passed, and I didn't figure I could block it if I wanted to. Besides, if he does get a good second-grade teacher, he should be OK."

June 5

Even though there were now only two days remaining in the school year, Mrs. Evans reorganized her reading groups. Her least advanced group, formerly called the Orange Group, was now called the Green Group. There were three students, Gloria, Paul, and Carolyn (there previously had been five). What follows was the last observed reading lesson for Gloria and her group.

Mrs. Evans calls the Orange Group over to the reading area. Gloria picks up her chair and moves it so that she is directly to Mrs. Evans's right. Gloria is asked to read first. Mrs. Evans follows along in Carolyn's book. (The book is from the S.R.A. Basic Reading Series, Level E, and is entitled *Kittens and Children*.) As Gloria reads, she needs much help. The teacher has to help her on about every third word. Carolyn reads next and does well. She needs almost no help as she reads a whole page. When it is Paul's turn, he says he doesn't want to read because the book is too hard. He slams the book shut. Mrs. Evans tells him to go back to his seat. When he does, he slams the book down on his desk. The reading group working with the teacher's aide in the hall comes back into the room. Gloria is reading, but Mrs. Evans is interrupted five times as other children come to tell her what they have read in their group. Gloria needs help also. She is having difficulty with words like "picture," "scraps," "kitchen" and "slept."

As the noise in the room rises, Mrs. Evans calls out, "Children, you're disturbing our reading group." The noise does not diminish. Carolyn reads another full page and Mrs. Evans then dismisses the group.

June 6: A Bus Ride

Several times during the year, I rode with the A.T. students from the school where they met in the morning to board the bus to where they disembarked some thrity minutes later at Brush School. The bus rides were generally uneventful. On the bus were the children, the driver, and a middle-aged black woman who had the task, as she put it, of "keeping the lid on." During this particular ride, there were two fights. One involved Alex from Mrs. Hill's room and Duke from Mrs. Daley's room. It began when Alex grabbed Duke's comb. Duke tried to get it back and a struggle ensued. The second fight was between two fourth graders over who was going to change the station on a transistor radio one of them had. In both instances, the bus driver had to stop the bus and help disentangle the participants. Other children on the bus shouted encouragement to one or another of the boys, but no one else got involved. Throughout the trip, the driver talked to the students, seeming to know them quite well. He was trying to strike a deal with them that if they would not eat candy on the bus today, they could eat it both ways tomorrow, the last day. Most of the students agreed, but Alex pulled out a long stick of licorice. An older boy immediately took it away from him and told him to put it away because they had all made a deal with the driver. When we reached Brush, the students all got off, and as I was doing the same, the driver commented, "Just one more day. I think I can hold out."

June 7: The Last Day

The routines and patterns at Brush persisted up to the very end of the school year. On this, the final day, I visited all three first-grade rooms. But before I got to the first of the rooms, I observed an interaction between the principal and Alex that demonstrated "business as usual" at the school.

As I am about to enter the principal's office to pick up the daily bulletin, I see the principal talking to a parent of one of the third-grade students in Mrs. Daley's room. Almost at the same time, Alex comes up the stairs toward the office. When he sees the principal, he turns and starts back down. The principal calls for Alex to come back, but he does not. The principal calls out again, and this time Alex turns and comes to the office. Alex is asked what he is doing and he says he has been sent to the office by Mrs. Hill. The principal asks why and Alex says he doesn't know. He then begins a long explanation of how the teacher told him to get started on an assignment, but he did not have any paper. Later, the teacher saw him not working and told him to go to the office. Alex is asked if that is the whole story, because, the principal says, when he was sent to the office yesterday, there was much more to the story than what Alex told him. Alex says there is no more. The principal takes him into his office and says he will check it out.

From the principal's office, I went to Mrs. Brown's classroom.

When I enter the room I am struck by how quiet and how hard-working the children are. I tell Mrs. Brown that I am surprised at how diligent they seem to be on this last day. "Oh, they all asked to be able to work today because they're racing to see how far they can get in their workbooks. This is their last big spurt." Since the children are all at their desks, Mrs. Brown and I have an opportunity to continue our conversation. She says some teacher at Brush next year is "going to be very lucky because Tim isn't going to be here." She adds, "That means that David is going to be gone, Pam is going to be gone, and Tim is going to be gone. How quiet it will be! You know what else this means. Donald is going to be easier to handle with Tim gone." While we talk, Mrs. Brown moves through the back of the room taking down pictures and displays. She says the only student she is going to retain is Trish, because "she is so young and immature that she needs another year at first grade."

Next, to Mrs. Evans's classroom.

When I enter, none of the children are involved in academic tasks. Most are up out of their seats talking to other students, or playing games at the front, or working on Father's Day gifts (felt bookmarkers). Gloria and Anne are playing dress-up. Mrs. Evans comes over and says something happened yesterday that she thinks I would want to know. She says Gloria was invited to dinner at Anne's house. "That's why they're playing together now. You know, I didn't think they were such good friends." (During the entire time I'm in the room, Gloria and Anne are together).

Later, when Mrs. Evans had dismissed the class to the playground, I asked if she planned to retain any of the students in her room. "No, I've had such a beautiful group this year. There's no one who needs another year in first grade. In fact, I think this is one of the best first-grade rooms I've ever had since I've been at Brush."

Last, to the classroom of Mrs. Wills.

When I enter, the room is absolutely silent. Mrs. Wills is in the front giving a math lesson on multiple addition (One example: blank + blank + 4 = 9). Jeff and all the other students seem very attentive. Mrs. Wills then passes out worksheets for all the students. I note, though, that Jeff is given a sheet different from the others. Once the children are all working on their sheets, Mrs. Wills comes to the back of the room, where I am seated. I ask her if she plans to retain any of the students from her room and she says there will be two — Jeff and John. She begins a rather lengthy explanation of why she has decided to keep back these two students, but the essential points are that Jeff is academically not ready and John is socially not ready to advance.

At 10:50 A.M., Mrs. Wills calls the names of the boy and girl who are to serve as the host and hostess in the lunchroom. The boy, Don, says he is not finished with his paper. Jeff asks if he can go in Don's place and Mrs. Wills says he can. So he and Ellen leave. Mrs. Wills says to me, *"I'm so proud of how he has come around. Last fall you saw how naughty and sleepy he was. Now he's really trying* [emphasis added]. It used to be such a struggle just to get through a day with him. I do hope I can keep him for next year."

After visiting the three rooms, I went back to the principal's office to make an appointment for an interview. In the outer office, Alex was asleep on one of the chairs. Another teacher entered about the same time and asked the secretary what had happened with Alex. She replied, "Nothing out of the ordinary. It was just another time that Alex had to come down for disciplinary action." The teacher said, "Did you know he was asleep?"

"I wouldn't be surprised," she answered. "He sleeps almost every time he comes down. I wonder if he ever gets enough sleep at home. That's what probably causes half of his trouble here."

The principal was meeting with a parent, so my interview was tentatively scheduled through the secretary. With that I left the school and ended the last observation of the year.

POSTSCRIPT: REFLECTIONS ON INTEGRATION AT BRUSH

I came back to Brush the week after school ended to conduct a series of interviews with the five teachers central to this study, the A.T. coordinator, and the principal. I also had interviews in the evenings with the parents of the seven remaining A.T. students in the five rooms. Here are excerpts from those interviews.

With the Principal:

Q. *What is your general impression of how the A.T. Program went this year?*

R. Only fair, because I believe the A.T. kids did not achieve the academic goals I had set for them. Most of them began in the bottom stanine and stayed there all year. Three fourths of the A.T. students did not achieve the goals I set for them.

Q. *What is your general impression of the adjustment of the A.T. students?*

R. On the whole, very good. But there were some problems. Take Henry, for example. He was suspended at two other schools before he came here, and you know, he made it the whole year without getting suspended. I came close to doing it once or twice, but he did make it.

Q. *What is your general impression of the adjustment of the white students?*

R. No problems. I do think some of them bent over backward to be friends. They were a little too careful not to offend the black students.

Q. *How would you characterize the response of the teachers to the A.T. program?*

R. I would say good.

Q. *How would you characterize the response of the black parents?*

R. Very receptive. Very cooperative. They want the best for their kids. I've said that all year long. They supported anything I wanted to do. They knew me and I think they respected me. The key thing was constant communication. I was always in touch with the parents.

Q. *How would you characterize the response of the white parents?*

R. They were receptive and accepted the black students. I don't think they were overly enthusiastic about having them here, but I know some were. Mostly, I would say they just tolerated them.

Q. *What would you consider the positive outcomes of the A.T. Program at Brush?*

R. The positive things are the white children having the opportunity to work with children of another environmental group and the black children having the opportunity to work with another economic group.

Q. *What would you consider the negative outcomes of the A.T. Program?*

R. All the problems that arise due to putting low achieving black students in rooms with high achieving white students. So many of the black students had such low ability that they just couldn't keep up. Then they started to cause problems because they were frustrated and discouraged. They never had an opportunity to succeed.

Q. *Have you seen any behavior on the part of either the white or black students that you would classify as race prejudice?*

R. Just once, and it was a minor thing when a white boy called a black boy a nigger. But the next day they both came to see me and told me they were friends.

Q. *How would you compare the disciplining of the black students with that of the white students?*

R. About the same, though I think I handled it a little differently with the white children. I could shame them into behaving easier than I could the black students. With the black students, I had to tell them the way it was going to be.

Q. *What would you consider the optimal number of black students you would want here at Brush to run the kind of integrated program you think best?*

R. This is where the mistake is made. Some schools try to do too much too fast. I think we need to move slow and begin with the primary grades. Then the white children can grow up with them. I don't think there should be more than just a few in any class. This school doesn't need any more than it has right now. We have a good number and I can handle them all right. Any more than this and it would be nothing but problems. This way, there can be the individual instruction so many of them need and I can have the time to build good relations with the parents.

Q. *What were you personally striving for this year in terms of building an integrated program?*

R. Minimum discipline problems and good achievement. I want satisfactory improvement in all my students.

In reviewing these responses of the principal, several issues are particularly important. First, though it is apparent that the principal had set goals for what he wanted accomplished during the year with respect to the A.T. students, there is no indication that he took any definitive measures to ensure they were met. One senses good intentions but a lack of follow-through. The reasons for this may be many, but it would be well to note that during the entire time of my study, I learned of no special efforts by the school system to work with principals or to try to train them in how to achieve desired outcomes in a desegregation program. He was left, it appears, on his own. Second, the racial assimilationist position remained strong. From the time before the first black students arrived to past the time the school year was completed, the principal remained convinced of the necessity for small numbers of black students who could be closely monitored. Finally, he seemed generally pleased with his year at Brush. Granted, he said, some of the black students did not perform well academically, but overall, the program was a success. And what problems there were, the black students brought with them—low ability, lack of shame, and differences of environment.

With the Teachers

Q. *Nowadays, one hears a lot about the term "culturally disadvantaged." Do you think that applies to any of the students in your room?*

R. Mrs. Evans: "Until I got Brian, I would have answered no. But he surely is. He has been shuffled around a lot, and he believes no one cares about him."

R. Mrs. Brown: "Yes, but not so much to someone like Donald as to Tim. His mother works and he has no father. Or maybe Trish. Her parents don't seem to be able to do much of anything for her."

R. Mrs. Hill: "Definitely. Look at Alex and Diane, but Alex more so. And there's Susanne. I wouldn't want her parents to know, but I think she's disadvantaged also."

Q. *Some people argue that most black people speak a dialect of English different from that spoken by most whites. Would say that is true of _____?*

R. Mrs. Evans: "I would say Gloria is bilingual. I suspect at home she speaks differently than she speaks here. Here she is the one who has to make all the adjustments."

R. Mrs. Wills: "With Jeff, yes. His grammar and English are very poor."

R. Mrs. Daley: "It's true of both Duke and Melvin. At the first of the year, there were students telling me they could not understand a thing those two were saying."

Q. *How would you compare _____'s motivation to do well in school with that of other students in the room?*

R. Mrs. Wills: "Jeff is lower than the others. But in P.E. he's good. He's one of the only boys who can jump rope."

R. Mrs. Brown: "I think Donald's is just as high. By the end of the year he was really trying and proud of what he could do."

R. Mrs. Hill: "Alex lacks motivation. And what makes it more difficult is that he doesn't respond to any kind of positive reinforcement. The only thing that will move him is a negative reinforcement. As for Diane, I would say she is average."

Q. *How would you compare your discipline of* _____ *to how you handled others in the room?*

R. Mrs. Brown: "I don't think I was as hard on Donald as I should have been. Sometimes I think I let him get away with murder."

R. Mrs. Wills: "I had to be very firm with Alex. I always had to carry out what I said I would do or he would catch me on it."

R. Mrs. Daley: "Both Duke and Melvin were not big problems. Duke sometimes would whine and sulk, that was no real problem to anyone else."

Q. *Have you seen any changes in* _____ *during the year and how do you feel about those, if any, that you have seen?*

R. Mrs. Brown: "Donald is now much more a part of the class since he quit taking things from others. I used to think of him as a vacuum cleaner, and he still takes things now and then. But he's doing much better. I think it has helped our relation too."

R. Mrs. Evans: "The biggest change in Gloria was when Joyce took her over. She was becoming Joyce's keeper. I think it's great that Joyce left. Gloria is a very sensitive little child and I like the good things I've seen in her."

R. Mrs. Hill: "Alex has, overall, changed very little. He still doesn't know much of classroom etiquette and he also continues to take things from others. It's Diane that I feel better about. When she first came last fall, she was lazy and wouldn't do her work. I think being in this atmosphere has been a big help because it has forced her to work harder. Now she's trying."

Q. *Do you think the A.T. Program has been worth having here at Brush?*

R. Mrs. Wills: "Sure. I know being here has helped Jeff. Just think what it would be like for him to stay in one of the ghetto schools."

R. Mrs. Brown: "At the first of the year, I wasn't sure. With all that stealing and fighting, I thought it wasn't working. But now I see how Donald's doing and figure it was worth it."

R. Mrs. Hill: "I don't know. I know the white students are getting something from it, but it's harder to see what the black students are gaining. I just can't believe it has been of any help to someone like Alex."

Like the principal, the teachers thought that in the long run the A.T. Program had gone rather well. It is unclear from these comments whether they thought any academic benefits had accrued to the black students who joined the program. Those benefits they did mention are behavioral—less stealing, less laziness, less sleepiness. But I also sensed that the teachers believed the black students had somewhat assimilated the dominant values at Brush—speaking more clearly, starting to be proud of one's work, and trying to do one's work well. And as a result of this perception of change in the A.T. students, the teachers generally expressed satisfaction with the endeavor.

With Mrs. Miller, the A.T. Coordinator

Q. *What is your general impression of how the A.T. Program went this year?*

R. I though it went all right. I haven't heard many complaints from the other teachers, especially considering this was the first year. I do wish we had had the discipline down better, especially with Alex and Henry. But what really helped was having so few students in the program. We were able to keep a pretty close eye on all of them.

Q. *Can you think of anything in retrospect that you wish had happened, but did not?*

R. The discipline. I don't like the way it was handled. It should have come sooner and firmer. Also, I would have liked more teacher-parent contact. There were some minor misunderstandings that more communication could have cleared up.

Q. *What is your general impression of the adjustment of the black students?*

R. I think things went well. Fortunately, the white kids here are so stable. Many of the black children became just like one of us.

Q. How would you characterize the response of the teachers to the program?

R. Since they had never dealt with them before, much of what the black kids did was shocking to them. It seemed like some of them really did not know how to cope with the black kids, especially someone like Henry. I got a kick out of some of their comments. They were so naive.

Q. Are there any of what you would consider positive outcomes to the program this year?

R. If anything, just having a year's experience with them. Hopefully, things should go better next year. The teachers should have more of an understanding of the need for structure for the A.T. students.

Q. Are there any of what you would consider negative outcomes to the program this year?

R. No.

These comments reflect a more utilitarian approach than those of the principal or other teachers. Here the concern is on learning how to discipline the black children, knowing that A.T. students need structure, and having experience with "them." Mrs. Miller also felt that better parent-teacher relationships would minimize friction. She does not mention academic goals, but talks only about behavioral changes. Her approach may have arisen in part because of her notion of what is was to be a "coordinator." One coordinates in order to assist the smooth operation of the schools; qualitative changes in the lives of children were left to the individual classroom teacher. But such a view neglects to consider the very real possibility, nay, inevitability, that the operational procedures of the school are directly related to and impinge upon the educational processes experienced by the children.

With the Black Parents

Finally, here is the year-end assessment by the black parents. These are the people who had made the decision that sending their children by bus to Brush was more desirable than keeping them in the neighborhood school. And as is evident from the past chapters, this decision resulted in their being almost completely isolated from the life of the new school their children attended. The costs were high. The issue is whether the parents perceived any benefits.

Q. *How do you think your child generally felt about going to Brush School?*

R. Mother of Melvin: "He really do like to go."

R. Mother of Gloria: "I think so, especially in comparison to my two other children. The only thing I know she didn't like was getting up so early."

Q. *Have you noticed any ways in which going to Brush School has changed your child?*

R. Father of Donald: "I think it has improved him intellectually. His learning habits are much better, and I think that is because it's a much better school."

R. Mother of Duke: "Yeah, he has improved in school. That whole new environment changed him for the better."

R. Mother of Gloria. "I can't really say. I haven't noticed any changes."

Q. *Can you think of any special help you would have wanted for your child that the school did not provide?*

R. Mother of Diane: "She got all the special attention she needed. I know the teacher was concerned about her."

R. Mother of Alex: "He still be needing more help with his reading. He needs help on that every day."

R. Mother of Duke: "No, they gave him lots of special help with tutors and all."

Q. *Do you think there were any benefits for your child in attending Brush School?*

R. Father of Donald: "Well, I can tell there was an improvement in his learning habits, but I better wait a year to say more."

R. Mother of Jeff: "Yeah, if there's a place where he be learning, that's it. Besides, the principal was breakin' him of all that fightin'."

Q. *Do you think there were any negative consequences in sending your child to Brush?*

R. Mother of Gloria: "Well, with them being out of the area, it was hard to keep contact with their friends here in the neighborhood."

R. Mother of Melvin: "It's too far and I have no way to get out there."

R. Mother of Diane: "I'm always worried about what could be happening to her. I don't like her being way down there."

Q. *Do you plan to send your child back to Brush in the Fall?*

R. Mother of Duke: "Yes, I'll send him back because I like the environment there. At first I was worried about the prejudice, but I've come to find out there wasn't any."

R. Mother of Gloria: "Yes, she will be there as long as there is a bus to take her."

R. Father of Donald: "Yes, I would like for him to stay there until he is ready to leave for high school."

R. Mother of Alex: "Yeah, he'll be back, but I sure do hope they be doing something about his reading."

Q. *A final question: if you had to do it all over again, would you start your child in the program at Brush?*

R. Mother of Jeff: "Yeah, I would."

R. Mother of Gloria: "I think the busing idea is a good one. She would be going there or somewhere else regardless."

R. Mother of Duke: "Yes, I wish I had known about Brush earlier. I would've tried to start him right away."

R. Father of Donald: "Yes, I would. The opportunity there is good."

R. Mother of Melvin: "It would be the same thing. There be no other school where they learn so much."

R. Mother of Diane: "Yes, I wish I could have gotten her there sooner."

R. Mother of Alex: "Yeah, he'd go again and I want to start my young one soon's I can."

This uniformly positive assessment by the parents of the busing of their children to Brush is striking. All the parents said they would send their children back, and they all said they would do it again if they had to begin anew. It may be argued that the parents in this study are not typical of other black parents at Brush, or of those who have their children in the A.T. Program in another school, or even of black parents in general. But what cannot be ignored is that every A.T. parent with a child in the five classrooms central to this study had a positive evaluation of the educational experience at Brush.

But whether the parents' assessment warranted their endorsement of the program is a different question. It could be argued that the parents were not "really aware" of what was happening to their children at Brush. If they were, they would not have responded as they did. But instead, a few phone calls and a paper to take home and tack on the wall was sufficient to give the parents a superficial and essentially false sense of the workings of the school. Or one could assume that in fact the parents did know the activities and socialization processes operating at Brush and endorsed them. From their viewpoint, the emphasis on academics plus the experiences their children were having in learning to live with white people, even if on white people's terms, made participation in the program worthwhile. Their children were gaining invaluable experience in dealing with whites that would not have been possible had they chosen to stay in a predominantly black school.

Or, perhaps, the black parents who sent their children to Brush School, much like parents everywhere, hardly paused to consider what happened to them when they got there. The parents' expectations may have been rather basic: so long as the teachers tried to teach and the children could stay out of trouble and away from the principal's office the school was doing a good job. This attitude is especially likely if the parents believed that in their neighborhood schools, which were predominantly black, the teachers did not teach and their children were more prone to get in trouble. If so, the black parents who were volunteering their children were framing the decision to do so not in terms of where they would be going, but what they were leaving. Black parents had to make a deliberate choice to have their children leave a neighborhood school; it was then happenstance whether the bus let them out at Brush or some other predominantly white school.

7.

Becoming Visible

I began this study with the contention that there are multiple perspectives concerning what constitutes an "integrated education." Furthermore, the perception of what constitutes a "successful" school program within the framework of one perspective may be antithetical to that within another. What I found was an apparent consensus at all levels of the Portland school system that the proper approach to school integration is one emphasizing racial assimilation. Whether focusing on the macro-level of the citywide system and those at the pinnacle of the decision-making process, or on the social and cultural milieu of the individual school, or even on specific classrooms, I found evidence of a pervasive attempt to implement a "color-blind" approach to integration.

The ultimate outcome of this definition of the situation is exemplified in the school experiences of Donald, or Gloria, or Diane. Day after day, they and the other black students came off the bus to a setting where the goal was to render them invisible. And the more invisible they became, the greater the satisfaction of the school personnel that the integration program was succeeding!

In assessing the integration program at Brush, one is immediately confronted with a series of value-laden decisions, political, pedagogical, and programatic. The fact that there are no "value-free" means by which to judge the Brush experience necessarily implies that there are no absolute answers. Instead, the imputing of "success" or "failure" to the program must be derived from the stance one takes *vis-a-vis* this question: Is the racial assimilationist approach a viable framework for implementing integrated education in the context of American society?

I think it is not. Racial assimilation makes demands of both black and white children that are unrealistic and presents them with an inaccurate and distorted understanding of the world. Black children must deny who they are and the cultural and historical roots from which they come. They are asked to become something and someone they are not. Furthermore, black children have no guarantee that they will be rewarded if they do attempt to transform themselves. It is as if white society dangles the perennial carrot of success and mobility in front of black children, telling them to reach just a bit further. For white children, the issues are not very different. They also are asked to believe something about the world that is not true. An emphasis on racial assimilation distorts the relative lack of importance of Anglo culture within the lives of many minority and ethnic groups within the United States. White flight from a recognition of the diversity of minority experiences in American society may be more comfortable and politically expedient in the immediate future, but reality has a persistent way of intruding, often with a jolt.

TEACHING AND LEARNING IN BRUSH

Here I want to point out several areas of activity where the educational experience at Brush would be amenable to change in order to move away from an assimilationist position. For those who remain convinced of the correctness of the assimilationist view, this may be the final parting of company. Here I interpret school integration and how well or how poorly it has succeeded from the position that a recognition and affirmation of the diversity of cultural life in American society is absolutely essential. Any integration program that avoids this affirmation I believe to be unsuccessful, regardless of the levels of achievement measured with paper-and-pencil tests. This is not to say that such achievement is not desirable and necessary, but simply that it is not sufficient. It is thus from this view that my most basic indictment of the assimilationist position derives: children are to be acknowledged and respected for who they are, not for what others say they must become.

The following recommendations for change in the patterns of Brush School will not dramatically alter the structure of education in American public schools. Dreary facilities, credentialing, compulsory attendance, and age segregation will all remain. But even within these constraints, there appear to be opportunities for some few modifications in the *processes* of education and in providing milieus for children in which they may live and grow. Jencks (1972:256) has spoken to this issue as well:

> Instead of evaluating schools in terms of long term effects on their alumni, which appear to be relatively uniform, we think it wiser to evaluate schools in terms of their immediate effects on teachers and students, which appear much more variable. Some schools are dull, depressing, even terrifying places, while others are lively, comfortable, and reassuring. If we think of school life as an end in itself rather than a means to some other end, such differences are enormously important. Eliminating these differences would not do much to make adults more equal, but it would do a great deal to make the quality of children's (and teachers') lives more equal. Since children are in school for a fifth of their lives, this would be a significant accomplishment.

The Teachers

Perhaps more than any other professional group in the schools, the teachers have the most pervasive and critical influence on the direction and content of a desegregation program. Although public attention and media coverage may focus on the angry citizens or on the children who ride the buses, it is the teachers who have to deal daily with the situation. Public hysteria will eventually recede, the sporadic fights among students will taper off as new informal norms are developed, and a routine and pattern of activity will emerge as a new *status quo*. For the teacher it is not so simple. To say that with quiet and order teachers can go back to teaching and the desegregation program will be on its way is much too facile. As Orfield points out (1975:318), "The teacher often faces a deeper and more persistent crisis — the professional crisis of realizing, consciously or subconsciously, that she doesn't know how to effectively teach children whose background is very different from that of the dominant group in her school. It is a particularly traumatic adjustment for older teachers who have long taught in strong middle class neighborhoods in schools which ignored the small minority of children with serious learning problems." Much the same view has been reported by Metz (1971) from her study of a newly integrated school in California. She wrote of the teachers (1971:113):

> They stressed academic material above all else, and they expected punctuality, neatness, and deference to be displayed by the students as a matter of course . . . These teachers were for the most part used to dealing with middle class children only. Many resented the influx of lower class children with fewer academic skills, less orderly behavior, and less acceptance of adults. The teachers, some of whom had come to Hamilton to get away from such children, often had few methods for coping with this kind of child and low motivation to set about acquiring such methods.

In reflecting on the teachers at Brush, it became apparent to me that they built their professional identities as "good teachers" around the successes of their students, most of whom were strongly motivated, high achieving, and generally well behaved in terms of the norms of school. I sensed a pride in the teachers arising from the long-term satisfactions they derived from the continual contact with tens and hundreds of what they saw as "model students." Yet it must be said that most of these students would succeed regardless of what the school did, given the enormous advantages that they brought with them from their homes and that they reinforced among one another. Teachers at Brush *facilitated* the performances of bright students, but they did not have to grope about to find some small spark of interest or ability.

In spite of Mrs. Brown's claim that fourteen of her twenty-two students had significant problems, the range of students at Brush was rather narrow. Overwhelmingly, they were as characterized above: bright, well attuned to the norms and goals of school, easily able to interact with adults, and, seemingly, personally confident. With the advent of the desegregation program there came a group of students, some of whom were bright and energetic like the majority of white students, but others of whom did not respond or perform at all well according to the norms at the school. With this latter group, the tendency on the part of the teachers was to interpret and explain their behavior as the result of individual deficits.

I am convinced that the attribution of deficits was made without consciously articulated racism, if one understands racism as implying the denigration of a *category* of people based on skin color. When a teacher had a student such as Jeff or Duke or Alex in the room, I think it would be inaccurate to say that her reaction was based on the assumption "You might as well expect as much: blacks are not as smart as whites." The teachers seemed to make a conscious effort to avoid attributing characteristics to categories. Not to have done so would have inevitably undercut their "color-blind" approach — after all, there were no categories in the school, just individual students.

Given these views, one could not alleviate the teachers' frustration with black nonperforming students by suggesting that the teachers needed to come to terms with personal prejudices. To say that the eradication of racism would enhance the learning milieu of Alex or Jeff or Lou is to miss the mark. The more fundamental problem would appear to be how to help teachers to learn new ways to reach and to teach students who do not respond to the normative patterns operating in a school where high academic achievement is the goal. In the absence of such new approaches, the outcome found at Brush could be anticipated: the year-long placement of so many of the A.T. students in low reading groups.

If the increased diversity of students in a school like Brush is to be responded to other than with a "business as usual" approach, which almost invariably results in the tracking of the black students into the low group, the teachers must develop a new classroom approach, one that allows the students to build on their strengths and work step by step to repair their weaknesses. The traditional approach of having all students work on the same material at the same pace and for the same length of time seems to be the classical formula for ensuring that at least some students will not succeed. Students in the same classroom need not march to a single drum. As St. John (1975:103) has noted: "Thus the factors that will probably determine whether the desegregated classroom is, on balance, academically facilitating rather than threatening are lack of interracial tension and either initial similarity in achievement level of black and white children or else supportiveness of school staff, availability of school academic policies that favor overcoming handicaps, avoidance of competition, and above all, individualization of instruction."

The fact that the teachers at Brush did not appear to change in any significant way their approach to classroom instruction does not necessarily imply that they were not aware of the situation. Clearly, teachers such as Mrs. Hill, Mrs. Brown, and Mrs. Wills were actively concerned with the progress and performance of their students. But what they seemed to lack was the knowledge of how to transform this sensitivity of student difficulties into a new classroom approach that would successfully deal with them. Yet they were not alone. In other studies of teachers trying to come to grips with teaching in desegregated classrooms, a similar sense of awareness of the situation and frustration at not having the techniques for addressing the students' needs has been voiced. In a study of a White Plains, New York, school that had recently integrated, a teacher is quoted as saying:

> How can we teach children of widely varying abilities and skills in one classroom without discouraging the less able and holding back the fast learners? This is a problem that arises in any classroom. In an integrated classroom, however, it is underlined by the racial issue. Children who are made to feel frustration and failure at the academic level and who are forced to

attend a class in which they cannot meaningfully participate
become bored and begin to look upon themselves as worthless.
(Schlesinger and D'Amore 1971:99)

As has been noted earlier, it is singularly inappropriate to
assume that the resolution of this situation in general, and at
Brush in particular, lies in an eradication of whatever prejudicial attitudes teachers might have. The Brush teachers' inability
to respond effectively to the very different academic needs and
skills of some of the black children should have necessitated their
learning new approaches and techniques for classroom instruction. Had they done this, they could have made a concerted effort
both to enhance the black students' academic participation in the
life of the class and to increase their status among their white
peers.

This latter point is worth emphasizing. The implication is that
the A.T. students' status position could have been greatly enhanced had their academic performance improved. What kept
students like Jeff, Alex, Lou, Joyce, and Duke at the fringe of
their classes was not segregation by color, but, more profoundly,
segregation by performance level. (The same argument could be
made for white students in the low reading groups—that their
status would improve as their performance increased.) The classroom organization at Brush worked to ensure the presence of a
group of low-status students differentiated on the basis of a hierarchy of presumed competencies. That many of the A.T. students came to Brush without some of the skills necessary for high
performance in the context of school norms meant that they
sifted to the bottom of the class. That they were left there be-
speaks the tragedy not only of the program at Brush, but of any
program that hierarchically ranks students.

This stress on the teachers' need to learn new skills for successfully incorporating black and other minority students into the
academic life of their classrooms is not to imply that there is not
also a need for attention to the multicultural and interracial
aspects of interaction in an integrated setting. The teachers at
Brush received precious little assistance in this regard. The previous chapters have documented the in-service training class that

was ostensibly to help teachers understand the viewpoints and cultural heritage of the black community. It was a project that offered too little and came too late. Not only had the teachers (and principal) to work through the first month of school with absolutely no assistance, but when the program did begin, its tenor was such that many teachers became extremely defensive and thought it was accusing them of being racist — a label they vehemently rejected.

Such short-term and sometimes emotional sessions seemed to produce two undesirable outcomes. First, there was no restructuring of whatever prejudices did exist — and perhaps these were even inadvertently strengthened as teachers reacted defensively to the training program (Carter et. al. 1967). Second, teachers received no factual information about either the history of black people or means of developing new teaching styles to respond to the presence of the black students. Had any been made to develop new teaching techniques, the teachers might well have accepted it as a program that responded to the "professional" activities of teachers in dealing with day-to-day classroom situations. After many training sessions at Brush, the teachers came away with little or no information that had direct applicability to their rooms. Instead, they saw themselves being maligned and accused of racist beliefs. The point is not whether they actually held such beliefs, but that no attempt was made to help them do well by their students.

A caveat here is necessary. It is sometimes assumed that a multicultural program can be created simply by introducing minority teachers into the classrooms. But widening the composition of the staff is not sufficient; one must also train them. At present few faculty members, whether majority or minority members, have had or are receiving any substantive training in those areas critical to the multicultural approach (see Rist 1972, 1973). For example, history and literature are disciplines that demand the same serious study and scholarship as do others, and it is not sufficient to say that minority teachers will be able to teach such topics simply because they are from the minority. As Orfield has commented in a similar vein (1975:330):

Even in districts with relatively good desegregation plans, the training effort in these fields (minority studies, history, literature, art, music) is often no more than a very few brief workshops. This is hardly adequate to re-orient teachers to some of the basic assumptions of their fields. Too frequently, the task of preparing new teaching units is assigned to teachers lacking adequate academic preparation in the fields. The result is often trivial or misleading material which does not become an integral part of the operative curriculum. Even when good materials are obtained or developed there is usually little or no serious effort to provide faculty members with the professional training they need to use and interpret the resources.

The situation at Brush, of course, was not even as good as that described by Orfield. There was no coherent curriculum that included a multicultural approach to the presence of black students in the classrooms, there was no division of labor to develop such a curriculum, and most basically, there was no impetus to do so.[1] Thus, it is not even possible to bemoan the poor use of good materials or the incomplete descriptions of innovative teaching methods, for neither new methods nor new materials were introduced. Had the number of black students at Brush been larger, perhaps teachers would have been forced to reexamine their teaching styles and rethink the content of the curriculum to eliminate any cultural biases and racism in it. The greater the number of black students, the more difficult it is to perpetuate their invisibility. But at Brush, neither the small black constituency nor the inadequate training program created the momentum necessary for social change.

The Principal

In the growing body of research literature on school desegregation, the central role of the principal is frequently emphasized.

---

1. Yet it need not necessarily be so. On March 13, 1975, the *Portland Observer*, the newspaper serving the black community, published an article entitled "White School Teaches Black History." The article was an account of how a white receiving school, through the efforts of several black staff and the PTA, began two black studies courses for seventh graders at the school.

While in normal circumstances the role may involve bureaucratic constraints, little real authority, and much routine, in times of desegregation there emerge pressures and demands that disrupt established patterns. And it is the principal who must directly confront and attempt to resolve them. The anxieties of parents, the uncertainties of the teachers, the early conflicts among students, the guidelines from the administration, the occasional inquiries from the media, and the heightened sensitivity of the neighborhood all necessitate the principal's attention as the process of desegregation begins. Demands are made on the principal to become a "change agent," an "arbitrator," and a "facilitator."

It would be well to note here several brief assessments of the role of the principal in the desegregation process. Willie (1973: 45) has written: "Much of the ease with which Highland approached this new situation of an enlarged nonwhite population was probably due to the kind of leadership which the principal gave." Writing of the METCO program in the Boston suburbs, Useem (1972:51) said: "In those schools where the principal was strong and positive supporter of METCO, there was increased likelihood of interracial harmony." Summarizing her examination of a number of studies in this area, St. John (1975:98) suggested: "Administrative sanction is probably the most important precondition of prejudice-reducing contact in schools. If central office staff is determined that integration shall be complete, the status of all school children made equal, and racial competition avoided, the other necessary ingredients of healthy biracial schools will probably follow." Finally, in his assessment of desegregation programs in a number of California schools, Wirt (1974:24) observed: "Principals appear in about every desegregating system who make a difference to the education of minorities, who bring all constituencies into their planning and implementation to produce an educational environment that literally bubbles with the excitement of learning."

A note of caution. Though this study and others have portrayed the principal as a key agent in the process of school integration, this does not mean that such social change must rest upon a "great man of history" theory. There are a variety of forces at work in American education, and in none of its institutional settings can one role encompass all the authority, all the decision-making options, or all the value assumptions necessary for its functioning. If we must wait for charismatic principals to ensure that schools allow learning to occur and provide a sense of satisfaction for both teachers and students, we may wait for Godot. As Orfield (1975:322) has noted:

> While it is obvious that principals with extraordinary talent and dedication are a great asset to any school system, it is hardly in the power of the court to expand the supply. What is important, for the standpoint of desegregation planning is that principals with certain attributes seem to handle the process of transition more effectively. Principals with positive attitudes towards desegregation, naturally enough, tend to handle the process better, as do principals able to help teachers successfully adapt their curricula and teaching styles.

In reflecting on the perceptions, activities, and pronouncements of Mr. Norris, I think it is fair to say he thought he was being honest and just in his dealings with the black students. If one were color-blind, there could be no discrimination. But there was a profound bifurcation in his approach that worked against his goals. While claiming that he treated "kids as kids" and that he knew "black parents want for their children what we want for ours," he spoke in ways that emphasized racial categories. He made distinctions between "them" and "us," between what "they want" and what "we want," and between "black troublemakers" and "good white students." It is as if he had said, "See those black and white students over there. I see no differences, just students." By trying to neutralize any emphasis on or attention to the presence of a new racial group in the school, he opted to continue in the same fashion as he had before integration came to Brush. Yet when problems arose precisely because of the presence of the black children, he had foreclosed the option to deal with them in that context. In a real sense, he had limited himself to approaching school integration with at best a philosophy of benign neglect and, at worst, an outright denial that it was even happening.

But regardless of whether one agrees or disagrees with this approach to school integration, one must ask whether integration at Brush School could realistically have been much different. I think not. There were many powerful forces working to reinforce the principal's notion of integration as color-blind assimilation, and few if any working to approach integration as a means of enhancing cultural pluralism. *So long as the city school administration opted for a program of one-way busing that sought to hide black students in the nooks and crannies of white schools without offending the sensibilities of the white parents and community members, so long as the personal views and attitudes of the principal were not examined or discussed with others, so long as the principal was left virtually isolated and unassisted in the implementation of his program, so long as the teachers were themselves unassisted and left to their own views, so long as the black parents had at best marginal contact with the life of the school, so long as the black staff was a single aide, the realities defined by Mr. Norris and the responses he encouraged came to constitute the sanctioned definition of the situation.*

What may have further crystallized the principal's views as the dominant motif for integration at Brush was that the school was not in any basic way disrupted by the influx of a few dozen black students. Had there been sufficient numbers of black students to jar established procedures or invalidate patterns and routines, then the principal and the teachers would have been forced to respond to their presence. But as it was, the numbers were so small and the students so widely dispersed that there were no disjunctures and no incidents necessitating new approaches. The problems that did arise could be interpreted as personal or idiosyncratic, and not as related to the institution. The new students were submerged in the established milieu of the school. They virtually became invisible. And nowhere in the social, political, or pedagogical context of Brush was there any push or encouragement to have it otherwise.

THE CURRICULUM

A number of historians of American education have noted that since its earliest days a common goal has been the conveying of an understanding of our institutions, our history, and our national character. The possessive "our," however, has had a rather specific connotation. As suggested earlier, those who traditionally have been in positions of authority and decision making have been white Protestants, and it is to them that I refer when mention is made of "our" institutions and "our" history. The main purpose of public education has been to promote Anglo-conformity and perpetuate the dominant Anglo cultural traditions, whether in language, law, religion, political values, or institutional arrangements. In large part this has been done by protraying white Americans devisers and implementers of phenomenally successful institutions, particularly those in the political arena, the sum of which have enabled this society to solve or come close to solving most, if not all, of its social problems.

At Brush School, this approach dominated the presentation of curriculum materials. One would be hard-pressed to discover, from what was available in the classrooms, anything about the contributions of minority groups to the life of the society. Perhaps even more basic, one would be hard-pressed to find any acknowledgment that minority groups even exist in American society. Other than the few black children coming to the school by bus, there was nothing in either the curriculum or the milieu of the school that would necessitate the recognition, let alone the affirmation, of the existence of nonwhite peoples. *It was as though history and reality stopped at the edge of white history and white reality.*

Perhaps even a few years ago, one could explain this situation by the fact that there were no appropriate materials dealing with the minority experience. But this is not the case now. Educators throughout the country have available to them a wide variety of integrated and minority-oriented materials. Furthermore, an extensive revision of curricular materials is under way at state and local levels. In such diverse states as California, South Carolina, Virginia, Michigan, and Florida, textbooks and teaching programs are being changed to include an affirmation of a more pluralistic approach to the study of American society. As one example, the South Carolina State Department of Education released in 1972 a booklet entitled *Ethnic Contributions to U. S.*

History. Developed by a biracial statewide committee, the booklet says: "No history course should leave an individual with a sense of inferiority. And every community and school district must rise above the conditions of mistrust which divide and destroy the fabric of any society. If one group insists in espousing superiority over another, we all lose."

The situation may be more subtle than is suggested by overt claims of white superiority and minority inferiority. For example, the lack of recognition and discussion of minority groups and their contributions can convey the message: "Minority groups are not important. It is not necessary to discuss them." The study of Brush School suggests that this is so. It is then an open question as to whether it is more destructive to the minority student to suggest his inferiority or his insignificance.

From the perspective of developing a culturally plural approach to integration at Brush, what is most desperately needed is the presentation and affirmation of the multiplicity of racial and ethnic groups that compose the American mosaic. In a very literal sense there must be a rewriting of history, a reevaluation of which events and persons are significant. In addition, there is needed a more open presentation of the failings of the nation, both past and present. For in large measure, the history of minority groups in American society has been inextricably linked to those failings and their consequences. It would also be beneficial to present a more diversified set of views about contemporary controversies. One can understand why racial assimilationists do not do this, but if Du Bois was correct when he wrote in *Souls of Black Folk* that "the problem of the twentieth century is the problem of the color line," then refusing to acknowledge its existence is a tremendous denial of one of the great cleavages of Western societies.

One further point. A viable program of school integration should be one that is sought by whites as well as by minority groups. White dominance of Brush School was so strong that the presence and contributions of black people were discounted. The black children confronted a school milieu that either rejected or ignored their existence. Furthermore, there appeared to be an

implicit assumption that school integration was proceeding
through the largesse of whites. It was they who were opening up
their schools and their facilities to the black children. Whites did
not go to blacks for integration; it was the other way around.
Never did anyone articulate the idea that white children would
benefit from the integration program. Whites were doing their
"good deed." Ironically, one of the strongest positions within the
black movement has been to refute and refuse to commit black
children to any integration program based on the assumption
that blacks have much to gain and nothing to give. Perhaps an
indication of the white community's commitment to integration
will come when the black community refuses to participate unless the white community actively tries to create an educational
climate where both black and white will benefit. If and when that
happens, Brush School may be on the way to becoming truly
pluralistic.

In a study of ninety-five school districts in the state of California, Mercer (1974) has provided a useful distinction between
what she terms "cultural integration" and "structural integration." The former she defined as follows:

> Cultural integration is the social process by which children,
> parents and teachers acquire an understanding and respect for
> the language, history, and cultural heritage of all ethnic
> groups through cultural sharing. Cultural integration does not
> imply monocultural Anglo conformity, but rather the develop-
> ment of the multicultural child who is able to participate in
> and be enriched by more than one cultural tradition. It in-
> volves developing an institution in which there is congruence
> between the behavior of all ethnic groups and teacher expecta-
> tions so that students of all ethnic groups like school, feel posi-
> tive about themselves, develop a positive identification with
> their own ethnic group, feel they are accepted by others in the
> school, and are not overly anxious about their school perfor-
> mance or school status.
>
> Structural integration, on the other hand, is the social pro-
> cess by which children, parents, and teachers of all ethnic
> groups acquire statuses and play roles in the school that are of
> equivalent power and prestige. Structural integration implies
> that there is a high level of involvement of the parents of all

ethnic groups in the school's social structure. It implies that staff members of all ethnic groups participate in the school structure at all status levels and play equally active roles in the social interaction matrix of the school. For pupils, structural integration implies a high rate of intra- and inter-ethnic friendships.

Though conceptually Mercer is correct in splitting apart the cultural and structural components of the integration process, these two have been fused throughout this study. This was done simply because it does not appear that one is likely without the other. The curriculum, the participation of the parents, the training and subsequent classroom practices of the teachers, and the interactions among the students are all interrelated. Furthermore, all of these must contribute if we are to create humane integrated settings. It also goes without saying that we are far from achieving such settings in any numbers. Mercer's study and those of a number of other researchers generally agree that the development and implementation of a cultural-structural approach to school integration is infrequent. As Mercer noted, "Clearly, the schools in our sample have not yet achieved a multi-ethnic climate in which there is a convergence between the teacher's values and children's behavior so that children from all ethnic backgrounds are perceived in an equally favorable light" (1974:47).

But all is not doom and gloom. The fact that the majority of schools in Mercer's study and in other studies have not reached a state of viable integration does not mean that they are not moving toward it. In many parts of the country and at many levels of school administration, there is a growing recognition of the need for more than simply an "Anglo-conformity" approach to school integration. But if schools like Brush are multiplied time and again throughout the United States, substantial change is necessary before a culturally pluralistic approach to school integration is anywhere near to becoming the normative pattern.

School integration at Brush and elsewhere is a relatively new phenomenon in American society. We have had, in actuality, little more than a decade to work toward transforming dual and discriminatory school systems into integrated ones. That we have

not transformed separate and unequal schools into viable integrated ones overnight does not mean that we should stop working
toward this goal. The moral, legal, and pedagogical reasons for
continuing are clear. And if we are not moved by the pursuit of
good works, then we should consider what will become of this
society if we choose not to act.

Epilogue:
Race and Education in America

A great schism exists between the realities of American education and our expectations for it. Our educational institutions have been successful in ensuring the continued prosperity and status of the middle and upper classes, but the poor and minorities have been systematically denied invitations to the American Feast. Not until 1954 and the monumental Supreme Court decision in *Brown v. Board of Education of Topeka* were the legal and social precedents of separating children by race for purposes of education outlawed. The *Brown* case provided a secure basis for the movement away from the inequality of segregated school systems, despite the fact that stipulating "all deliberate speed" surely slowed the process for at least a decade. But in the short time span since the *Brown* decision, the United States has undertaken major efforts to transform discriminatory dual systems into a single educational system.

Though the changes encouraged by the desegregation of much of American public education have been profound, few if any serious analysts believe that we are yet close to achieving comparable educational opportunities for all our citizens. As the problems in the years after the Court decision of 1954 were confronted, new ones of equal complexity and tenacity arose. During the 1960's we made a massive commitment of federal funds to programs designed to improve the educational opportunities of minority and low-income children, seemingly with mixed results. It must still be said, unequivocally, that the major unresolved issue facing American education remains how to improve significantly the education of minority and poor children. Despite years of social change (or at least efforts in that direction), large-scale funding, innovations of all types, and radical departures in school governance, it is safe to conclude that there are no panaceas, no quick and painless solutions, no single, short-term strategy that can be counted on to enhance the educational experiences and opportunities of minority children in any significant way.

Millions of dollars and the efforts of countless teachers, administrators, and researchers throughout the country have provided no clear breakthrough ensuring all children equal access to educational benefits. As a result, it is increasingly evident that we are faced with a set of policy options, none of which in and of itself will provide the solutions to the problems at hand. And in addition to the educational costs and benefits of any policy decision (which are not always clearly established), political factors must also be considered. Perhaps one of the major realizations emerging in the debate over the form and content of education for poor and minority students is that it is a false dichotomy to separate the political from the pedagogical. They are inextricably intertwined. Only with an analysis of their interrelations can one generate policies that fit the realities of the society.

In the pages to follow, an effort is made to move beyond the immediate implications of the situation at Brush School and discuss some of the more general issues raised by this study concerning race and education in the United States. These topics are necessarily applicable to Brush and grow from the work there, but are also pertinent to a larger discussion of school integration and the directions it might take. The comments here have been set off from the main text in order to indicate that the analysis now moves beyond the data — but not the questions — generated by the Brush study.

INTEGRATION AND MINORITY TOKENISM

The Administrative Transfer Program at Brush, from the vantage point of one encouraging racial assimilation, was correct to keep the number of black students small. But if the goal had been cultural pluralism, the effort was clearly tokenism *par excellence.* As suggested previously, when one takes several dozen black children and distributes them among hundreds of whites in a school, there are a variety of interpretations as to whether that constitutes an integrated educational setting. And beyond such judgments, there is the question of the effort and toll tokenism takes on the black child, both psychologically and academically.

A variety of researchers have written on this point, and their conclusions are not encouraging. Pettigrew (1974:59), for instance, says:

> Tokenism is psychologically difficult for black children. Without the numbers to constitute a critical mass, black students can come to think of themselves as an unwanted appendage, and white students can overlook the black presence and even perceive it as a temporary situation. But once the minority percentage reaches about 20 to 25%, blacks become a significant part of the school to stay. They are now numerous enough to be filtered throughout the entire school structure, on the newspaper staff, and in the honor society as well as in the glee club and on athletic teams. Substantial minority group representation, of course, does not guarantee intergroup harmony, but it is clearly a prerequisite for integration.

There is a central but somewhat ambiguous element in the discussion of the impact of tokenism on black students, and Pettigrew alluded to it when he mentioned the concept of "critical mass." In assessing the social-psychological impact of varying numbers of black students within a school setting on their own self-perceptions and self-esteem, Pettigrew implied that at least 20 to 25 percent were needed in order for the black students to become a "significant part of the school." By implication, such a range would supply the necessary numbers for enhanced self-identity. Likewise, in her assessment of Blalock's (1967) analysis, St. John (1975) posited a 15 to 40 percent minority enrollment as optimal. This figure would allow a situation where minority numbers would be sufficient to exert pressure without constituting a power threat to the majority.[1]

Attempts to assess the impact of varying percentages of minority students on their academic achievement have resulted in mixed data and interpretations. And though there have been many studies of the relation of desegregation to achievement, few have attempted to specify exact percentages or even ranges within which one could, with a strong degree of certainty, project achievement outcomes. But one study that has sought to do precisely this is that of Jencks and Brown (1975); they worked with data collected in the mid-1960s from the national cross-section Equality of Educational Opportunity Survey (EEOS). They suggested that "in general, blacks gained ground relative to whites in all schools where they were more than 10 percent and less than 75 percent of total enrollment." This conclusion applied only to the elementary grades because when Jencks and Brown analyzed high school scores, they concluded that none of the findings were "large enough to be of much pedagogic importance." They spoke of the differences in high school black-white scores related to school composition as generally "trivial."

In this context, it would be well to mention briefly the impact of desegregation on white achievement. Most studies have focused on white attitudes and tolerance rather than on performance, but St. John (1975) did assemble twenty-four studies that had at least some applicable data. Having surveyed them, she concluded: "The evidence appears convincing that the achievement of white students is not adversely affected by the addition of a few black students in their classrooms."

In assessing studies on black and white achievement as they re-

---

1. Without stating a specific figure, Farley (1975:15) followed much the same line of reasoning when he wrote, "Presumably the opposition of whites to integration is proportional to the percentage of students black. That is, white parents may accept desegregation more willingly if 7, instead of 67, percent of the students are black." Downs (1968) came to a similar conclusion when he developed his "Law of Dominance": "A vast majority of whites of all income groups would be willing to send their children to integrated schools or live in integrated neighborhoods, as long as they were sure that the white group concerned would remain in the majority in those facilities or areas" (p. 1,338).

late to classroom and school composition, the conclusion appears to be that we do not yet have enough data to posit a causal relation. As St. John (1975:36) says: "More than a decade of considerable research effort has produced no definitive positive findings. In view of the political, moral, and technical difficulties of investigation on this question, it is doubtful that all the canons of the scientific method will ever be met or a causal relationship ever established. Suggestive trends have been uncovered, however, as has one important negative finding: desegregation has rarely lowered academic achievement for either black or white children."

In sum, a discussion of the relation of tokenism to school integration appears best served if the achievement issue is put aside.[2] At the present time, we cannot definitively tell whether causality exists or in what direction it might point. What we can grapple with are the social-psychological outcomes. Here the evidence is more direct: black students who serve as tokens in a white milieu tend to suffer. Put in a situation conducive to estrangement and loneliness, black students single-handedly bear the brunt of achieving what, for some, constitutes the optimal integrated setting. Again we have a situation in which the costs of social change to the majority are much less than the costs to the minority. In specific terms, it was students like Diane, Alex, Duke, and Gloria who paid more than their share to create the "integrated" classrooms of Brush school.

To change this situation requires solving problems of great magnitude. In a city where the black community is in a minority, how do we move the white community to accept more than tokenism? How do we assess the aspirations and intentions of the black community? Can we provide situations of either tokenism (if we

2. There is perhaps another set of circumstances where the entire discussion of tokenism *per se* can be put aside: the situation where blacks are not numerically fewer than whites. This situation is becoming more and more common in cities, especially the large ones. As Farley (1975:21) has noted: "When the nation's twenty-five largest cities are considered, we find that by 1972, blacks comprised the majority of public school students in ten cities. In another nine cities blacks accounted for 30 to 50 percent of the public school enrollment, and given current migration trends, schools in these cities will be predominantly black in the foreseeable future."

assume that some parents want to push their children towards assimilation) or more substantial minority representation in schools without running afoul of both state and federal guidelines about the legal racial composition of schools? How do we approach multicultured education in this context? Is it only to be offered in places with sizable minority student populations, or should token programs include it as well?

There are obviously no pat answers to these questions. But I suggest that, in spite of possible political and social resistance, we base future educational decisions on a key consideration laid down in *Brown v. Board of Education:* that blacks should have access to an educational system that provides *them* with benefits. Thus, I would not advocate programs like that at Brush unless black parents clearly understood the program and agreed to it. As it was, they volunteered their children to a program they knew nothing about. Black parents had not the slightest say in several key decisions made about their children at Brush. The principal alone decided that they should be dispersed and become one or two among twenty or thirty. The principal and teachers alone decided that the school would retain its exclusive white orientation.

It is one thing to tell black parents that they will have a "quality education" for their children when they volunteer to send them to white schools. It is quite another then to create a situation where the children may loose more than they gain. In my view, a city like Portland should refrain from its policies of token dispersal (unless black parents specifically request it) and allow a fewer number of predominantly white schools to integrate so that they would have larger percentages of minority children. Some white students would be deprived of integrated settings, but black students would no longer have to pay all the costs of giving whites the experience of integration.

Still other problems must be solved if we are to have better integration programs. Though I have argued here for the incorporation of the black parents into the planning and implementation of the integration process (and have suggested that no program cannot long succeed without their involvement), it is very difficult to find ways of stimulating white parent involvement that go beyond the simple affirmation of white dominance. What is it going to take to bring white parents to support a pluralistic approach to integration?

I think two arguments might encourage such support. The first is that a pluralistic approach to integration would provide benefits for the white children in learning how to "live with others." When earlier I mentioned the "hidden curriculum" in schools, I emphasized the socialization component within it. But parents want the schools not only to socialize their children to pursue academic rewards, but also to teach them to manage good personal relations, as is evidenced by report card categories such as "gets along well with others" and "displays good classroom citizenship." School integration can be presented as a program that helps develop interpersonal relations.

The second way of gaining white support is to affirm that there are cultural diversities and strengths in white communities as well as in minority communities. In their curricula, American schools have ignored the contributions of white ethnic groups almost as much as they have ignored those of racial minority groups, and it may well be that many in white ethnic communities resist school integration because they believe that they are now the "odd men out." If present school programs emphasize Anglo-Protestant values, and if integration means the introduction of awareness of racial minorities into the curriculum, then white ethnics are the new invisible group. But if a pluralistic approach to integration affirms the cultural contributions and diversities of all groups in society, then it should attract white ethnics. Integration would then serve as a means of introducing their own cultural heritages into the school curriculum. Social change is easier to support when one perceives personal benefits, as opposed to benefits for others. If school integration remains under the control of white administrators and governmental officials, on the one hand, and black parents, on the other, continued resistance from segments of the white community can be anticipated.

One final issue here is when and how to grant to Anglo-conformity the same legitimacy as cultural pluralism. It could be

argued from what has been presented in this book that an education based on that world-view is not in the least culturally pluralistic, but instead is monolithic in its value system. The issue here
is not the substantive one of whether one "believes in" competition, achievement, striving, and assimilation, on the one hand, or
tolerance, diversity, and caring, on the other, but rather the
practical issue of what to do about a substantial segment of the
nation (perhaps the majority) who at least claim to espouse the
Protestant ethic. In short, what arrangement for schooling can be
created that allow those who do not believe in racial equality and
tolerance and those who strongly wish to be assimilated the option of not participating in pluralistic and integrated education?

I am not sure such arrangements can be made. In an ideally
pluralistic situation, everyone, including those who do not sub-
scribe to pluralistic goals, would have perfect freedom of choice.
But where, as in this country, the government has established a
monopoly over education, there can ultimately be no freedom of
choice. The government declares certain options illegal, such as
efforts by white parents to avoid desegregation through establishing "freedom of choice" transfer plans and parental decisions not
to send a child to school at all. The best we can hope for is that
government will provide several legal options to parents and students. Educational "vouchers," "educational income tax deduc-
tions" or even "community control of schools" might appropri-
ately be offered. But no plan should be created that denies a
child entrance to a learning situation simply on the basis of race.
Age might be a criterion for admittance, or religion, or even educational philosophy (traditionalist versus noncompetitive, graded
versus nongraded classrooms, and so on), but race and ethnicity
could not be. Guaranteeing the rights of minority children cannot be left to the good will of whites. Such approaches would
offer opportunities for choice among a variety of educational orientations. And in contrast to the present situation, where only
the few have the means for private or parochial education, an ex-
pansion of public school options would increase the choices available to all parents, regardless of their social class, religion, or
racial background.

SERVICE/STATUS-EQUALIZATION STRATEGIES AND INTEGRATION

In the writings on implementing school integration, it has become a part of the conventional wisdom that remedial services are a necessary component in any workable program. Academicians (Pettigrew 1974, Mercer 1974, Willie 1973, and St. John 1975), practitioners (Smith et al. 1973, and Foster 1973), and various branches of the federal government, including the U.S. Commission of Civil Rights, the Congress, and the Department of Health, Education, and Welfare, have all noted the importance of providing remedial services. The most general rationale for such services is that newly integrated minority students will need additional assistance in order to compensate for the past inadequacies of the segregated schooling process. Further, if such services are not provided, the minority students will almost inevitably find themselves lumped at the bottom of the class in terms of academic achievement; and having few if any resources with which to change their position, they will simply remain there.

A major impetus for the establishment of remedial programs in desegregating schools (particularly those that were formerly all or overwhelmingly white) has been the financial support of the federal government through Title VII of the Emergency School Aid Act (P.L. 92-318). In Portland, the money was designed "to improve the basic skills among academically disadvantaged students and to *provide basic skills and remedial instruction for receiving schools* in the voluntary Administrative Transfer Program" (emphasis added). At Brush School in particular, the funds were used to support several teacher aides, one teacher half-day to provide remedial instruction, and the work of Mrs. Miller as the program coordinator.

If the problem is really that in desegregating schools, many minority students cannot successfully compete with white students, then programs such as those at Brush are totally inadequate solutions. To assume that one can remedy past educational neglect through twenty or thirty minutes a day is tenuous at best. What makes the whole discussion of remedial services so important is that there is a significant body of research literature that suggests that minority students will never achieve more than the most minimal acceptance by white students so long as their achievement levels remain very low. (see Katz 1964, McPartland 1968, Lewis and St. John 1974). And further, the lack of acceptance and sense of rejection that minority students experience further inhibits their academic performance. A classic example of the vicious cycle. And to carry the argument yet further, it becomes difficult to argue that desegregation benefits black students if their acceptance and popularity depends on their academic achievement.

But if we are committed to creating and sustaining integrated classrooms where both white and minority students can flourish and develop, then we must develop *means* of doing this. And such an approach does not hinge its validity on whether one can scientifically "prove" the benefits of integration. Instead, if the moral, political, and ethical commitment is made to create multiracial educational settings for children, the task is to make those settings as humane, lively, and supportive as possible. A new and much expanded notion of school "services" is warranted.

The belief that a bit of remedial tutoring and perhaps a few pictures of black people on the classroom walls will be sufficient to overcome both the unequal academic skills black children bring to the school and the subsequent unequal status that lack of skill affords them is naive at best and malicious at worst. What must be addressed, instead, are the *interrelations* of racial, social, and academic statuses, because all three are inextricably interwoven in the integrated school and its classrooms. Thus, any attempt to deal with one as though it were isolated from the others is thwarted by the realities of their interdependence. It was the refusal at Brush School to recognize the centrality of this triad of racial, social, and academic statuses that both created and perpetuated a situation where the black children were placed in the lowest reading groups and concomitantly experienced low acceptance by and frequently high rejection from their peers. At Brush it was as though there had been a collective and tacit

agreement that race did not exist and that the social-status rami-
fications of an intensely competitive academic setting were nil.

In the effort to posit methods of changing school practices so as
to minimize as much as possible the distresses and hazards of
school integration, little assistance is forthcoming from the research literature. While there are measures upon measures of
self-esteem, hundreds and hundreds of reports on academic
achievement, and while scale after scale assesses racial tolerance,
there is little to tell us how to increase any of them. Yet we are not
completely without guideposts. In my estimation, the most promising avenues of investigation are associated with the following
topics: teacher expectations, production of equal status in students, and classroom instructional processes. Consider, for example, the following comments by Cohen (1975: 296-297). They
reflect one significant line of research that clearly recognizes the
interdependence of the various processes at work in an integrated
setting.

> Continuing theoretical and laboratory work had made us
> realize that bringing together groups of children separated by
> a wide social gulf in a school setting where there is competition
> of scarce rewards and where there are typically large achieve-
> ment differentials on conventional academic skills, makes the
> problem of producing "equal status experience" just about
> *twice* as difficult. In the first place, even if the children were all
> of the same race but entered schools with differential skills and
> aptitude for the conventional curriculum, a status order based
> on classroom achievement would emerge which would be just
> as effective in triggering self-fulfilling prophecies as race. In
> other words, the achievement status which emerges in competi-
> tively structured classrooms is capable of infecting new situa-
> tions so that those who have low achievement status will expect
> to do less well on any new task when combined with those stu-
> dents who have a higher achievement status in the classroom
> . . . In addition, from another laboratory study, we had
> grounds for believing that competition aggravates the effect of
> diffuse status characteristics such as age or race . . . We now
> realize there are still several other factors which make the de-
> segregated school a very difficult place in which to produce

equal status interaction. Of prime importance is the narrowness of the conventional curriculum . . . This means that if students enter the desegregated situation with a lower level of skills they are fated to be perceived as having little academic ability in almost every class they attend—there is no escape from this fate. This will occur even if there is no tracking or ability grouping . . . Still another factor may have been of vital importance: success of the cooperative treatment in the field experiment has led to the hypothesis that a key factor may well have been the presence of interracial classroom teams of teachers and a school administrative structure which was carefully balanced between black and white throughout its ranks (starting with black and white co-directors). Not only were the students shown a rare organization where power and authority were shared between blacks and whites, but classroom teams modeled "equal status behavior" every day of the summer school.

Building on these past seven years of research, Cohen and her associates now plan "to experiment with a non-competitive small group curriculum featuring multiple human abilities, combined with a strictly non-competitive, but individualized program in the basic skills area. We would hypothesize that if the academic and racial status problems are effectively treated, we should not only see equal status behavior, but improvement in black achievement."

I have quoted Cohen at some length to demonstrate the multi-faceted approach that I believe necessary if prevailing patterns of academic and status inequalities, such as those fround at Brush, are to be changed. Paper-and-pencil tests and sporadic interventions cannot fundamentally alter the dynamics of the classroom situation. Instead, we urgently need to find new ways to deal with classroom heterogeneity that neither demean the minority student nor create antagonisms and stereotypes for the majority student. St. John (1975) writes of the need for new patterns of "social engineering" in integrated classrooms. She is correct. The participants in such settings need to learn new ways of relating to one another. Without such changes, the present situation will perpetuate itself.

INTEGRATION: A METROPOLITAN OR
NEIGHBORHOOD SOLUTION?

In the aftermath of the "long hot summer" of 1967, the National Advisory Commission on Civil Disorders began its report with the following "This is our basic conclusion: Our Nation is moving toward two societies, one black, one white — separate and unequal." Though it would have been more accurate to say that the United States already exists as two separate societies, this statement nevertheless has a profound implication for any discussion of school integration: to integrate schools in American society necessitates crossing the boundaries between distinctive social groups in the system. And perhaps the most visible indication of such boundaries is the overwhelming racial segregation in housing patterns. The racial composition of American cities has changed radically in the last three decades: they used to be almost exclusively white; now seven of the ten largest have black populations of at least 30 percent. And in the suburban rings around the central cities, the population remains overwhelmingly white. By 1970, six tenths of all black people were central-city residents, while only 5 percent were living in suburbs.

It is only belaboring the obvious to say that a city like Portland, Oregon, with a black population of 5 or 6 percent faces quite different problems in desegregating its schools than does, for example, a city like Washington, D.C., where the black population is 75 percent. Yet both have something in common — residential segregation. If one opted for neighborhood schools in both cities, white children would overwhelmingly go to school only with other whites and black children only with other blacks. While Portland could successfully desegregate its schools within the boundaries of the city, this would not be possible in cities like Washington, D.C., Detroit, Newark, New Orleans Parish, or St. Louis. All have more than a 65 percent black enrollment. Here the only apparent solution to racial separation is metropolitan consolidation. But the Supreme Court said no to this solution in its 1974 decision in *Milliken v. Bradley,* a case in Detroit.

By refusing to endorse litigation directing the metropolitan approach to the desegregation of the Detroit public schools, the Court reaffirmed its stance of supporting desegration only so far as it can be accomplished within school districts. It was faced with one of two alternatives: to support the constitutional right of children to an education not encumbered by segregationist practices or to support the widely acknowledged right of local communities to manage their own affairs. In the end, the Court opted for local autonomy, saying: "No single tradition in public education is more deeply rooted than local autonomy over the operation of schools; local autonomy has long been thought essential both to the maintenance of community concern and support for public schools and to the quality of the educational process" (Milliken v. Bradley, S.Ct. 73-434, 1974).

In the aftermath of this decision, some attention has been paid to the seeming loophole for future metropolitan remedies found in the comments of Justice Stewart, the "swing" justice, who in this instance voted with four Nixon appointments to the Court:

> This is not to say, however, that an inter-district remedy of the sort approved by the Court of Appeals would not be proper, or even necessary, in other factual situations. Were it to be shown, for example, that state officials had contributed to the separation of the races by drawing or redrawing school district lines . . .; by transfer of school units between districts . . .; or by purposeful, racially discriminatory use of state housing or zoning laws, then a decree calling for transfer of pupils across district lines or for restructuring of district lines might well be appropriate.

Stewart indicated that he found no evidence suggesting the school officials either in or outside Detroit were involved in any of the activities listed above. Rather, he invoked his own notion of the dynamics of urban growth as an explanation for the separation of the races between city and suburbs: "It is this essential fact of a predominantly Negro school population in Detroit—caused by unknown and perhaps unknowable factors such as in-migration, birth rates, economic changes, or cumulative acts of private racial fears—that accounts for the 'growing core of Negro schools,' a 'core' that has grown to include virtually the entire city."

The implication appears to be that if Stewart could be shown that the causes of racial separation were not "unknown and perhaps unknowable," he would be willing to switch his vote and favor metropolitan solutions. Yet the question remains as to what level of inference and proof Stewart would require, for though much in human societies may be "unknown and perhaps unknowable," it is surely the case that "the tight, unremitting containment of urban blacks over the past half-century within the bowels of American cities is not one of them" (Pettigrew 1974: 62). If there is one subject in the study of American race relations where extensive research has led to the fruitful understanding of social processes, it is the subject of housing segregation. In fact, it is now so well understood that mathematical models have been developed that can explain and predict with high degrees of accuracy the trends and outcomes resulting from current patterns (Hermalin and Farley 1973, Farley and Taeuber 1974, Farley 1975, Pettigrew 1975). It remains uncertain, however, to what degree Stewart would base a reversal in his position on social science data alone. He appears to have constructed a personal "social theory" of urban race relations based on a belief that the key factors are "unknown and perhaps unknowable." In this context, one "theory" becomes as good as another in trying to explain what is occurring in the cities of America.

Is there an alternative to simply waiting for Justice Stewart to change his mind? I believe there is, and I believe it is applicable not only to cities like Detroit, Washington, D.C., and St. Louis, where there are large black central-city populations, but also to cities like Minneapolis, Portland, Los Angeles, Harrisburg, and Charlotte, where the black population is considerably smaller. What appears both feasible and desirable is to develop a concerted effort to residentially desegregate our metropolitan areas. To encourage the desegregation of the suburbs in particular is to encourage housing to share with schools the task and responsibility of moving toward new goals in our society.

Three factors make this alternative attractive: (1) economic factors no longer adequately account for the concentration of black people in the central city and their absence in the suburbs; (2) with metropolitan desegregation there would be an increase in integrated neighborhood schools; and (3) the burden of integrating society would not fall exclusively on the schools. Each of these factors deserves brief discussion.

A conventional wisdom sometimes used to explain why black people are underrepresented in suburban communities is that they have been unable to afford the expensive housing found there. It has not been racism or blatant discrimination that has kept them out, but economic factors. Though there may well be some historical validity to this claim, it no longer holds true. Hermalin and Farley (1974) found that on the basis of data collected from the 1970 Census, economic factors can no longer account for the disproportional concentration of blacks in the central city. Pettigrew (1974:14) has worked from the same data and tabulated the following: "In metropolitan Chicago, 54% of the whites live in the suburbs compared with only 8% of the blacks though 46% of the area's blacks would be expected to do so on economic grounds alone; in metropolitan Detroit, the comparable figures are 73%, 12% and 67%; in metropolitan Washington, D.C., 91%, 20% and 90%; in metropolitan Minneapolis, 58%, 7% and 49%; and in metropolitan Baltimore, 58%, 5% and 51%."

The economic gains of black Americans in recent years are reflected in these data, which indicate a substantial potential market of black people for suburban housing. In addition, various opinion polls indicate that a majority of whites now favor integrated neighborhoods and favor sending their own children to integrated schools, so long as busing is not involved. Together, these findings suggest that residential integration can lead to the emergence of schools that are both integrated and neighborhood based. But it must be emphasized that all suburban communities must be involved, not simply those on the fringe of the black central city, for example, East Cleveland, Ohio, or University City, Missouri. As St. John (1975:131) has noted: "The type of neighborhood that would contribute to the achievement of integrated schools and society would not be the familiar, racially changing, lower class neighborhoods on the edge of the black ghetto . . . the benefits of desegregation have rarely been realized in such neighborhoods. Not a single sector but the whole suburban ring — stable working-class and middle-class areas alike — would have to be opened to racially mixed housing."

A second benefit of residential integration would be a growth in the number of integrated neighborhood schools, an emphasis on "neighborhood." I say this even though I am somewhat skeptical of the importance of neighborhood schools for at least two reasons: that millions of students each day travel long distances to schools, distances beyond any conceivable definition of neighborhood, with no demonstrable negative effects on either them or the endeavors of schooling; and second, that with one of every four families moving each year, the notion of "neighborhood" as a long-term place where one puts down roots and establishes "community" seems spurious. But even with these reservations, there is much that appears beneficial in having integrated schools that have been created naturally as a result of residential integration. It may be that only such schools can satisfy the desire for educational institutions that are both responsive and small enough so that students do not feel lost in a mass. The alternative is the aggregation and centralization of school systems and the implementation of large-scale transportation programs.

Residential integration minimizes the need for court orders that seek to overcome residential segregation in order to create integrated schools. It appears that a decision in the white suburbs will soon have to be made — either open up housing to black and other minority peoples and thus keep neighborhood schools, or else keep the housing market closed and confront court orders for the rolling of the buses. For many years, the suburbs have been able to have the best of both. How much longer they will be able to maintain this situation is a matter of speculation, but that it will last indefinitely is a tenuous assumption at best. Again, the more neighborhoods do integrate, the greater the likelihood that neighborhood schools can flourish.

Finally, there is the issue of how seriously this society wishes to create and sustain integrated milieus for children. To date, the responsibility has fallen almost exclusively on the schools, with all the limitations that implies for the variety and duration of such settings. Creating integrated residential areas would greatly expand the number of situations, both formal and informal, in which interaction between races could occur. To inhibit and thwart interracial interaction through the perpetuation of residential segregation means making the school, for many children, the sole source of cross-racial contact. And unless we want another generation of children to grow up in the violent and fearful atmosphere of a Boston, or experience the smug racism of white superiority, we need to change our ways. To do so would be no mean achievement.

References

Addams, J. 1914. *Twenty Years at Hull House.* New York, MacMillan.

Allport, G. 1954. *The Nature of Prejudice.* Cambridge, Mass., Addison-Wesley.

Amir, Y. 1971. "Contact Hypothesis in Ethnic Relations." *Psychology Bulletin,* vol. 71.

Armor, D. J. 1972a. "The Evidence on Busing." *The Public Interest,* no. 28.

———— 1972b. "School and Family Effects on Black and White Achievement." In F. Mosteller and D. Moynihan, eds., *On Equality of Educational Opportunity* (New York, Random House).

Baratz, S., and J. Baratz. 1970. "Early Childhood Intervention: The Social Science Base of Institutional Racism." *Harvard Educational Review,* vol. 40, no. 1.

Becker, H. S. 1952. "Social Class Variations in Teacher-Pupil Relationships." *Journal of Educational Sociology,* vol. 25.

Berger, P., and T. Luckman. 1967. *The Social Construction of Reality.* Garden City, N.J., Doubleday.

Bettleheim, B. 1972. "Middle Class Teacher and Lower Class Child." In *Rethinking Urban Education* (San Francisco, Jossey-Bass).

Biehler, R. F. 1954. "Companion Choice Behavior in the Kindergarten." *Child Development,* vol. 25.

Blalock, H. 1967. *Toward a Theory of Minority-Group Relations.* New York, Wiley.

Blauner, R. 1972. *Racial Oppression in America.* New York, Harper and Row.

Boocock, S. S. 1969. "Toward a Sociology of Learning: A Selective Review of Existing Research." *Sociology of Education,* vol. 39.

Boudon, R. 1973. *Education, Opportunity, and Social Inequality.* New York, Wiley.

Bowles, S. 1972. "Unequal Education and the Reproduction of the Social Division of Labor." In M. Carnoy, ed., *Schooling in a Corporate Society* (New York, McKay).

Brophy, J., and T. L. Good. 1974. *Teacher-Student Relationships.* New York, Holt, Rinehart and Winston.

Carithers, M. W. 1970. "School Desegregation and Racial Cleavage, 1965-1970: A Review of the Literature." *Journal of Social Issues,* vol. 26.

Clark, K. B., and M. K. Clark. 1947. "Racial Identification and Preference in Negro Children." In T. Newcomb and E. Hartley, eds., *Readings in Social Psychology* (New York, Holt, Rinehart and Winston).

Cohen, D., T. Pettigrew, and R. Riley. 1972. "Race and the Outcomes of Schooling." In F. Mosteller and D. Moynihan, eds., *On Equality of Educational Opportunity* (New York, Random House).

Cohen, E. 1973. "Modifying the Effects of Social Structure." *American Behavioral Scientist,* vol. 16, no. 6.

———— 1975. "The Effects of Desegregation on Race Relations: Facts or Hypothesis." *Law and Contemporary Problems,* vol. 39, no. 2.

Cohen, E., and S. Roper. 1972. "Modification of Interracial Interaction Disability." *American Sociological Review,* vol. 37, no. 6.

Coleman, J. S. 1972. "Class and the Classroom." *Saturday Review of Education,* vol. 55, no. 22.

Coleman, J. S., et al. 1966. *Equality of Educational Opportunity.* Washington, D.C., U.S. Government Printing Office.

Committee on Race and Education. 1964. *Report of the Citizens Committee on Race and Education* Portland, Ore.: Board of Education.

Corwin, R. G. 1965. *A Sociology of Education.* New York, Appleton-Century Crofts.

Davis, A. 1952. *Social Class Influences upon Learning.* Cambridge, Mass., Harvard University Press.

Downs, A. 1968. "Alternative Futures for the American Ghetto." *Daedalus,* vol. 97.

Eddy, E. 1967. *Walk the White Line.* Garden City, N.J., Doubleday.

Edgar, D. 1974. *The Competent Teacher.* Melbourne, Angus and Robertson.

Esposito, D. 1973. "Homogeneous and Heterogeneous Ability Group-

ing: Principal Findings and Implications for Evaluating and De-
signing More Effective Educational Environments." *Review of
Educational Research,* vol. 43, no. 2.

Farley, R. 1975. "Racial Integration in the Public Schools, 1967-1972:
Assessing the Effect of Governmental Policy." *Sociological Focus,*
vol. 8, no. 1.

Farley R., and A. Taeuber. 1974. "Racial Segregation in the Public
Schools." *American Journal of Sociology,* vol. 79, no. 4.

Foster, G. 1973. "Desegregating Urban Schools: A Review of Techniques." *Harvard Educational Review,* vol. 43, no. 1.

Fuchs, E. 1969. *Teachers Talk: Views from Inside City Schools.* Garden
City, N.J., Doubleday.

Gittell, M., and T. Hollander. 1968. *Six Urban School Districts.* New
York, Praeger.

Goffman, E. 1961. *Asylums.* Garden City, N.J., Doubleday.

Goodman, M. 1964. *Race Awareness in Young Children,* rev. ed. New
York, Collier.

Gordon, M. 1964. *Assimilation in American Life.* New York, Oxford
University Press.

Gouldner, A. W. 1970. *The Coming Crisis in Western Sociology.* New
York, Basic Books.

Hamilton, C. V. 1972. "The Nationalist vs. the Integrationist." *The
New York Times Magazine,* Oct. 1.

Hauser, R. M. 1971. *Socioeconomic Background and Educational Performance.* Washington, D.C., American Sociological Association.

Hermalin, A. I., and R. Farley. 1973. "The Potential for Residential
Integration in Cities and Suburbs: Implications for the Busing
Controversy." *American Sociological Review,* vol. 38, no. 5.

Henry, J. 1963. *Culture against Man.* New York, Random House.

Hodgson, G. 1973. "Do Schools Make a Difference?" *The Atlantic,* vol.
231, no. 3.

Hollingshead, A. 1949. *Elmtown's Youth.* New York, Wiley.

Jackson, P. 1968. *Life in Classrooms.* New York, Holt, Rinehart and
Winston.

Jencks, C. S. 1972. "The Coleman Report and the Conventional Wisdom." In F. Mosteller and D. Moynihan, eds., *On Equality of Educational Opportunity* (New York, Random House).

Jencks, C. S., et al. 1972. *Inequality: A Reassessment of the Effect of
Family and Schooling in America.* New York, Basic Books.

Jencks, C. S., and M. Brown. 1975. "The Effects of Desegregation on
Student Achievement: Some New Evidence from the Equality of
Educational Opportunity Survey." *Sociology of Education,* vol. 48.

Johnson, D. A. 1974. "Race, Peer Preferences, and Perceptions of Competence in an Integrated School." Paper presented to the Pacific Sociological Association, San Jose, California.

Kallen, H. M. 1924. *Culture and Democracy in the United States.* New York, Liveright.

Katz, I. 1964. "Review of Evidence Relating to Effects of Desegregation on the Intellectual Performance of Negroes." *American Psychologist,* vol. 19.

———— 1969. "Factors Influencing Negro Performance in the Desegregated School." In M. Deutsch, I. Katz, and A. Jensen, eds., *Social Class, Race, and Psychological Development* (New York, Holt, Rinehart and Winston).

Katz, M. 1971. *Class, Bureaucracy, and Schools.* New York, Praeger.

Kuper, L., and G. M. Smith, eds. 1969. *Pluralism in Africa.* Berkeley, University of California Press.

Leacock, L. 1969. *Teaching and Learning in City Schools.* New York, Basic Books.

Lewis, R. G., and N. St. John. 1974. "Contributions of Cross-Racial Friendship to Minority Group Achievement in Desegregated Classrooms." *Sociometry,* vol. 37, no. 1.

Lohman, M. 1970. "Changing a Racial Status Ordering by Means of Role Modeling." Technical Report #2. Stanford, Stanford University School of Education.

Mosteller, F., and D. P. Moynihan, eds. 1972. *On Equality of Educational Opportunity.* New York, Random House.

McGinley, P., and H. McGinley. 1970. "Reading Groups as Psychological Groups." *Journal of Experimental Education,* vol. 39, no. 2.

McPartland, J. 1968. *The Segregated Student in Desegregated Schools: Sources of Influence on Negro Secondary Students.* Baltimore, Center for The Study of Social Organization of Schools, The Johns Hopkins University.

Mercer, J. 1973. "Racial/Ethnic Segregation and Desegregation in American Public Education." Mimeo. University of California at Riverside Program Research in Integrated Multi-Ethnic Education.

Metz, M. H. 1971. "Authority in the Junior High School: A Case Study." Ph.D. diss., University of California at Berkeley.

Newman, W. M. 1973. *American Pluralism.* New York, Harper and Row.

Ogbu, J. U. 1974. *The Next Generation.* New York, Academic Press.

Orfield, G. 1973. "School Integration and its Academic Critics." *Civil Rights Digest,* vol. 5, no. 5.

———— 1975. "Desegregation and the Educational Process." *Law and*

Contemporary Problems, vol. 39, no. 2.

Perry, G. 1973, "A Better Chance: Evaluation of Student Attitudes and Academic Performance, 1964-1972." Unpublished report, ABC, Boston, Mass.

Pettigrew, T. 1971. *Racially Separate or Together?* New York, McGraw-Hill.

——— 1974. "A Sociological View of the Post *Milliken* Era." Paper presented to the U.S. Commission on Civil Rights in hearings, Washington, D.C.

———, ed. 1975. *Racial Discrimination in the United States.* New York, Harper and Row).

Pettigrew, T., E. L. Useem, C. Normand, and M. S. Smith. 1973. "Busing: A Review of the Evidence." *The Public Interest,* no. 30.

Porter, J. D. 1971. *Black Child, White Child: The Development of Racial Attitudes.* Cambridge, Mass., Harvard University Press.

Portland Public Schools. 1971. "Portland Schools and Integration— Some Alternatives." Portland, Ore., Portland Public School System.

Proshansky, H. M. 1966. "The Development of Inter-Group Attitudes." In L. W. Hoffman and M. L. Hoffman, eds., *Review of Child Development Research* (New York, Russell Sage).

Proshansky, H. M., and P. Newton. 1968. "The Nature and Meaning of Negro Self-identity." In M. Deutsch, I. Katz, and A. Jensen, eds., *Social Class, Race, and Psychological Development* (New York, Holt, Rinehart and Winston).

Ravitch, D. 1973. *The Great School Wars: New York City, 1805-1973.* New York, Basic Books.

Riessman, F. 1962. *The Culturally Deprived Child.* New York: Harper and Row.

Rist, R. C. 1970. "Student Social Class and Teacher Expectations: The Self-Fulfilling Prophecy in Ghetto Education." *Harvard Educational Review,* vol. 40, no. 3.

——— 1972. "Social Distance and Social Inequality in a Ghetto Kindergarten Classroom: An Examination of the 'Cultural Gap' Hypothesis." *Urban Education,* vol. 7, no. 3.

——— 1973. *The Urban School: A Factory for Failure.* Cambridge, Mass., The M.I.T. Press.

——— 1974. "Race, Policy, and Schooling." *Trans-Action/Society,* vol. 12, no. 1.

——— 1975. "Ethnographic Techniques and the Study of an Urban School." *Urban Education,* vol. 10, no. 1.

Rosenberg, M., and R. G. Simmons. 1972. *Black and White Self-Esteem: The Urban School Child.* Washington, D.C., American

Sociological Association.

Schlesinger, I., and M. D'Amore. 1971. *Children in the Balance.* New York, Citation Press.

Silberman, C. 1970. *Crisis in the Classroom.* New York, Random House.

Smith, A., A. Downs, and M. L. Lachman. 1973. *Achieving Effective Desegregation.* Lexington, Mass., Lexington Books.

Smith, L., and W. Geoffrey. 1968. *Complexities of an Urban Classroom.* New York, Holt, Rinehart and Winston.

Smith, M. 1972. "Equality of Educational Opportunity: The Basic Findings Reconsidered." In F. Mosteller and D. P. Moynihan, eds., *On Equality of Educational Opportunity* (New York, Random House).

St. John, N. H. 1972. "Social Psychological Aspects of School Desegregation." In H. Walberg and A. Kopan, eds., *Rethinking Urban Education* (San Francisco, Jossey-Bass).

———— 1975. *School Desegregation: Outcomes for Children.* New York, Wiley-Interscience.

Stein, A. 1971. "Strategies for Failure." *Harvard Educational Review,* vol. 41, no. 2.

Teplin, L. 1972. "A Study of Sociometric Choice and Rejection Behavior among Sexually, Racially, and Ethnically Integrated Groups of Elementary School and High School Students." Ph.D diss., Evanston, Ill., Northwestern University.

U.S. Commission on Civil Rights. 1967. *Racial Isolation in the Public Schools.* Washington, D.C., U.S. Government Printing Office.

Useem, E. 1972. "White Students and Token Desegregation." *Integrated Education,* vol. 10, no. 5.

Valentine, C. A. 1971. "Deficit, Difference, and Bicultural Models of Afro-American Behavior." *Harvard Educational Review,* vol. 41, no. 2.

———— 1972. *Black Studies and Anthropology: Scholarly and Political Interests in Afro-American Culture.* Reading, Mass., Addison-Wesley.

Warner, W. L., R. Havighurst, and M. Loeb. 1944. *Who Shall Be Educated?* New York: Harper and Row.

Wilcox, P. 1970. "Integration or Separatism in Education, K-12." *Integrated Education,* vol. 8, no. 1.

Willie, C. V., and J. Reker. 1973. *Race Mixing in the Public Schools.* New York, Praeger.

Wirt, F. M. 1974. "Contemporary School Turbulence and Administrative Authority." Paper delivered at Northwestern University Conference on Problems in the Politics and Governance of the Learning Community.

Index